SPANISH
CITY
PLANNING
IN NORTH
AMERICA

SPANISH
CITY
PLANNING
IN NORTH
AMERICA

Dora P. Crouch,
Daniel J. Garr,
and
Axel I. Mundigo

The MIT Press
Cambridge,
Massachusetts
London, England

This book was set in VIP
Sabon by DEKR Corporation
and printed and bound by
Halliday Lithograph
in the United States of
America.

Library of Congress
Cataloging in Publication
Data
Crouch, Dora P.
   Spanish city planning in
North America.
   Bibliography: p.
   Includes index.
   1. City planning—North
America—History.
I. Garr, Daniel
J.   II. Mundigo, Axel I.,
1935–   III. Title.
HT169.N68C76   307.7′6′097
81-18595   AACR2
ISBN 0-262-03081-0

To the slow ripening
of understanding
that makes history
come alive
A. M. and D. C.

To my parents
D. G.

CONTENTS

Scene from the market at
Tenochtitlan/Mexico City (figure
31)

LIST OF ILLUSTRATIONS

**Part III
Disintegration in
California**

**Chapter 3
Church-State
Boundary Disputes**

A foreword is meant to bring the audience to order and secure for what follows what medieval rhetoricians called benevolent attention (*captatio benevolentiae*).

It may be a principle of historical writing that the past itself becomes less pleasurable as the sum of knowledge increases. A corollary would then be that new subjects of historical discourse are the most entertaining for writer and reader alike. This is not to say that North American urbanism since Discovery is new, but only that in the repertory of the design of towns it is a subject less ploughed over.

Most appropriately, *Spanish City Planning in North America* begins with the Laws of the Indies in 1573 governing settlement in the Western Hemisphere. The authors note American variances from the laws, and they proceed directly to discuss Santa Fe in New Mexico, St. Louis, and Los Angeles as embodying the Vitruvian and Renaissance principles of the sixteenth-century laws. Seen from the point of view of Spain rather than of the English plantations, these cities emerge in an unexpected light as displaying traces—varying from faint to substantial—of the radiation of an urban design decreed at Madrid. The final third of the book tells of the disintegration of Spanish principles in California, both before the independence of Mexico from Spain and after the annexation of Alta California by the United States. San Diego, San Jose, Monterey, and Santa Barbara are the case histories.

It is an unhappy fact that urban design in our *fin de siècle* has become unhistorical. Urbanists are employed by regional and town authorities to make what order they can in cities disrupted by poverty, immigration, and motor traffic. Urbanists are not expected to review the history of what they are doing to us, and it is lamentable that historians are not urbanists. This book, by an urban sociologist, a planning historian, and an architectural historian writing in harmony, is manifestly one of the ways to bring urbanists and historians together.

Rarely do we think as did those who preceded us in the plundering of the planet. If we could hear the robber barons, the gold prospectors, the buccaneers, or the *conquistadores* confronted with twentieth-century excesses, their indignation might shame us all. As it is, the Laws of the Indies, bound as they are to their limitations, still carry the voice of a moral authority lacking in today's opportunistic legislation.

George Kubler
Yale University

ACKNOWLEDG-MENTS

To R.P.I. and S.A.H., who brought us together.

To John Reps, pioneer of American urban history, who shared his visual material with us.

To Richard Morse, Francis Violich, Dan Stanislawski, Charles Peterson, Norman Neuerburg, and others who preceded us, but especially to George Kubler, whose deep understanding of all the art of Mexico and its neighbors has been our inspiration.

To Michael Kannen, who stimulated our interest in colonization.

To all those who might have granted us awards to pursue these studies but didn't.

To Anna Mundigo, who prepared the index.

To Virginia Fitzgerald, Shirley Weiner, and Maria Villa-Nueva, who typed the manuscript.

Very few purely Renaissance cities exist in Europe. This statement bears some examination, since we are accustomed to think of Europe, especially Italy, as the home of the Renaissance. Born in Florence in the early years of the fifteenth century, the Renaissance affected every facet of intellectual and aesthetic life—philosophy, sculpture, poetry, cartography, painting, exploration, politics. And certainly the impact of this ferment on the physical fabric of cities was considerable. Handsome palaces were built by the wealthy as well as the noble; churches were remodeled and built anew; plazas were regularized.

But almost everywhere, these physical manifestations of Renaissance thought were merely inserted into the existing medieval fabric of the towns. As we have rediscovered in our own day, there is an inescapable lag between the new urban concept and its actualization. Buildings are far more durable than paintings, fashions of dress or thought, or even sculpture. If a sculpture is no longer pleasing, you can move it away or hide it behind shrubbery. But if the Victor Emannuel Monument is out of fashion, how can it be hidden? Only a Haussmann dares to tear down three sevenths of the housing stock of a city so that the boulevards necessary for the new urban concept may be driven through the old crowded quarters. Renaissance urban developers had to accommodate the intractability of settlements that were both densely built up and vital. The thirteenth century had been one of urban expansion and foundation in Europe, so that in many cases this fabric was relatively recent and in good condition.

Occasionally, and with marked success, patrons and architects could insert Renaissance ensembles into late medieval organic cities. One thinks of the plaza at St. Mark's in Venice, regularized over a long period and with much squabbling. Or of Michelangelo's reorganization of the Capitoline Hill in Rome, where political vacuum and physical disarray were followed by stately symbolism. Beyond the edges of these orderly plazas, however, during the fifteenth and sixteenth centuries the medieval city was left largely undisturbed.

True, there were a few foundations, such as Palma Nuova, that were created out of whole cloth and embodied to the fullest extent the urban ideas of Alberti and others. Even these, however "modern" their form, followed the

medieval tradition of a geometric pattern for military settlements, like the bastides of southwestern France in the
twelfth and thirteenth centuries (see figure 7). So far as we
know, there were no Renaissance attempts to impose such
order on an entire existing city. It was left to the Baroque
era to make wholesale alterations to European cities (as
Gideon has shown for Rome).

In the New World, however, the Europeans found an
essentially blank slate to be filled in by their ideas about
urban form. At Mexico City and at Cuzco, the conquerors
found great Indian cities at least equal in size, splendor,
and sophistication to European cities, but several factors
combined to offset the potential impact of these capitals
on their conquerors: the supine weakness of their rulers in
the face of European aggressiveness; the abhorrent super-
abundance of human sacrifice, which made the Aztecs
seem morally subhuman; and the destruction of Tenochtitlan by fire, so that none but the first group of *conquistadores* ever saw it in its prime. If one adds Spanish hubris
and sixteenth-century ethnocentricity, then it is compre-
hensible that the New World was perceived as an area
without culture where the latest Renaissance ideas about
urban form might not only be safely and easily imposed
but also be considered the perfect solution to an enormous
set of problems.

Not since the days of the ancient Romans or the Muslim
explosion of the seventh century had one small peninsular
people set out to conquer and colonize an immense area
beyond its own borders. Roman ideas about urban form
were known to the Spaniards from existing Roman foundations such as Barcelona (see figure 3), where the core of
the city still retained the Roman pattern, central open
space and gridlike pattern of blocks. The Islamic impact
on Spanish urban thought, which is being studied by our
colleague François-Auguste de Montêquin, will not be examined here, though its effects seem to have been both
profound and subtle. As for the interplay of ancient Roman and recent Renaissance urban thought, by the late
sixteenth century the rulers and intellectuals of Spain were
acquainted with the writings of the Roman architect Vitruvius, as published in the fifteenth century by Alberti,
and with Alberti's own book, with its discussions of proper
urban form. Some recent Spanish examples, such as Santa

Fe de Granada, established in 1491 by Isabel and Ferdinand (see figures 8 and 9), served as urban experiments, easily accessible for thoughtful review, embodying Renaissance notions of clarity, regularity, order, and harmony.

The Renaissance quality of Spanish New World cities was gradually developed through a "feedback" system that responded to the needs of conquest and settlement. At first, in keeping with Renaissance ideas of individual action and responsibility, orders from Spain were relatively brief and loosely framed. Since the reconquest of Spain from the Moors had proceeded city by city, it was natural to assume that conquest of the New World would also be urban. If cities did not exist, they would be created, each new one serving in turn as the base for further conquest and settlement.

As experience accumulated during the sixteenth century, the rights of individual conquerors were balanced against the needs of Spanish society and the demands of the crown. Order and predictability were necessary both for the individuals accomplishing this enormous feat who required psychological security, and for the Spanish crown, which wanted ease of administration and maximum return on its investment. Renaissance principles of legal, social, and physical order through hierarchical organization were not only acceptable but essential for the expansion and stability of the empire. In Europe the new urban ideas following from these principles had to compete with the existing fabric, but in the New World they could be and were imposed without resistance and without argument.

We can learn about Renaissance urban thought by careful study of three aspects of New World cities: their physical fabric, their maps and plans that mirror those physical entities, and the laws that controlled Spanish conquest. Indeed, the understanding of Renaissance urban thought to be derived from such study cannot be gained by studying the history and development of Florence or Rome or any other single European city. The uniqueness of such European examples militates against general understanding. In addition, European Renaissance cities have a semiconscious organic quality, part of their medieval legacy, that is natural to their historical context and contrasts strongly with the conscious, regular pattern of colonial cities. The very fact that one general set of edicts applied to more than 350 Spanish colonial cities differentiates them from their European counterparts.

Our own study has concerned itself mainly with the city planning ordinances issued by the Spanish King Philip II in 1573. A compilation of all previous planning edicts issued since the beginning of the Conquest, these regulated every aspect of conquest and settlement in the New World. Until now, an inadequate translation in an obscure periodical* has provided the only access to them for English-language readers. Besides an amplified and corrected translation, we offer here the insights of an urban sociologist, a planning historian, and an architectural historian. Each of us has asked different questions of this material, and together we offer insights into not only the urban history of this region but also the larger history of cities, the nature of urbanism, the historiography of urban history, and the relation of provincial examples to a major period of human thought.

The city planning ordinances of the Laws of the Indies mandated orderly procedure and orderly layout, with ample provision for growth. These ordinances were designed to direct amateurs in laying out and settling new towns. Each settlement was linked to the provincial governor, who was a direct representative of the crown. Each settlement was to extend the empire, enrich the crown and its local representatives as well as the founding settlers, and add thousands of converts to Christianity.

In theory and law, little was left to chance, though, as we shall see, politics, personality conflicts, and lack of money eroded the force of law, especially at the frontier. In this book, we are dealing mainly with frontier settlements located within what is today the continental United States. There are two reasons for this. The first is intellectual: If the forceful results of the operation of the Laws of the Indies can be seen even in these provincial examples and even after all this time, then our presumption is that in cities founded earlier and more centrally located to the Spanish presence in the New World, the impact of Renaissance urban thought can be observed even more viv-

---

* Z. Nuttall, "Royal Ordinances Concerning the Laying Out of New Towns," *The Hispanic American Historical Review*, Vol. 4 No. 4 (Nov., 1921), pp. 743–753. Reprinted in *Planning & Civic Comment*, Vol. V, pp. 17–20.

idly. The second is practical: Now that the pious myth of the founding of the United States only by Puritans at Plymouth and Cavaliers at Jamestown is generally questioned, the time is ripe for an examination of this other major strand in American history. The present eminence of Houston and Los Angeles makes a history centered only on Boston and New York untenable.

The first part of the book was written by Axel Mundigo with some assistance from Dora Crouch. It presents a new translation of the city planning ordinances of 1573 and a commentary on them. The problems involved in founding cities—site selection, relations with natives, political organization, layout of the plaza and streets, assignment of lands, and so on—are dealt with in these ordinances, all very clearly and definitely, in spite of the archaic verbalisms of the sixteenth century Spanish. The following chapter sets these ordinances in context and, among other things, raises the issue of Indian input into Spanish colonial urbanism. Both the Indian and Muslim substrata have been largely unacknowledged components of the theory and practice of city building in the New World, so that previous explanations of the observed reality have had a curiously incomplete quality.

The second part of the book studies three American cities. Urban ideas of the Spanish colonial period are evident in the physical fabric of these cities—the arrangement of their buildings and spaces—which, in turn, may be investigated as the embodiment of the laws by which they were founded. Also embodied here are the ambitious dreams of the founders and of the central government, for these buildings and spaces reflect these dreams as well as serve the needs of everyday life. One way to understand these dreams is to study the maps and plans of the settlements, such as those required by law to be sent to the Council of the Indies at Seville. These papers reveal not only the actual state of cities at various stages of growth, but also what was hoped for them. The book is therefore illustrated with plans, maps, and early views, all of which manifest this kind of urban thought in another way from either the laws or the physical form of the city. This part was written by Dora Crouch, except that the chapter on Los Angeles was coauthored by Daniel Garr. Most of the pictures were selected and their captions written by Crouch.

From an analysis of Spanish New World cities we can arrive at the characteristic features of Renaissance urbanism. Rationality dominated both plan and execution. The city was clearly organized and orderly. Blocks and streets formed an orthogonal pattern. Since political and social life were organized in a double hierarchy whose two ordering principles were church and state, ecclesiastical, administrative, and private buildings related to each other and to the open spaces in a way that mirrored this double balance. In particular, the names and uses of buildings related directly to the sovereign and his central government, which fostered growth not only by supplying capital but by requiring a central location for important buildings, so that expansion was not impeded. Like the colonial cities of the Roman Empire, those of the Spanish Empire were conceived and executed as propaganda vehicles, symbolizing and incarnating civilization.

From the fifteenth century through the eighteenth, historical circumstances permitted the development and proliferation of Renaissance thought in many fields of human endeavor. As late as the early 1950s, in fact, those art periods that we now characterize separately as Mannerist, Baroque, Rococo, and Neo-Classic were grouped as phases of the Renaissance. With the Industrial Revolution, however, these modes of thought as well as old technologies, were swept away. The Spanish colonial empire tottered and gave way under this onslaught. The third part of the book, written by Daniel Garr, examines the demise of the empire, the last gasp of Renaissance urban thought, as it may be seen in specific events and examples of early California history. As late as the 1830s, some Renaissance ideas of urbanism inspired attempts to strengthen and beautify the California settlements, but these ideas were short on money and energy, and they faded away almost like dreams before the vigor of the invading capitalistic and industrial American culture.

Spanish colonial cities, whether founded in the sixteenth century or later, seem to combine simplicity of form with complexity of social structure. By contrast, one may cite the Portugese experience in Brazil.* Here, Baroque urban

---

* R. M. Delson, *New Towns for Colonial Brazil,* U. Microfilms International, 1979.

ideas of the city as the creature of the state, of order as
beauty, of axiality, which gives a dynamic quality to even
the simplest settlement, are embodied in the physical arrangements of the town. In the attempt to integrate Indian,
Negro, and Portugese settlers, too, Portugal's New World
experience seems more dynamic than Spain's, the hierarchical character of which was naturally more static. An
extended study comparing Spanish and Portugese urbanism in the New World would be both useful and
interesting.

This book, then, serves as an introduction to the study
of an aspect of urban history that lasted nearly 500 years
and extended over more than one continent. Impinging
upon urban life today in California, Arizona, New Mexico,
Texas, and Florida, it calls us to new consciousness of how
the events and decisions of the past still affect the arrangement and content of our buildings and spaces. Moreover,
the New World cities defining this aspect of urban history
provide today's scholar or traveler with several hundred
Renaissance cities deserving of at least as much attention
as Ferrara or Bologna! In discussing the changes at Tenochtitlan, then the meager and almost pathetic realization
of Santa Fe, St. Louis, and Los Angeles, and finally the
disintegration at Monterey, we see the adolescence, old
age, and death of a set of urban concepts. We venture to
claim that in terms of the scope of their application, the
city planning ordinances of the Laws of the Indies are the
most influential body of urban law in human history.

In the future, we would like to see detailed studies of
this aspect of urban history. Already perceived as being
necessary are compilations of, and changes in, the Laws
of the Indies; comparisons of Spanish and Portugese colonial cities; investigations of the influence of Islamic city
patterns and municipal law on Spanish urban thought and
the Laws of the Indies; examinations of American Indian
settlement patterns, with particular regard for the extent
to which they were adapted and adopted by the colonizers;
the character of different colonial city types, such as seaports, forts, capitals, etc.; differences between North
American and South American Spanish cities in general,
and between Mexican and Californian/New Mexican cities
in particular; and comparisons of Greco-Roman coloni-

zation of the Mediterranean with Spanish colonization of the New World. Each of these studies can help us to recover, and also to reconstitute, the past.

Don Felipe, by the Grace of God, King of Castille . . . let it be known: That in order that the discoveries and new settlements and pacification of the land and provinces that are to be discovered, settled, and pacified in the Indies be done with greater facility and in accordance with the service to God Our Lord, and for the welfare of the natives, among other things, we have prepared the following ordinances.

Thus begins a document that has left a formidable physical imprint on, and social heritage in, all the areas of Spanish influence in the Americas. The ordinances referred to by Philip II are part of the Laws of the Indies and concern the founding of towns in the sixteenth century. They formed a set of decrees devised to extend across an entire continent an urban tradition and spatial arrangement that was to be repeated throughout the span of Spanish colonization.

Spanish city planning in the New World was not always uniform or regular. Since the arrival of Columbus, and for approximately thirty years thereafter, settlements had been started, but no specific pattern had been followed. A few of these early towns were built on the ruins of conquered towns and in some cases on the old foundations of pre-Columbian cities, such as Incan Cuzco. It was not until 1513, when Pedrarias Dávila received the first royal orders concerning the planning of cities in the New World, that a new phase of regulated urban development was initiated. These first instructions, presumably to be applied in the city of Panama, were also incorporated in the rebuilding of Mexico City by Cortés. Cortés arrived at Tenochtitlan in 1519. After the conquest and destruction of the Aztec capital, he set out to build what has remained one of the most important cities of the New World, a city whose appearance, and especially its plaza, drew great praise from a 1559 visitor: "Look carefully, please and note if you have ever seen another equal to it in size and grandeur. . . . What order! What beauty!" [1]

The translation and some of the commentary in this part first appeared in Axel Mundigo and Dora Crouch, "The City Planning Ordinances of the Laws of the Indies Revisited, I", *Town Planning Review*, vol. 48, July 1977, pp. 247–268. Reprinted by permission.

As city building and planning followed city founding, the gridiron, and especially the checkerboard system of square blocks, appeared as the most characteristic imprint that the Spaniards imposed in the New World. As Stanislawski has noted, there were some important considerations that made the grid the most practical layout for the new cities of Hispanic America: "(1) a complete new city to be built; (2) the city planned as a unity according to preconceived specifications and patterns; (3) centralized control; (4) the desire of measured apportionment of property; (5) knowledge of the grid." [2]

Caplow,[3] Stanislawski,[4] and Morse,[5] among others, have noted the Roman and classical planning ideas embedded in the various city planning ordinances issued by the Spanish kings. These ordinances were the product of a process of rationalization undertaken by a highly centralized government extending its domains into hitherto unknown lands. As the conquest proceeded, they were revised and improved several times during the sixteenth century. With every revision, their dependence on Roman city planning increased. The grid pattern for a city's plan became a mold that was to be applied with increasing rigor throughout the recently discovered continent. The 1513 ordinances given by Ferdinand to Pedrarias Dávila already contained the basic suggestions for this rational city layout. These ordinances were made more specific in 1523, but it was not until fifty years later, on 13 July 1573, that Philip II issued a comprehensive compilation expanding and incorporating the previous decrees by Ferdinand and Charles V. What emerged was a set of 148 ordinances dealing with every aspect of site selection, city planning and political organization; in fact they were the most complete such set of instructions ever issued to serve as a guideline for the founding and building of towns in the Americas and, in terms of their widespread application and persistence, probably the most effective planning documents in the history of mankind. In short, Philip's compilation reinforced the unilateral objectives of conquest, emphasized the urban character of Spanish colonization, and specified clearly the physical and organizational arrangements that were to be developed in the new cities of America. Above all, the ordinances stressed a Christian ideology and a cultural imperialism designed to provide the Spaniard in the New World with an urban environment that would include recognizable features while remaining adaptable to a variety of geographical locations.

The ordinances issued by Philip II for the laying out of new towns have remained largely unknown to the English-speaking public. The only translations available date from 1921 and 1922 and were made available by Zelia Nuttall and published in *The Hispanic American Historical Review*.[6] It is important to remark on the existence of two sets of translations, as some researchers have come upon one and not the other. The 1921 translation was published while Mrs. Nuttall was in Europe, but the actual translation was not her work. Mrs. Nuttall tells us of the "remarkable document I came across in the National Archives in Madrid in 1912. Being particularly impressed by the wisdom and foresight revealed in the set of Ordinances relating to the choice of the sites and the laying out of new towns, I copied these for future reference and use."[7] The Nuttall translations begin with ordinance 110, which is the first concerning the laying out of new towns, but interesting aspects concerning the founding of cities, choice of sites, and related information are also contained in ordinances 1–109, which, as far as we know, have never been translated before into English.

If the reader consults the Nuttall translations, the 1922 revision should be avoided except for the corrections made to the 1921 Spanish text. In the 1922 edition, Mrs. Nuttall edited the 1921 translation, completely eradicating the flavor of these sixteenth-century edicts. It is difficult to convey into English this old-fashioned language and its peculiar legalistic overtones, but in our view the ordinances should be presented to the reader in a fashion that is as true to the text as possible. Undoubtedly the English will read awkwardly—the Spanish reads equally awkwardly to a modern-day Spaniard. As an example of the difference between the 1921 and 1922 Nuttall versions, ordinance 114 can be cited:

[1921 translation] From the plaza shall run four main streets, one from the middle of each side of the plaza; and two streets at each corner of the plaza. The four corners of the plaza shall face the four principal winds. For the streets running thus from the plaza, they will not be exposed to the four principal winds which cause much inconvenience.

[1922 revision] From the plaza the four principal streets are to diverge, one from the middle of each of its sides and two streets are to meet at each of its corners. The four corners of the plaza are to face the four points of the compass, because thus the streets diverging from the plaza will not be directly exposed to the four principal winds, which would cause much inconvenience.

Furthermore, there are a number of minor interpretational errors in the 1921 translation as well. It is not our intention here to quarrel over the interpretation of this or that word, but in view of such discrepancies, we had to modify our earlier objective of including only those ordinances not translated by Mrs. Nuttall. Basically we present here a new and more complete translation beginning with ordinance 1 and ending with ordinance 148, but presenting in summary form those ordinances of lesser interest to the planner, sociologist, or urban historian. Ordinances omitted include those on crew size on ships, modes of approaching the Indians, punishment for taking Indians aboard ship, and so forth. In all, we add about thirty new ordinances and have revised the 1921 Nuttall translation whenever necessary. The objective has been faithfulness to the Spanish text. It should be noted that Mrs. Nuttall's dating of the ordinances is wrong. The correct date is 13 July 1573, not 3 July. In fact, the entire document closes with the following paragraph (following ordinance 148):

Because we order you to see to it that these Ordinances, as presented above be incorporated, complied with, and executed, and that you make what in them is contained be complied with and executed, and never take action or move against them, nor consent that others take action or move against either their content or form, under penalty of our Lord. Dated in the Woods of Segovia, *the thirteenth of July, in the year fifteen hundred and seventy-three*. I the King . . . [Italics added]

Mrs. Nuttall's translation begins with "I the King . . .," but, in fact, the ordinances end with the king and his assistants' call to compliance (see end of present translation). The actual beginning of the document is quoted at the start of this article, where we only omit the long list of titles of Philip II. Our revised translation of Philip's ordinances now follows.

1 Richard Morse, "Some Characteristics of Latin American Urban History," *American Historical Review*, Vol. LXVII (October 1961–July 1962), p. 321; hereafter cited as Morse, 1962.

2 Dan Stanislawski, "Early Spanish Town Planning in the New World," *The Geographical Review*, Vol. XXXVII, No. I (January 1947), p. 94; hereafter cited as Stanislawski, 1947.

3 Theodore Caplow, "The Modern Latin American City," in *Acculturation in the Americas— Proceedings and Selected Papers of the XXXIX Congress of Americanists*, ed. Sol Tax (Chicago: University of Chicago Press, 1952), pp. 255–260.

4 Stanislawski, 1947, pp. 94–105.

5 Morse, 1962, pp. 317–338.

6 Zelia Nuttall, "Royal Ordinances Concerning the Laying Out of New Towns," *The Hispanic American Historical Review*, Vol. 4, No. 4 (November 1921), pp. 743–753; *idem*, "Royal Ordinances Concerning the Laying Out of New Towns," *The Hispanic American Historical Review*, Vol. 5, No. 2 (May 1922), pp. 249–254.

7 Nuttall, 1921, p. 743.

We have prepared the following ordinances:

1

No person, regardless of state or condition, should on his own authority make a new discovery by sea or land, or enter a new settlement or hamlet in areas already discovered. If he were found without our license and approval or by those who had our power to give it, he would face a death penalty and loss of all his possessions to our coffers. And, we order to all our viceroys, *audiencias*, and governors and other justices of the Indies, that they give no license to make new discoveries without previous consultation with us and only after having obtained our permission; but we do consent that in areas already discovered, they can give license to build towns as necessary, adhering to the order that in so doing they must keep to the laws of February regarding settlements in discovered lands, [and] then they should send us a description.

2

Those who are in charge of governing the Indies, whether spiritually or temporally, should inform themselves diligently whether within their districts, including lands and provinces bordering them, there is something to be discovered and pacified, of the wealth and quality, [and] of the peoples and nations who inhabit there; but do this without sending to them war personnel nor persons who can cause scandal. They [the governors] should inform themselves by the best means available; and likewise, they should obtain information on the persons who are best suited to carry out discoveries—and with those who are best fit for this purpose, they [the governors] should confer and make arrangements, offering them the honors and advantages that justly, without injury to the natives, can be given them—and—before carrying out what has been arranged or has been learned, give narratives to the viceroy and the *audiencias* and also send them to the Council, which, after looking at the case, will issue a license to proceed with the discovery, which should be carried out in the following order:

3

Having made, within the confines of the province, a discovery by land, pacified it, [and] subjected it to our obedience, find an appropriate site to be settled by Spaniards—and if not, [arrange] for the vassal Indians so they be secure.

4

If the boundaries of the settlement are populated, utilizing commerce and ransom, go with vassal Indians and interpreters to discover those lands, and with churchmen and

Spaniards, carrying offerings and ransoms and peace, try to learn about the place, the contents and quality of the land, the nation(s) to which the people there belong, who governs them, and carefully take note of all you can learn and understand, and always send these narratives to the Governor so that they reach the Council [Consejo de Indias].

5
Look carefully at the places and ports where it might be possible to build Spanish settlements without damage to the Indian population.

6–12
[These ordinances concern discoveries that are made by sea as well as details of crew size, provisions, and related matters.]

13
Persons who participate in discoveries, whether by land or by sea, should take possession, in our name, of all lands and provinces they might reach and, upon setting foot on to land, perform the necessary ceremonies and writs, thus providing public evidence and faithful testimony.

14
Once the discoverers arrive at newly discovered provinces or lands, together with the officials, they should name each land, each province, and the mountains and principal rivers they might encounter as well as the settlements and towns they might find or that they may begin.

15–31
[These ordinances express a serious concern for the fate of the Indian population, exhorting the Spaniard to treat the locals in a friendly way, but emphasize finding out what metals there are and of what quality (15); local foods (16); possibilities for religious indoctrination (17); dangers of running out of foodstuffs and what to do (18); approaching unknown land with large ships (19); avoiding war, mutiny, and problems with the locals (20); informing the governors and council of the Indies (21, 22, 23); punishment by death for taking Indians aboard ship or bringing them back in voyages (24); expenditures for discoveries (25); proper treatment of priests who might discover and preach in new lands (26); the conversion of Indians (27); discoveries by foreigners (28); peaceful discoveries (29); adherence to these ordinances (30); and problems of discovery and possible conflicts (31).]

32

Before discoveries are duly recognized, no new population settlements are permitted, whether in the discovered areas or in those still to be discovered, but in those parts which are already discovered, pacified, and subjected to our mandate, population settlements, both of Spaniards and of Indians, should be ordered having permanence and giving perpetuity to both groups as specified in the fourth and fifth books [of the Laws of the Indies], especially in those parts dealing with population settlements and with land allotments.

33

Having populated and settled the newly discovered area, pacified it, and subjected it to our mandate, efforts should be made to discover and populate adjacent areas that are being discovered for the first time.

34

In order to populate those areas that are already discovered, pacified, and under our mandate, as well as areas that might be discovered and pacified in the course of time, the following sequence should be adhered to: choose the province, county, and place that will be settled, taking into consideration the health of the area, which will be known from the abundance of old men or of young men of good complexion, natural fitness and color, and without illness; and in the abundance of healthy animals of sufficient size, and of healthy fruits and fields where no toxic and noxious things are grown, but that it be of good climate, the sky clear and benign, the air pure and soft, without impediment or alterations and of good temperature, without excessive heat or cold, and having to decide, it is better that it be cold.

35

And they should be in fertile areas with an abundance of fruits and fields, of good land to plant and harvest, of grasslands to grow livestock, of mountains and forests for wood and building materials for homes and edifices, and of good and plentiful water supply for drinking and irrigation.

36

And that they should be populated by Indians and natives to whom we can preach the gospels since this is the principal objective for which we mandate that these discoveries and settlements be made.

37

And they should have good access and outlet by sea and by land, and also good roads and passage by water, in

order that they may be entered and departed easily with
commerce, while bringing relief and establishing defenses.

38

Once the region, province, county, and land are decided
upon by the expert discoverers, select the site to build a
town and capital of the province and its subjects, without
harm to the Indians for having occupied the area or because they agree to it of good will.

39

The site and position of the towns should be selected in
places where water is nearby and where it would be possible to demolish neighboring towns and properties in order to take advantage of the materials that are essential
for building; and, [these sites and positions should be
suitable] also for farming, cultivation, and pasturation, so
as to avoid excessive work and cost, since any of the above
would be costly if they were far.

40

Do not select sites that are too high up because these are
affected by winds, and access and service to these are
difficult, nor in lowlands, which tend to be unhealthy;
choose places of medium elevation that enjoy good winds,
especially from the north and south, and if there were
mountains or hills, these should be in the west or in the
east, and if there should be a need to build in high places,
do it in areas not subjected to fogs; take note of the terrain
and its accidental features and in case that there should be
a need to build on the banks of a river, it should be on the
eastern bank, so when the sun rises it strikes the town first,
then the water.

41

Do not select sites for towns in maritime locations because
of the danger that exists of pirates and because they are
not very healthy, and also because in these [locations] there
are less people able to work and cultivate the land, nor is
it possible to instill in them these habits. Unless the site is
in an area where there are good and principal harbors,
among these, select for settlement only those that are necessary for the entry of commerce and for the defense of
the land.

42

Having selected the site for capital towns in each county,
determine the areas that could be subjected and incorporated within the jurisdiction of the head town [English
approximation: county seat] as farms, granges, and gardens, without detriment to Indians or natives.

43

Having selected the area, province, and site where the new settlement is to be built, and having established the existing opportunities for development, the governor in whose district [the site] is or borders upon should decide whether the site that is to be populated should become a city, town, or village settlement. In compliance with his decision, it should form a Council [and] commonwealth [*república*] and name corresponding officials and members in accordance with stipulations in the "Book of the Republic of Spaniards" [Libro de la República de Españoles]. Thus in case it were to become a metropolitan city, it should have a judge with title and name of *adelantado* [title often given to the governor of a province, probably interim governor], or governor, or principal mayor; a *corregidor*, or ordinary mayor, who would have *insolidum* jurisdiction and who jointly with the regiment would carry on the administration of the commonwealth [with the help also of] three officers of the Royal Exchequer [*Hacienda Real*], twelve magistrates [*regidores*], two executors, two jurors for each parish, one general procurer, one scribe for the Council, two public scribes [one for mines, another for registers], one main town crier, one broker for commercial transactions, two ushers to diocesan or suffragan bishops, eight [lower] magistrates, and other such essential officials. For the towns and villages, [there should be] an ordinary mayor, four magistrates, one constable, one scribe for the Council and a public scribe, and a majordomo.

44–108

[Ordinances 44–108 deal in detail with a variety of legislative, legal, and fiduciary regulations, generally introduced in ordinance 43, approximately in the following sequence: government, justice, settlement rights, and registration of the settled population (44–46); distribution of land, plots, and areas for cultivation, workers in the land, and their duties to farm owners and to officials of the town (47–51); names, titles, and officials for new towns, and inheritance of these positions (52–57); the *encomienda* system (58–62); mining, governance, land subdivision, and matters concerning the royal exchequer (63–71); counting of new towns and their populations and other groups for the purpose of pacification and for building additional towns (72–78); taxation and governor's succession (79–82); on duties toward the governor (83–85); on discoveries, pacification, and settlement (86–88). Ordinances 89 and 90 are of interest to our study:]

The persons who were placed in charge of populating a
town with Spaniards should see to it that within a specified
term, assigned for its establishment, it should have at least
thirty neighbors, each one with his own house, ten cows,
four oxen or two oxen and two young bulls and a mare,
five pigs, six chickens, [and] twenty sheep from Castille;
and it should have [also] a clergyman who can administer
sacraments and provide the ornaments to the church as
well as the necessary implements for the divine service; if
this is not accomplished, he should lose everything already
built or formed and he will incur a fine of a thousand gold
pesos.

90
The aforesaid stipulations and territory should be divided
as follows:
Separate first the land that is needed for the house plots
[*solares*] of the town, then allocate sufficient public land
and grounds for pasture where the cattle the neighbors are
expected to bring with them can obtain abundant feed,
plus another portion for the natives of the area.
The rest of the grounds and territory should be divided
into four parts: one is for the person in charge of building
the town; the other three should be subdivided into thirty
lots for the thirty neighbors of the town.

[Ordinance 91 deals with the location of new towns by the
sea. The next deal with who is to be counted as a neighbor
(92); on extension of the building term (93); common
grounds (94); town officials (95–96); nearby mines (97);
and taxes on items carried along to start a new town (98).
Ordinance 99 continues the trend from ordinance 90:]

99
Those who have made a commitment to build the said
new town, who after having succeeded in carrying out its
settlement, as an honor to them and to their descendants
[and in] their laudable memory as founders, we pronounce
them *hijosdalgo* [illustrious men of known ancestry]. To
them and to their legitimate heirs, in whatever place they
might reside or in any other part of the Indies, they will
be *hijosdalgo*, that is, persons of noble ascendancy and
known ancestry.

100
Those who should want to make a commitment to building
a new settlement in the form and manner already prescribed, be it of more or less than 30 neighbors, [know
that] it should be of no less than twelve persons and be

awarded the authorization and territory in accordance with the prescribed conditions.

101

If there were not enough people to start a settlement and to commit themselves to building a new town, but if there is an abundance of married men who volunteered to agree to start a settlement in a place already selected for this purpose, it could be done if at least ten of them were married; in this case proper authorization and territory should be granted and they should choose among themselves an ordinary mayor and officials for a Council and for their annals.

[Ordinances 102 and 103 deal with the need to adhere to the regulations for town settlement and to write down everything concerning the distribution of city plots, grazing, and farm lands, and state that no settler is to receive more than five *peonías* and three *caballerías* (103). A *peonía* is a plot of 50 feet in width and 100 feet in depth (102), and a *caballería* is a plot to build a house of 100 feet in width and 200 feet in depth (105). In addition to the plots, grains, cereals and seeds were given to the settlers. These plots were to be well delineated and with clear and closed boundaries (106). Those who accept *caballerías* and *peonías* have an obligation to build a house, work the land, and acquire herds, grasslands, and so forth within a particular time period (107–108).]

109

The governor who authorizes the settlement of a new town or concedes rights for an existing town to be populated anew, by means of his own authority or by making a request, should ascertain that those who have made a commitment to settle in a new town comply with the taking of seat in a proper manner. This should be done with great diligence and care. Also, the magistrates and Council procurer should initiate due process against the settlers who are bound up by a specified term and who have not complied with it to make them meet the terms, and those who might have left should be prosecuted, seized, and brought back to the town in order that they comply with the terms of settlement, and if they were in another jurisdiction, a requisitioning order should be issued in order that justice be done under penalty of Our Lord.

110

Having made the discovery, selected the province, county, and area that is to be settled, and the site in the location where the new town is to be built, and having taken possession of it, those placed in charge of its execution are to do it in the following manner: On arriving at the place where the new settlement is to be founded—which according to our will and disposition shall be one that is vacant and that can be occupied without doing harm to the Indians and natives or with their free consent—a plan for the site is to be made, dividing it into squares, streets, and building lots, using cord and ruler, beginning with the main square from which streets are to run to the gates and principal roads and leaving sufficient open space so that even if the town grows, it can always spread in the same manner. Having thus agreed upon the site and place selected to be populated, a layout should be made in the following way:

111

Having made the selection of the site where the town is to be built, it must, as already stated, be in an elevated and healthy location; [be] with means of fortification; [have] fertile soil and with plenty of land for farming and pasturage; have fuel, timber, and resources; [have] fresh water, a native population, ease of transport, access and exit; [and be] open to the north wind; and, if on the coast, due consideration should be paid to the quality of the harbor and that the sea does not lie to the south or west; and if possible not near lagoons or marshes in which poisonous animals and polluted air and water breed.

112

The main plaza is to be the starting point for the town; if the town is situated on the sea coast, it should be placed at the landing place of the port, but inland it should be at the center of the town. The plaza should be square or rectangular, in which case it should have at least one and a half its width for length inasmuch as this shape is best for fiestas in which horses are used and for any other fiestas that should be held.

113

The size of the plaza shall be proportioned to the number of inhabitants, taking into consideration the fact that in Indian towns, inasmuch as they are new, the intention is that they will increase, and thus the plaza should be decided upon taking into consideration the growth the town may experience. [The plaza] shall be not less than two hundred feet wide and three hundred feet long, nor larger than eight hundred feet long and five hundred and thirty-two feet wide. A good proportion is six hundred feet long and four hundred wide.[1]

114

From the plaza shall begin four principal streets: One
[shall be] from the middle of each side, and two streets
from each corner of the plaza; the four corners of the plaza
shall face the four principal winds, because in this manner,
the streets running from the plaza will not be exposed to
the four principal winds, which would cause much
inconvenience.

115

Around the plaza as well as along the four principal streets
which begin there, there shall be portals, for these are
of considerable convenience to the merchants who generally gather there; the eight streets running from the plaza
at the four corners shall open on the plaza without encountering these porticoes, which shall be kept back in
order that there may be sidewalks even with the streets
and plaza.[2]

116

In cold places the streets shall be wide and in hot places
narrow; but for purposes of defense in areas where there
are horses, it would be better if they are wide.

117

The streets shall run from the main plaza in such manner
that even if the town increases considerably in size, it will
not result in some inconvenience that will make ugly what
needed to be rebuilt, or endanger its defense or comfort.

118

Here and there in the town, smaller plazas of good proportion shall be laid out, where the temples associated
with the principal church, the parish churches, and the
monasteries can be built, [in] such [manner] that everything may be distributed in a good proportion for the
instruction of religion.

119[3]

For the temple of the principal church, parish, or monastery, there shall be assigned specific lots; the first after the
streets and plazas have been laid out, and these shall be a
complete block so as to avoid having other buildings
nearby, unless it were for practical or ornamental reasons.

120

The temple of the cathedral [principal church] where the
town is situated on the coast shall be built in part so that
it may be seen on going out to sea and in a place where
its buildings may serve as a means of defense for the port
itself.

Next, a site and lot shall be assigned for the royal council and *cabildo* house and for the custom house and arsenal, near the temple, located in such a manner that in times of need the one may aid the other; the hospital for the poor and those sick of noncontagious diseases shall be built near the temple and its cloister; and the hospital for the sick with contagious diseases shall be built in such a way that no harmful wind blowing through it may cause harm to the rest of the town. If the latter be built in an elevated place, so much the better.

122
The site and building lots for slaughter houses, fisheries, tanneries, and other business which produce filth shall be so placed that the filth can easily be disposed of.

123
It shall be of considerable convenience if those towns that are laid out away from seaports, inland, be built if possible on the shore of a navigable river, and attempts should be made to place the town on the side from which the cold north wind blows and that buildings that cause filth be placed on the side of the river or sea below the town.

124
The temple in inland places shall not be placed on the square but at a distance and shall be separated from any other nearby building, or from adjoining buildings, and ought to be seen from all sides so that it can be decorated better, thus acquiring more authority; efforts should be made that it be somewhat raised from ground level in order that it be approached by steps, and near it, next to the main plaza, the royal council and *cabildo* and customs houses shall be built. [These shall be built] in a manner that would not embarrass the temple but add to its prestige. The hospital for the poor who are not affected by contagious diseases shall be built near the temple and near its cloister, and the [hospital] for contagious diseases shall be built in an area where the cold north wind blows, but arranged in such a way that it may enjoy the south wind.

125
The same plan shall be observed in any inland place without shore, taking considerable care to ascertain the availability of those conveniences that are required.

126
In the plaza, no lots shall be assigned to private individuals; instead, they shall be used for the buildings of the church and royal houses and for city use, but shops and houses for the merchants should be built first, to which all

the settlers of the town shall contribute, and a moderate tax shall be imposed on goods so that these buildings may be built.

127

The other building lots shall be distributed by lottery to the settlers, continuing with the lots closer to the main plaza, and the lots that are left shall be held by us for assignment to those who shall later become settlers, or for the use that we may wish to make of them, and so that this may be ascertained better, the town shall maintain a plan of what is being built.

128

Having made the plan of the town and having distributed building lots, each of the settlers shall set up his tent on his plot if he should have one. For this purpose the captains should persuade settlers to carry them, and those who did not bring one should make their huts of easily available local materials, so that they may have shelter, and everyone as soon as possible shall make a palisade or ditch encircling the plaza[4] so that they may not be harmed by Indians or natives.

129

Within the town, a commons shall be delimited, large enough that although the population may experience a rapid expansion, there will always be sufficient space where the people may go to for recreation and take their cattle to pasture without them making any damage.

130

Adjoining the commons there shall be assigned pasture ground for the work oxen and for the horses as well as for the cattle for slaughter and for the usual number of cattle that the settlers must have according to these Ordinances, and in a good number so they can be admitted to pasture in the public lands of the Council; and the rest [of the adjoining land] shall be assigned as farm lands, which will be distributed by lottery in such a number that the [farm lots] would be as many in number as the lots in the town; and if there should be irrigated lands, lots shall be cast for them and they shall be distributed in the same proportion to the first settlers according to their lots; the rest shall remain for ourselves so that we may assign it to those who may become settlers.

131

In the farmlands that may be distributed, the settlers should immediately plant the seeds they brought with them and those they might have obtained at the site; to this effect it is convenient that they go well provided; and in the pasture lands, all the cattle they brought with them or gathered should be branded so that they may soon begin to breed and multiply.

132

Having planted their seeds and made arrangements for the cattle in such number and with good diligence in order to obtain abundant food, the settlers shall begin with great care and efficiency to establish their houses and to build them with good foundations and walls; to this effect they shall go provided with molds or planks for building them, and all the other tools needed for building quickly and at small cost.

133

They shall arrange the building lots and edifices placed thereon in such a manner that when living in them they may enjoy the winds of the south and north as these are the best; throughout the town arrange the structures of the houses generally in such a way that they may serve as defense or barrier against those who may try to disturb or invade the town, and each house in particular shall be so built that they may keep therein their horses and work animals and shall have yards and corrals as large as possible for health and cleanliness.

134

They shall try as far as possible to have the buildings all of one type for the sake of the beauty of the town.

135

The faithful executors and architects as well as persons who may be deputed for this purpose by the governor shall be most careful in overseeing that the above [ordinances] be executed; and they shall hurry in their labor and building so that the town may be completed in a short time.

136

If the natives should resolve to take a defensive position toward the [new] settlement,[5] they should be made aware of how we intend to settle, not to do damage to them nor take away their lands, but instead to gain their friendship and teach them how to live civilly, and also to teach them to know our God so they learn His law through which they will be saved. This will be done by religious, clerics, and other persons designated for this purpose by the governor and through good interpreters, taking care by the best means available that the town settlement is carried out peacefully and with their consent, but if they [the natives] still do not want to concur after having been summoned repeatedly by various means, the settlers should build their town without taking what belongs to the Indians and without doing them more harm than it were necessary for the protection of the town in order that the settlers are not disturbed.

137

While the town is being completed, the settlers should try, inasmuch as this is possible, to avoid communication and traffic with the Indians, or going to their towns, or amusing themselves or spilling themselves on the ground [sensual pleasures?]; nor [should the settlers] allow the Indians to enter within the confines of the town until it is built and its defenses ready and the houses built so that when the Indians see them they will be struck with admiration and will understand that the Spaniards are there to settle permanently and not temporarily. They [the Spaniards] should be so feared that they [the Indians] will not dare offend them, but they will respect them and desire their friendship. At the beginning of the building of a town, the governor shall name one person who will occupy himself with the sowing and cultivation of the land, planting wheat and vegetables so that the settlers can be assisted in their maintenance. The cattle that they brought shall be put out to pasture in a safe area where they will not damage cultivated land nor Indian property, and so that the aforesaid cattle and its offspring may be of service, help, and sustenance to the town.

138–148

[These last eleven ordinances pertain to the way in which the settlers are to deal with the Indians and convert them to Catholicism as a means of bringing them under the aegis of the Spanish crown.]

138

Having completed the erection of the town and the buildings within it, and not before this is done, the governor and settlers, with great care and holy zeal, should try to bring peace into the fraternity of the Holy Church and bring on to our obedience all the natives of the province and its counties, by the best means they know or can understand, and in the following manner:

139

Obtain information of the diversity of nations, languages, sects, and prejudices of the natives within the province, and about the lords they may pledge obedience to, and by means of commerce and exchange, [the Spaniards] should try to establish friendship with them [the Indians], showing great love and caressing them and also giving them things in barter that will atract their interest, and not showing greediness for their things. [The Spaniards] should establish friendship and alliances with the principal lords and influentials who would be most useful in the pacification of the land.

140

Having made peace and alliance with [the Indian lords] and with their republics, make careful efforts so that they get together, and then [our] preachers, with utmost solemnity, should communicate and begin to persuade them that they should desire to understand matters pertaining to the holy Catholic faith. Then shall begin our teaching [efforts] with great providence and discretion, and in the order stipluated in the first book of the holy Catholic faith, utilizing the mildest approach so as to entice the Indians to want to learn about it. Thus you will not start by reprimanding their vices or their idolatry, nor taking away their women nor their idols, because they should not be scandalized or develop an enmity against the Christian doctrine. Instead, they should be taught first, and after they have been instructed, they should be persuaded that on their own will they should abandon all that runs contrary to our holy Catholic faith and evangelical doctrine.

[Ordinances 141–147 continue with details on how to attract the Indians so that they will accept the Catholic faith. Ordinance 148, the last, reads as follows:]

148

The Spaniards, to whom Indians are entrusted [encomendados], should seek with great care that these Indians be settled into towns, and that, within these, churches be built so that the Indians can be instructed into Christian doctrine and live in good order. Because we order you to see to it that these Ordinances, as presented above, be incorporated, complied with, and executed, and that you make what in them is contained be complied with and executed, and never take action or move against them, nor consent that others take action or move against either their content or form, under penalty of our Lord. Dated in the Woods of Segovia, the thirteenth of July, in the year fifteen hundred and seventy-three. I the King; the Licenciado Otalaza; the Licenciado Diego Gasca de Alazar; the Licenciado Gamboa, the Doctor Gomez de Santillán.

1 Ordinances 117–118 in the original manuscript of the Laws of the Indies. Page 86 is reasonably clear, facilitating translation in this case. (Courtesy of the Archivo General de Indias, Seville)

124

125

126

2 Ordinances 124–126. Page 89 of the Laws of the Indies. Unlike the page shown in figure 1, this page is unclear and points to the difficulties involved in translation. (Courtesy of the Archivo de Indias, Seville)

1 The 1921 Nuttall translation says "thirty two feet wide," the 1922, "three hundred feet wide," indicating that the mistake originates when Mrs. Nuttall copied the Spanish version in Madrid in 1912. The original manuscript of the ordinances was consulted for the present translation, and the measurements given here are the correct ones.

2 In most Latin American cities the plaza is surrounded by porticoes (i.e., colonnades or portals, *portales* in the MS), and often there is a sidewalk (pavement) between these and the street. The plaza, around its rim, also has a sidewalk that coincides in width and is aligned with the sidewalk of the streets that begin at the corners of the plaza. In earlier cities the streets start at the corners of the plaza but are not continuations of the street around the plaza.

3 There is a reversal of ordinances 119 and 120 in the Spanish version copied by Mrs. Nuttall. The original manuscript of the ordinances obtained from the Consejo de Indias in Seville is the source for the order followed here.

4 Some manuscripts say "town" here, but the original says "plaza."

5 The Spanish original is ambiguous here; it reads, "Si los naturales se quisiesen poner en defensa de la población, se les de a entender como se quiere poblar . . . ." Mrs. Nuttall's 1921 translation (p. 752), interprets this to mean, "Should the natives care to place themselves under the defense of the town, they must be made to understand that it is desired to build a town. . . ." However, Mrs. Nuttall's 1922 translation (p. 253) reverses this interpretation as follows: "If the natives should wish to oppose the establishment of a settlement, they are to be given to understand that the settlers desire to build a town. . . ." We have adopted the second meaning because later on in the ordinance it is declared that "if they still do not want to concur. . . ," which would be out of context if the Indians had decided to place themselves *under* the protection of the town in the first place.

There is some confusion concerning the actual sources available to scholars for the study of the city planning ordinances of the Laws of the Indies. The original manuscript is available at the Archivo General de Indias (AGI) in Seville, and it is entitled "Ordenanzas de Descubrimiento, Nueva Población y Pacificación de las Indias, Dadas por Felipe II en 1573." This document is located in the Indiferente General, legajo 247, libro XIX, folio 63–93, in the AGI. The translation is based on a Mexican reprint of this document, which has the advantage of being legible. It was published in Mexico's *Boletín del Archivo General de la Nación* Tomo 6(3) (May–June 1935):321–360, under the title "Fundación de Pueblos en el Siglo XVI." We have checked it against the original manuscript and found no appreciable difference.

This version of the city planning ordinances circulated in the New World until the end of the seventeenth century, when the first completed compilation of the Laws of the Indies was issued by the Council of the Indies in Seville. The 1573 ordinances were in themselves a small compilation in one of the many areas—in this case the planning and building of new towns—for which legislation was dictated for the Indies by the Spanish kings. These ordinances were not entirely new since many had been issued already during the sixteenth century, notably during the reign of Charles V: "Cédula" of 1521;[1] "Nuevas Instrucciones" of 1526; and "Instrucciones y Reglas para Poblar" of 1529.[2] The history of efforts to compile the Council of the Indies legislation is interesting since it explains why Philip II issued the city planning ordinances separately. Their rapid publication was part of their success.

The first efforts to codify the bulk of legislation that had been issued by the Consejo de Indias were started during the reign of Philip II,[3] under the supervision of Juan de Ovando, president of the Supreme Tribunal, but he was not able to complete the task despite his great zeal. Ovando died 8 September 1575. The first two books of his compilation were actually finished at the time of his death, and their subject was the "Spiritual and Temporal Government of the Indies." These two books were never printed, but Philip II later issued much of their content as separate sets of ordinances, and several sections (*títulos*) of the books were actually published: the "Statutes of the Royal Council of the Indies" on 24 September 1571; the ordinances for the "Descripciones" on 3 July 1573; on 13 July of the same year the ordinances on "Descubrimiento, Nueva Población y Pacificaciones" extracted from the second book of Ovando. Finally, on 1 June 1574, the ordinances of the Regio Patronato, taken from title fourteen of the first book, were also issued. The Ovando compilation was never finished, and its plan was abandoned by the Council of the Indies.

In 1582 the Supreme Tribunal entrusted Diego de Encinas, a minor but hard-working official of the Council of the Indies, with the task of gathering the principal legislation relating to the Indies, from the time of discovery to that time. Encinas was somewhat overwhelmed by the task and was only able to put together a collection of *cédulas* and other legal edicts, which were published in four volumes in 1596. Encinas's work is entitled *Provisiones, Cédulas, Capítulos de Ordenanzas, Instrucciones y Cartas, Librados y Despachados por Sus Majestades.*[4] Encinas's *Provisiones* is not a real compilation since he assembled existing documents without eliminating duplication or unnecessary material. The city planning ordinances of 1573 appear in volume four of Encinas's *Provisiones.*

The reign of Philip II ended without achieving the objective of a fully organized body of legislation that could have helped to guide further conquest and population of the Indies. Over the next half-century, only minor efforts at organizing these materials took place—one of them is the *cuadernos* of Diego de Zorrilla, which was not well received and has in fact disappeared. Apparently it was not well done, lacking proper titles and other information. After Zorrilla, the council assigned Rodrigo de Aguiar y Acuña to prepare summaries of these *cuadernos.* The *Sumarios de la Recopilación* were published by Aguiar in 1628 in incomplete form.

In the year 1622, Juan de Villela became president of the Council of the Indies, and a lawyer, Antonio de León Pinelo, who had been working on a compilation of Spanish legislation in Lima, Peru, arrived in Madrid to present his work to the Spanish king. In Madrid he discovered that Aguiar was also working on a general compilation, a task to which he had already dedicated thirteen years. Taking note that Aguiar, who was a member of the council, did not have the necessary time to devote to the work of codification, León Pinelo proceeded to offer his services to the council in a presentation that extolled his own work, of which two books were already completed. The council accepted his offer, thereby resolving Aguiar's problem and giving León Pinelo a free hand. León Pinelo had no other duties, and was totally dedicated to his professional pursuit. He believed that his mission was to codify and revise the laws—summarize them; eliminate from them whatever was repetitious and unnecessary; and fully annotate them as to sources, dates, places, and so forth—with the council assuming responsibility for resolving any difficulties or problems of interpretation. León Pinelo's original plan for the compilation that he had begun in Lima included nine volumes of codified laws. On 19 April 1624, a council decree officially entrusted León Pinelo with the work of the compilation. (The tenth of May 1624 is considered as the official beginning of the codifying work of the council.) León Pinelo started afresh the work of compiling the council's legislation but following his own scheme. He was to devote five more years to it. He left aside all other existing codifications, including Aguiar's work (although presumably still under Aguiar's supervision). But he did have all previous manuscripts at his disposal, including Ovando's and Encinas's. León Pinelo's work advanced rapidly after this point. Aguiar—the superintendent in charge of the work—died in the year 1629 and the council appointed Juan de Solórzano Pereira to replace him. León was not greatly affected by this change, however. He continued his work alone and uninterrupted until 1634 when he agreed to council requests that he finish his work in one year. León Pinelo completed his nine volumes, as promised, on 20 October 1635. He included a list of 600 points of doubt that the council had to resolve before the work could be printed. The council then asked Juan de Solórzano to review León Pinelo's work. Solórzano was also assisted by D. Pedro de Vivanco, who seems to have had a minor part in the revision since he was soon named president of the Casa de Contratación. Solórzano finished his revision in seven months, but the council had to approve it through a careful scrutiny and censorship. This took about two years, ending on or about September 1637. Philip IV then named a special commission to end the revision of León Pinelo's work. This commission included three people: Solórzano, Palafox, and Santelices. León Pinelo's work—following the revisions of 1636—was left intact, and the compilation was now ready for publication. However, there were insufficient funds to publish the work, and León Pinelo died in 1660 with his work still unpublished. A successor to León Pinelo was named, Fernando Jiménez Paniagua, but his contribution to the work which León Pinelo had completed was minimal, although he took credit for the entire work. The *Recopilación de Leyes de los Reynos de las Indias*, ordered to be printed by his Catholic Majesty Charles II, was published in four volumes containing nine books and over 3,000 laws, in Madrid in 1681. Of the 3,300 sets published, 1,646 were sent to the council in Seville for distribution to the Indies, and the other 1,654 remained in Madrid. Of these, 1,326 were sent to the Council of the Indies in 1695. By 1740 only 10 sets remained in Seville.

The next edition of the *Recopilación* was ordered by the Council of the Indies and it was published in 1791 by the widow of Don Joaquín Ibarra, the printer of the council. It is important to note that the principal difference between it and the 1681 edition is that the text is not divided into three volumes but that the nine books remain and that the name of Charles II (by then long deceased) remains (as in the original), in the cover of this new edition.

In both these editions of the *Recopilación*, the city planning ordinances appear in the libro III, títulos IV, V, VI, and VII. León Pinelo organized the ordinances differently and presented them in the following categories: "Concerning Peace Making" (*pacificaciones*), "About the Populations," "About the Discoverers, Peace makers, and Inhabitants," and "About the population of Cities, Villages, and Communities." By this time, most of the important cities of Hispanic America had been founded, and the earlier ordinances, despite their problems of repetition and consistency, had served as the main guide in the founding of new towns.

There is also a doubt concerning the use of the title of "Laws of the Indies" for the 1573 city planning ordinances. Since the *Recopilación* of 1681 was the first complete text of Spanish legislation for the Indies, this work has become generally known as the Laws of the Indies. What we prefer is to accept that all council or royal ordinances are part of the Laws of the Indies and that as long as we include the specific subject and the date, scholars will have no quarrel with this usage, hence the title of this chapter.

Spanish colonization of the New World occupied a vast period of time and extent of territory. The first settlement was made at Hispaniola in the West Indies in 1493, and the last surviving settlements in California in 1781. In North America, Spanish influence is evident from Florida in the east to Louisiana on the Gulf and as far north as St. Louis, and all across the continent to California. The earliest Spanish city of North America, St. Augustine, Florida, was begun in 1565, and was already more than 200 years old when Philip de Neve, governor of Alta California, founded Los Angeles in 1781.[5] During these 200 years, Spanish urban policy had time to grow, develop, and be codified.

Most of the important cities of Latin America were founded between 1506 and 1570 (sixteen of the twenty largest cities were dedicated by 1580), according to a centralized system of royal planning that encouraged concentration of power, wealth, and resources. Rather than creating a system of cities, each principal city was administratively linked to, and thus dependent on, the government in Spain, and trade among them was not encouraged.[6] We still see the fruits of this dependence in the trade and growth patterns of these cities.

The Spaniards defined a city as the urban area plus the neighboring hinterland,[7] a concept that dates back to the Greeks and the Romans. During the colonial period, however, a new emphasis on the relation of smaller towns to their capital city lessened the importance of communication and links with their hinterland. Increasingly, the towns served as gateways of communication with foreign ports.

The Laws of the Indies specified that cities were to "have good access and outlet by sea and by land, and also good roads and passage by water, in order that they may be entered and departed easily with commerce, while bringing relief and establishing defenses," (37).*

This led to cities being founded along the coast, linked to inland cities that acted as loading and storage centers. Some developed as pairs, an old inland city plus a port, such as Caracas and La Guaira, Callao and Lima, and others.[8] The result was a double system, with the old Indian towns of Central America and the Andes competing with the commercial cities of the coast from the colonial and modern periods. According to Violich, the evolution of Latin American cities has gone through four planning periods:[9]

1. Pre-Columbian–Maya, Aztec, and Inca cities—before 1530;
2. Laws of the Indies—ca. 1530–1820;
3. Post-Revolution—1820–1900; and
4. Industrial expansion and European immigration in the twentieth century.

Violich remarks that of these four periods, Inca planning was best. It embraced both physical and socioeconomic planning, and was based on an excellent communication system of roads and bridges and stopping places; and since the welfare of the group was the primary value, the Incas planned development of resources to benefit all.

The Spanish conquest, however, proved enormously successful in developing an urban network, cultural hegemony, social makeup, and physical imprint that was recognizable throughout the New World. The Laws of the Indies were an important planning tool of the Spanish crown for the achievement of these objectives.

It is important to note for our purposes that the Laws of the Indies had a relatively slight impact on North America because these territories were marginal to the Spanish and settlements there were always undermanned and underfinanced.[10] Theoretically, the Laws of the Indies applied to *pueblos* (civic settlements) in North America and not to missions (religious) or presidios (military), neither of the latter being permanent settlements, but in practice there seems to have been little distinction between them in North

---

*All numbers in parenthesis from here on refer to the corresponding ordinance.

America, and often the familiar ordinances were applied equally to all, after a fashion.[11]

While the Spanish crown was in the process of preparing a compilation of existing city planning laws, cities in Hispanic America did not hesitate to supplement decrees from the central government with laws of their own devising. As early as 1534, in Mexico City, we find the municipal government enforcing aesthetic uniformity and being responsible for public hygiene and public utilities such as water supply.[12] Lima in 1553 required walling in of all property, tree planting, street cleaning, washing animals and clothes in restricted areas so as not to contaminate the drinking supply, and separate settlement for Indians with smaller buildings and narrower streets.[13] Even after the promulgation of the laws, cities retained the right to make purely local decisions and to amend and resist the decisions of the central government. As Violich has pointed out, cities were (and are) focal points of the decision-making process. He notes also that the "provision of a physical plant shaped to facilitate this dominance was a matter of critical importance."[14]

A combination of religious zeal with a spirit of adventure characterizes the Spanish conquest. The Spanish kings, aware of the potential wealth and empire-building possibilities in the New World, attempted to orchestrate the slow but steady expansion of Spanish settlements in a way that each act of conquest would result in the effective extension of the highly centralized power structure of the Spanish government. Previous translations of the ordinances have not included the first 100 or so edicts, which are essential to an understanding of the spirit of the enterprise of discovery and settlement undertaken by the Spaniards. The tight centralized controls imposed by the Spanish crown on all New World activities is evident from the first ordinance, which made it clear that the task of discovery was to be carried out in an orderly manner, for who is "found without our license. . .would face a death penalty and loss of all his possessions to our coffers" (1). Only viceroys, royal governors, or other high officials directly responsible to the Spanish crown "can give license to build towns" (1), the most symbolic act of conquest and possesion of new lands.

Throughout the conquest and before decisions were made on sites for settlement, especially as the opening up of the southern regions of the New World proceeded, there was substantial pressure to maintain and keep good records, especially when "there is something to be discovered and pacified, of the wealth and quality, [and] of the peoples and nations who inhabit there" (2) The importance of this point was stressed over and over: "Try to learn about the place, the contents and quality of the land. . . and carefully take note of all you can learn and understand, and always send these narratives to the Governor. . ." (4). The building of towns was to be done in an orderly manner and be tightly controlled: Before discoveries are duly recognized, no new population settlements are permitted" (32); this can only be done in those areas "already discovered, pacified, and subjected to our mandate" (32).

Once a site has been selected for a future new town, "The governor in whose district [the site] is or borders upon should decide whether the site that is to be populated should become a city, town or village settlement" (43). Depending upon the decision, the town would have various types and numbers of officials, such as a mayor or corregidor, "three officers of the Royal Exchequer, twelve magistrates, two executors, two jurors for each parish, one general procurer, one scribe" (43). By contrast, a smaller town would have only "an ordinary mayor, four magistrates, one constable" (43), in all, a much reduced administrative structure. The detail of these administrative arrangements is contained in ordinances 44–108, only some of which are included in the present translation. It is important to note the honors accorded the first settlers of a town: "[As an honor] to them and to their descendants [and in] their laudable memory as founders, we pronounce them *hijosdalgo* [illustrious men of known ancestry]" (99).

In this fashion, an urban elite was created and additional motivation was provided to further the conquest of new regions and the founding of new cities. With fame and status went also the probability of wealth, either by acquiring gold from the natives or from the large tracts of land that first settlers could secure. Important among the many systems of land distribution was the *encomienda*, which later gave rise to the *latifundia* system still predominant in many Latin American countries.

The minimum population size necessary for the beginning of a new settlement was established at "thirty neighbors, each one with his own house, ten cows, four oxen or two oxen and two young bulls and a mare, five pigs, six chickens [and] twenty sheep from Castille" (89). Under some special circumstances as few as "twelve persons [could] be awarded the authorization and territory in accordance with the prescribed conditions" (100). There was concern also with one of the essential conditions of an urban settlement: "permanence" (32); thus when less than the ideal thirty settlers set out to start a new town, this "could be done if at least ten of them were married" (101). Surprisingly little was said in these ordinances about the role of women, perhaps already symbolic of the *machismo* subculture that was to develop throughout Latin America.

Once the governor gave his permission to go ahead with the starting of a new town, he was responsible to "ascertain that those who have made a commitment to settle in a new town comply with the taking of seat in a proper manner" (109). When Francisco Pizarro decided to transfer his capital from Jauja, a cold inhospitable spot that was not appropriate as the permanent capital of Peru, he decided to look for a site that would meet the royal instructions given him by Charles V (earlier but similar ordinances). The soldiers he sent to reconnoiter returned with news of a site on the Rimac River shielded by an ample valley and with lush vegetation. Plantations, especially of maize, had been developed there by the natives in well-irrigated fields. It had woods, and from a neighboring hill a flat expanse—enough for a large city—could be appreciated.[15] Pizarro arrived at the site on 18 January 1535 and named his city "City of Kings." "The Book of the First City Council" ("Libro Primero de Cabildos de la Ciudad de Lima") lists the names of the twelve first settlers (including Pizarro) and gives a detailed account of the founding activities.[16]

These proceedings were repeated over and over again in the founding of towns throughout the New World:

As an act of founding the city, at the church to which the name of Our Lady of the Ascension is given by the governor and captain general of his Majesties, [Pizarro], after indicating the city plan, made and ordered to be built the above-named church, to which effect he placed, with his own hands, the first stone and the first piece of wood in order to take possession for his Majesties of these kingdoms, of the sea and the land, and of future discoveries, after which he proceeded to give *solares* [sites] to the people with him. . . .[17]

The actual plan of Lima was drawn on paper by Don Rodrigo de Agüero, following the king's ordinances. The checkerboard plan was divided into 117 square blocks. The streets of Lima were marked off with a string by Pizarro himself, assisted by his entourage, who seem to have enjoyed the task.

What were the sources that the Spanish government turned to for ideas on laying out the settlements of their new empire?

The heavy dependence of Philip II, as well as his predecessors, on the Roman city planner Vitruvius has been documented by Stanislawski.[18] There is very little doubt that the more complete the ordinances became, the more they relied on Roman principles of city planning. The objectives of conquest and expansion of the Roman Empire and of the sixteenth-century Spaniards were very similar but for one aspect: the strong apostolic mission that infused every step of the Spanish conquest of the New World.

The Roman land-tenure system, as implanted by the Spanish in the New World, was actually a deterrent to urbanization, but the concept of the city plan as a package of necessary elements for the functions of the city—theater, arena, stadium, baths, aqueduct, in the case of the Roman city—had great impact on the Spanish planners.[19]

The ideas of Vitruvius were very influential in the development of sixteenth century urban planning. The manuscript of his *Ten Books on Architecture* had been "rediscovered" in the fifteenth century, and published by Alberti, toward the end of the century. Some of Vitruvius's prescriptions are found almost word for word in Alberti and a century later in the Laws of the Indies.[20]

Let us take site selection as one example of the parallelism of thought. Vitruvius recommended that towns need a healthy site, not misty or frosty, not hot or cold but temperate, avoiding marshes. It is stagnant marshes, he said, that are harmful, but that one may utilize a site in marshes if it has a north or northeast exposure and is above the level of the seashore, so that one may dig drainage ditches and utilize storm water from the sea to kill the harmful marsh creatures.[21] Ordinance 111 of the Laws of the Indies is strikingly similar. Ordinances 35 and 37 parallel Vitruvius's remarks (book I, chapter IV) that the site that enables food to be grown locally is best, especially if serviced by good roads, rivers, or a seaport. With but slight reordering, Alberti made many of the same recommendations: "Earth and water can be improved," he tells us in book I, chapter III, "but not air." The Alps and the desert were not recommended, but rather an area with all the necessities of life and good transportation facilities in all seasons. The site was to be neither moist nor parched, though cold and dry were preferrable to warm and moist. This compares well with ordinance 34, which states the same requirements almost word for word.

Other important Vitruvian ideas were totally ignored, however, such as his ideal street pattern, a radial plan with the eight main streets laid out according to the prevailing winds and converging on a central plaza. This ideal was adapted and modified by Alberti, but not included by the more pragmatic Spaniards in their ordinances, probably because radial streets would be too difficult for amateurs to lay out.

Vitruvius wrote at a time when the Roman Empire had been founding colonial towns for at least three centuries, basing their practice on theories drawn from Greek experience going back at least to the seventh century B.C. (figure 3) Thus, the Laws of the Indies are based on elements of a Renaissance philosophy of city planning whose origins date back to earliest planning traditions of classical times. But, whereas this philosophy could not be applied to the Old World in the sixteenth century, the New World provided a set of unparalleled opportunities.

Of all the decisions the Spaniards had to make in the urban development of the New World, none was more important than site selection. Thus, a substantial number of ordinances were concerned with the criteria for selecting "an appropriate site to be settled by Spaniards" (3). Geographical maps and inventories were essential first steps in identifying places and ports suitable for Spanish settlements (5). Part of the task was to "name each land, each province, and the mountains and principal rivers" (14). Site to be considered "should have good access and outlet by sea and by land, and also good roads and passage by water" (37). Defense was also a consideration, especially in seaside locations: "Do not select sites for towns in maritime locations because of the danger that exists of pirates" (41). When harbor sites were available, the settlers were to "select for settlement only those that are necessary for the entry of commerce and for the defense of the land" (41). The question of immediate survival was also important, as the first year the settlers could not expect supplies from elsewhere. Thus, at the site there had to be "sufficient public land and grounds for pastureation where the cattle the neighbors are expected to bring with them can obtain abundant feed" (90). Ordinance 111 summarized the necessary or ideal site conditions for the new towns: "an elevated and healthy location; with means of fortification; fertile soil. . .; fuel, timber, and resources; fresh water, a native population, ease of transport, access and exit; open to the north wind." The winds were thought to be enormously important in determining layout. The plaza was to be situated so that "the four corners. . .face the four principal winds, because in this manner, the streets running from the plaza will not be exposed to the four principal winds, which would cause much inconvenience" (114). Since strong recommendations were made for the selection of elevated sites, which are windier, the combination of these two criteria made good sense.

Inland towns should "be built if possible on the shore of a navigable river, and attempts should be made to place the town on the side from which the cold north wind blows and that buildings that cause filth be placed on the side of the river or sea below the town" (123). Indeed, many cities in Latin America are built on the banks of rivers (to name a few: Santiago (Chile) on the Mapocho; Asunción (Paraguay) on the Paraguay; Buenos Aires (Argentina) on the Rio de la Plata; and, Guayaquil (Ecuador) on the Guayas).

As early as the second ordinance, one of the most frequent concerns of the conquest was expressed: the possibility of abusing or treating badly the native population of the New

World. Those who were to carry out discoveries were to do so "without injury to the natives" (2). The objective was to "pacify" the Indians "so they be secure" (3), that is, subject to Spanish control and obedience. The same considerations were to guide the steps in selecting "the site to build a town. . .without harm to the Indians for having occupied the area" (38). While the town was going up, "the settlers should try, inasmuch as this is possible, to avoid communication and traffic with the Indians, or going to their towns" (137). Having sexual intercourse and amusing oneself with Indians in any way was prohibited, as was taking Indians aboard ships, which was to be punished by death (24).

The concern for the Indians reflected a more serious concern for the Spaniards themselves, and their welfare and safety prompted a thorough consideration in the ordinances of the environment in which they might settle. For example, settlers were instructed to take "into consideration the health of the area, which will be known from the abundance of old men or of young men of good complexion" (34). Among the environmental factors to be weighed in making a decision were "healthy fruits"; "no toxic and noxious things"; "good climate"; "air pure and soft"; "good temperature" without excessive "heat or cold" (34). Further instructions had to do with the type of land: its crops and its potential for a good harvest and other agricultural qualities. Of course, the essential environmental resource necessary for the success of any human settlement, a "good and plentiful water supply for drinking and irrigation" (35), was not forgotten.

A great deal of the decision-making concerning site selection, then, was made to secure environmental health. This made particularly good sense given the climatic, topographical, and general geographical diversity that the New World offered. "Do not select sites," the settlers were instructed, "that are too high up because these are affected by winds, and access and service to these are difficult, nor in lowlands, which tend to be unhealthy; choose places of medium elevation" (40). One of the more interesting clauses concerns the location of river towns. These should be built " on the eastern bank, so when the sun rises it strikes the town first, then the water" (40). Since many market areas were near the water, early shoppers would have been blinded by the rising sun as it hit the water first. Settlers were also urged to avoid areas subject to fogs (40).

This concern for the health and welfare of the inhabitants of the new towns, implicit in the attention to environment, is quite explicit throughout Philip's ordinances. There are provisions for "hospitals for the poor and those sick of noncontagious diseases" as well as for a "hospital for the sick with contagious diseases [that] shall be built in such a way that no harmful wind blowing through it may cause harm to the rest of the town" (121). As in the siting of the town (123), the influence of the winds in selecting the directions of streets or the locations of certain facilities was of prime importance: "The [hospital] for contagious diseases shall be built in an area where the cold north wind blows, but arranged in such a way that it may enjoy the south wind" (124). In addition, houses and other buildings were to be placed so as to avoid bad winds and enjoy good ones "in such a manner that when living in them they [the occupants] may enjoy the air of the south and north as these are the best" (133).

In the political organization of the new cities, the Laws of the Indies drew upon Spanish experience in the reconquest of Spain from the Moors.[22] In fact, the Iberians became a municipal people during the reconquest. As the reconquest proceeded, a set of municipal ordinances that proved workable for Toledo in the twelfth century was then transferred to Seville in the thirteenth, becoming eventually the basis of municipal legislation for the New World (figure 4). The Spanish experience of reconquest also enfused their conquest of the New World with a desire to transplant Spanish culture, principally its Catholic doctrine. Thus, new settlements were to be built in areas "populated by Indians and natives to whom we can preach the gospels since this is the *principal objective* [italics added] for which we mandate that these discoveries and settlements be made" (36).

The most successful road to the acculturation of natives was seen to be through religious indoctrination: "Having made peace and alliance with [the Indian lords]. . . make careful efforts so that they get together, and then [our] preachers, with utmost solemnity, should communicate and begin to persuade them that they should desire to

understand matters pertaining to the holy Catholic faith"
(140). The Spanish settlers planned their townscapes in
part to reinforce the more subtle activities of Indian conversion to Catholicsm by the physical impressiveness of
the buildings. Of these, the one designed to impress the
natives the most was the main cathedral, which was to be
built according to precise specifications that would result
in it "acquiring more authority" (124). Just as the former
Moorish sites in Spain had been taken over, transformed,
and Christianized, so too in the New World, Indian sites
were reused, expressing the dominance of the new culture
over the old. This even went so far, in Mexico City for
example, as the substitution of the new cathedral for the
old Temple of the Sun, on the same foundations and made
from the same stones.

The almost rectangular Tenochtitlan, the Aztec capital,
agreed fully with the Renaissance ideals of city planning
that the conquerors brought with them much more than
it did with their own experience in the medieval cities of
Spain. Once they had had the opportunity of living in a
regularized city, they went on to establish this as the norm
for colonial settlement. In his narrative of life in the Americas at the time of the arrival of the Spaniards, Bernal Díaz
tells us about Tenochtitlan:

The plan of the city, shows the original area divided into
four symmetrical parts. Each ward contained a variable
number of subdivisions, remnants of an older organization, based on clans, on which the imperial state had been
superimposed. The boundaries of the four original wards
met at a central point, which was the area occupied by the
great temple, the imperial palaces, and the homes of some
of the lords. From each of the four gates of the enclosure
of the great temple, there ran a street that marked one of
the boundaries of the wards. Three of these streets became
causeways built of stone and supported by rows of stakes
driven into the lake bottom, and thus they crossed the
water to the mainland.[23]

Tenochtitlan was, then, a very orderly city, laid out on
a quadrangular plan. It has not been well understood by
modern historians that this great Aztec city had been built
following a pattern that contained elements that would
later be the essence of Spanish city planning. Tenochtitlan
was planned with care; a public official was responsible
for ensuring that the houses were duly aligned along the

streets and canals, so that these would be straight, with well-defined boundaries.

Tenochtitlan made a great impression on the conquerors. This is evident from Diaz's writings:

And when we saw so many cities and villages built in the water and other great towns on dry land and that straight and level causeway going towards Mexico, we were amazed and said that it was like the enchantments they tell of in the legend of Amadis, on account of the great towers and temples and buildings rising from the water, and all built of masonry. And some of our soldiers even asked whether the things that we saw were not a dream.

Tenochtitlan, built on a lake, had filled-in land between the original islands and had grown to about five square miles by 1521. By calculating the available land surface and the amount of tribute collected by the Aztec Empire, Díaz believed that it must have had about 80,000 inhabitants. Ignacio Bernal comments, "This number, which seems so low today, is greater than that of the majority of *contemporary* European cities, since only four of these— Paris, Naples, Venice, and Milan—had more than 100,000 inhabitants. The largest Spanish city, Seville, had only 45,000 in 1530."[24] Therefore, it was not an exaggeration on the part of the conquerors that they were impressed by Tenochtitlan's size and beauty, as this statement by Díaz indicates:

Some of the soldiers among us, who had been in many parts of the world, in Constantinople and all over Italy, in Rome, said that so large a market-place and so full of people, and so well regulated and arranged, they had never beheld before.

The first instructions concerning the building of towns in the New World were given in 1513 to Pedrarias Dávila, "the first Spaniard to arrive in America with precise royal orders regarding the setting out of cities. . . ."[25] The grid plan, which was to have a great deal of influence and be the most salient characteristic of numerous towns throughout Spanish America, was already contained in these instructions. They were applied first to old Panama City: "Let the city lots be regular from the start, so that once they are marked out the town will appear well ordered as to the place which is left for a plaza, the site for the church and the sequence of the streets; for in places newly established proper order can be given from the start. . . ."[26]

Thus, there is little question that after the haphazard settlements developed during the earlier stages of the conquest, the Spanish kings, as Stanislawski has remarked, "finally realized the necessity for a plan, and for this [they] turned to [their] neighbors [Italy, France], and beyond them to the Roman and Greek sources from which they had profited."[27] In a later article, he remarked that "the instructions to Pedrarias Dávila *imply* [italics added] the use of the grid plan" and that "the lack of a definite and detailed description of the grid may be the reason for its failure to appear in the New World for years after these instructions were given."[28] As the conquest proceeded, the instructions became clearer. These were modelled after classical Roman practice and had been tried in Spain by Ferdinand and Isabella, first in Santa Fe, about ten miles from Granada, built as a fortified rectangle intersected by the crossing of two perpendicular axes and approached by four cardinal gates[29] (figures 8 and 9). Later, only a few years before Columbus's first voyage, the Catholic kings built Puerto Real, their royal port, which "followed the same layout though in a larger scale" than Santa Fe.[30]

These are both gridiron plans, and both may have been influenced by the semimilitary bastide towns of southern France, which go back to the thirteenth century[31] (figure 7). Both the French and the Spanish examples share a context of military necessity that made rational organization more important than organic growth. Something of this necessity seems to have been transferred to the urban foundations of the New World, and accounts perhaps for the similarity of form.

Some fifty years later, Philip II's ordinances strongly reinforced both the importance of the plaza as starting point and the use of rectangular blocks for the laying out of new towns. For example, ordinance 112 stated, "The main plaza is to be the starting point for the town; . . . [it] should be square or rectangular, in which case it should have at least one and a half its width for length"; ordinances 114 and 117 reinforced the matter: "From the plaza shall begin four principal streets: One [shall be] from the middle of each side [as in the case of Guatemala City], and two streets from each corner of the plaza" (114); "The streets shall run from the main plaza" (117). Meanwhile, in Europe, Philip II had built the monastic town of San Lorenzo el Real del Escorial, begun in 1563, and one of the greatest and most regular of such cities.[32] The success of this venture was undoubtedly fresh in the king's mind as he directed the settlement of the New World.

In the New World, the first successful use of the grid was at Mexico City, where the existing foundations and street pattern from the Indian period were already arranged in a grid. The Spanish surveyor Alonso Garcia Bravo, who drew up the plan, seems to have known also about Vitruvian principles of classical planning, as planners of the mid-sixteenth century routinely turned to Vitruvius as their oracle.[33] Smith remarked that "in devising their plan the Spaniards were obeying the trend established by Italian humanists of the 15th century, who revived in theory, if not in fact, the orderly layout of classical cities, for none of their designs were actually carried out. Men like Alberti and Filarete based their plans for ideal cities upon the monumental concept they obtained from reading the text of Vitruvius . . . but they used these features on a radial rather than a grid iron basis."[34] Smith concluded that "none of the town plans of the Italian humanists which came to be known in Spain by the early years of the sixteenth century can be considered precise models for the master plan of the Laws of the Indies."[35] Smith assumed, as have many others, that Virtuvius advocated the use of the grid, but in fact that grid was not the latter's preferred plan, although it had an important place in both Greek and Roman planning practice. Vitruvius actually recommended a radial city plan. It seems that the Spanish crown required that the ancient sources be studied directly by the architects but with greater concern for orderliness and imperial expansion than for Renaissance refinements. Thus the ordinances drafted by the Spanish advisors on city building were closer to Roman practice and, undoubtedly, attractive to a crown bent on efficient conquest.

The grid system of city planning had been introduced into Spain during the Roman conquest of the Mediterranean. "Dozens of Spain's major cities can attribute at least their cores to Roman planners. . . . Among them are Merida and Zaragoza, whose very names are mere contractions of their Roman names, Emerita Augusta and Caesar Augusta."[36] The later application of classical principles to

Santa Fe de Granada and Puerto Real gave real evidence to the Spanish planners involved in drafting and compiling the city planning ordinances of the Laws of the Indies, of the practical worth of these ideas—their foolproof application and their simplicity—and this would explain their indifference to Renaissance innovations. Moreover, in understanding Spain's conservative attitude, it must not be forgotten that, unlike the other Renaissance states, Spain was embarked on a colonial venture for which there was no other precedent but the Roman experience. The Spanish colonist, the man who would build new cities, the dreamer/adventurer in search of fame and fortune, needed a standard, a format, a set of guidelines readily understandable and readily applicable to a variety of environments. The Roman formula for imperial expansion provided a suitable model. In particular the Spanish crown needed an urban model of proven merit and found it in the Roman grid with central open space.

We think the grid was chosen because it had worked well for the Romans and also because it can be easily applied by people without any previous experience in the founding or laying out of cities. No special symbolic significance is or should be attached to the gridiron plan; rather, it should be seen as one of the more practical elements of a cluster of ingredients that were being implemented in a more or less standard form by those defining the future urban shape of the New World.

The Laws of the Indies—in particular, ordinances 115–118—include details concerning town layout but do not actually prescribe street patterns. Apparently, the pervasive grid was adopted spontaneously as the simplest way to carry out the laws' provisions, and came to be universally applied as if it had been required (figure 10). Thus a gridiron or checkerboard plan resulted from the combined application of royal edicts and the perceived advantages of such a plan.[37]

In Spain itself, different city forms had developed in response to different conditions (figure 5). The military towns of the earlier period, in the shape of forts with a simple church at the center, gave way after the reconquest (from about 1248 on) to a more elaborate form with the large cathedral dominating the city, the municipal palace nearby, and more direct streets leading to them from the gates. This urban form found support in the writings of Vitruvius and Alberti, who both grouped the principal temple (church), government buildings, granary, treasury, and arsenal at the center of the city, and from a number of sixteenth-century treatises on fortification (some based on Roman texts or surviving Roman examples) that recommended a checkerboard plan with an open plaza at the center.[38] These ideas were followed in the New World cities laid out according to the Laws of the Indies (ordinances 120, 121, 124, and 126).

The town that resulted from these ideas was both flexible and expandable, largely because no buildings at the city edge had a specific function. No markets or storehouses were sited at the periphery. At first, the settlement had only one focus, the plaza. Commerce took little space, being considered a necessary evil rather than a reason for existence; its facilities were modest and at first only temporary. These ephemeral arrangements eventually gave way to more permanent ones, however, as the city grew, and commerce began to invade the buildings around the plaza and along the adjacent streets. Also associated with urban growth was the expansion of the various religious orders, which increased their urban holdings by bequests and by requesting land from the town councils. The poverty of some of these new settlements was reflected in the very slow gain of municipal wealth, typified by the early history of Santa Fe. Many new settlements were very slow to build a town hall, a slaughter house, or a jail. Few of them were walled, at least at first, although questions of defense were a great concern of the Laws of the Indies (ordinances 37, 41, 120, and 133).

The importance of the main plaza in the history of the cities and towns of Hispanic America cannot be overemphasized, for its role as the center of civic life has endured ever since its creation as the pivotal space around which the entire town's plan evolved. Indeed, from the early days of the Spanish conquest, the plaza was a center for secular, religious, political, social, and other ceremonial activities, so that it was not merely the point of convergence of main streets, but was also the point at which civic identity was expressed (figure 11). In fact, there was no better symbol of a town's stature than its plaza and the buildings that framed it. And at the center of small and poor settlements, the plaza reflected not only their wealth but also their hopes, or, rather, the hopes of the central government about their future development.[39] The ordinances spared no detail in defining the role of the plaza; it "should be at the center of the town" (112), or in port cities be "placed at the landing place" (112), and it should be rectangular because "this shape is best for fiestas in which horses are used" (112). It should also be large in scale and "proportioned to the number of inhabitants [of the town]" (113), but conforming to minimum and maximum lengths and widths: "not less than two hundred feet wide and three hundred feet long, nor larger than eight hundred feet long and five hundred and thirty-two feet wide" (113). Surrounding the plaza were to be porticoes (115), and "the temple [cathedral] in inland places shall not be placed on the square but at a distance" (124).

The placing of the cathedral or main church has been the subject of considerable controversy. Smith believed that there seems to be a discrepancy between the codified instructions and the actual practice because the laws specifically direct that the cathedral was to be erected not in the principal square, but "in some separate and prominent place."[40] Gakenheimer argued correctly that the problem is linguistic and the confusion due to poor translations.[41] Ordinance 124 stated that the cathedral "shall not be placed on the square," but nowhere did it advise that the cathedral should be built at any other location not immediately adjoining. In practice, most main cathedrals and churches in Hispanic American towns (with rare exceptions), are built on sites surrounding the main plaza. Several ordinances dealt with this point; for instance, ordinance 119 stated that "the temple of the principal church, parish, or monastery. . .shall be assigned to specific lots; the first after the streets and plazas have been laid out" (119). "[It] shall be separated from any nearby building . . . and ought to be seen from all sides" (124), and "efforts should be made that it be somewhat raised from ground level in order that it be approached by steps" (124).

Secular buildings such as those housing the council or the *cabildo* were to be built "next to the main plaza", but "in a manner that would not embarrass the temple but add to its prestige" (124). The strong link between plazas and churches as natural complements of built-up and open spaces is clearly stated in the ordinances: "Here and there in the town, smaller plazas . . . shall be laid out, where the temples associated with the principal church . . . can be built" (118). However, the directive that really settles the matter as to the use of the space around the square and the siting of the main church is ordinance 126, which reads that: "in the plaza [read: around the plaza], no lots shall be assigned to private individuals; instead, they shall be used for the building of the church and royal houses."

Finally, a word should be said about the nature of civic life in these early towns. There is no doubt that the plan worked and that it created the psychological security it intended. But there was a gap between the plan for settlement and the settler's reality. The effort to get organized and build from nothing was strenuous. Add to this unfriendly Indians, hostile environments, cold climates in the mountain areas, and the uncertainty of a future in a vast unknown continent. To people in these circumstances, untrained city builders at best, the ordinances must have been a practical "how to" manual of procedure that they followed willingly and enthusiastically. Morse argued that this enthusiasm or drive "was externally induced by threats of foreign attack upon coastal cities, by deprivation from famine, and by geographical isolation.[42] These threats were recognized by Philip and his advisors, who stated that "at the beginning of the building of a town, the governor shall name one person who will occupy himself with the sowing and cultivation of the land" (137). The case of Buenos Aires, which was founded for the second time in 1580, reveals some of the hardships involved: "Its penurious inhabitants often went without salt, oil, vinegar, and even wine for Mass."[43] In spite of hardships, life went on, cities prospered, the Spanish grip over the newly conquered territories strengthened, and by the seventeenth century, an alien urban culture was well entrenched throughout the area of domination extending up to St. Louis in North America and down to Buenos Aires and Santiago in the Southern Hemisphere.

Among southern cities, Lima, founded by Pizarro, had particular importance as the capital and commercial center of such a vast and rich territory as Peru. By the seventeenth century, the city could count among its inhabitants an assortment of Frenchmen, Italians, Germans, Flemish, Greeks, Dalmatians, Genoese, English, Hindus, and Chinese. Life was always gay and commerce thrived. One of the first accounts of early Lima is an anonymous document written by a Portuguese Jew and addressed to the Dutch States. This man had lived in Lima for over fifteen years during the early part of the seventeenth century and had been married to the granddaughter of a well-known physician in town. His picture of Lima reveals some aspects of life in these early times.[44] "There were numerous fiestas and processions, and a great deal of dancing that made much noise and was accompanied by instruments and inventions that do not exist in any city in Spain, nor are there streets with such riches and wealth." The palace of the viceroy is also described as

containing great luxury in its interior, [and] was built around two enormous courts, one to the east where a staircase ascended to the Viceroy's private rooms, which were permanently guarded by thirty uniformed guards. . . . Also around the east court were the Viceroy's chapel and the offices of the treasury. In front of the palace there was a garden, and behind the palace the servants' quarters. . . . In the center of the plaza was a water fountain of stone, to the east the cathedral could be seen, which was ugly by comparison to the principal church of Seville [after which the cathedral was actually modeled], but which had many side chapels and was decorated with much gold and silver. . . .

He described life in the bustling streets of Lima, among which the most important was, as it still is today,

that of the Merchants (Calle de Mercaderes), which began from the plaza going south between the porticoes of the Scribes and that of the Haberdashers. In this street there were at least forty stores, filled with merchandise from the world over. Here was the commercial center of Peru, and there were merchants who had a working capital of over a million pesos . . . and who invested their money in Spain, and in Mexico, and other parts, even entering in business with Great China.

By no means were the colonial towns replicas of the usual Spanish city type—mainly because there was no basic Spanish city type, but rather a proliferation of types. What the Laws of the Indies did was to incorporate familiar elements into an organized plan that would be easily applied to a variety of terrains by unskilled city builders. For example, the plaza was an important feature of the towns of Spain and the Western Hemisphere, but in different ways. In Spain there were several kinds of plazas: the market, the "organic", and the monumental. From the eleventh century on, market plazas had grown up at sites outside the gates. These tended to be irregular. Irregularity was also a characteristic of the organic plazas, which were integral parts of slowly developed communities. Historically, monumental plazas were laid out in the great cities, particularly in Castille. These had little or no functional relation to the streets, having been carved out of the urban fabric and typically being closed. First of this type was the plaza at Valladolid, 1592. It had the town hall on one side, and no other public building; it was not adjacent to a cathedral or church. The plaza had a ceremonial use, for executions, *autos de fe*, bullfights, and festivals, but did not have a daily social function (figure 15).[45] In contrast, the New World plaza, built according to the Laws of the Indies, was much like the organic plaza in having functional attributes that made it an integral and central part of the new community, but it was more regular and geometric. Thus by design it bore a relation to the street system, to which it was linked at the corners and, in a few cases (for example Guatemala City), from the middle of each side as well (ordinance 114). The principal church and civic buildings were deliberately laid out along its edges (ordinances 118, 119, 121). Further, the plaza was an essential part of the daily life of the community and was used for the evening promenade and many other activities. Often, the market was set up in this plaza, rather than being relegated to the outer edge of town (compare with figure 5).

The laws prescribed a Vitruvian orientation of the plaza. Ordinance 114 was explicit on this point. In Hispanic America, streets spread out from a square or oblong central plaza and intersect at right angles, forming rectangular blocks of great neatness, much like small midwestern communities in the United States. Foster noted that the grid's principal characteristics exemplify the new cultural forms that are not traditional in the donor country, but which are called into being as a result of contact [with the Indian cultures of the New World]. The "grid-plan" or "chess-board" design which marks nearly all Spanish American communities is the most striking example of this. Most Spanish towns are relatively formless. In Spanish America, however, streets radiate from a square or oblong central plaza and intersect at right angles to form rectangular blocks of great neatness, much like small mid-western communities in the United States. Usually, the important buildings face the plaza: church or cathedral, municipal hall, homes of important political and religious leaders, and other structures central to the life of the inhabitants. Commercial life takes place in coffee shops or on the benches of the plaza itself, and in the late afternoon and evening people come to stroll and relax, to greet friends, or to court. In villages and small towns, a periodic market may be held in the plaza, while in larger communities a separate square, often covered, shelters a daily market.[46]

Foster also pointed out that the emerging culture of the New World, characterized by its application of a generalized value system appeared almost as strange to those who had emigrated from Spain as to the native Indians. In fact, the very multiplicity of Spanish cultures made such standardization and codification necessary in dealing with the new environment. The city planning ordinances of the Laws of the Indies contributed significantly to the establishment of this generalized value system by mandating the use of a viable and enduring physical form.

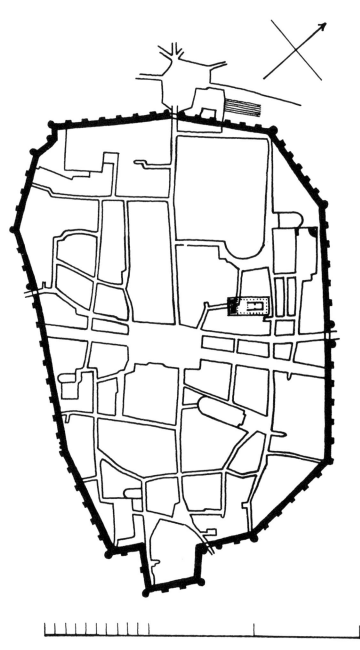

3 The Roman core of Barcelona, Spain. The regular Roman street and block pattern is still discernible today. Such extant Roman cities were one source of Spanish urban ideas at the time of the Renaissance. (Reprinted, by permission, from E. Gutkind, *International History of City Development*, vol. 3, New York: The Free Press, 1967, p. 218. Copyright 1967 by The Free Press, a division of Macmillan Publishing Co., Inc.)

4 Islamic street pattern of Toledo, Spain. Medieval street pattern with "organic" quality that developed during centuries of Moorish occupation. Islamic culture placed a high value on the privacy of the home, which is designed to present a blank, planar wall to the street; this quality of the urban landscape was transferred to the conquering Spaniards, and from them to their American possessions (compare figure 29). Perhaps more important, sets of municipal laws that served well at Toledo were transferred to Seville and from there to the American colonies. (Reprinted by permission from E. Gutkind, *International History of City Development*, vol. 3, New York: The Free Press, 1967. Copyright by The Free Press, a division of Macmillan Publishing Co., Inc.)

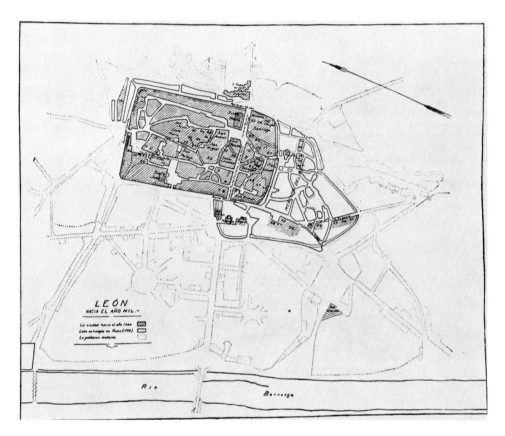

5 Expansion pattern at Leon, Spain. The oldest city is shaded. Outside the gate to the right, an informal market under the king's special protection was eventually formalized with a colonnade. The quarter around the market was later included within the circuit of walls. At the bottom of the plan, the same process seems to be repeating. As commerce became more important toward the end of the Middle Ages, the densely built-up towns could not allow enough space for it within their walls, so this add-on solution was frequent. In addition, merchants who were often strangers were therefore almost "enemies" and needed to be kept outside the wall, in their own quarter. (Reprinted by permission from E. Gutkind, *International History of City Development,* vol. 3, New York: The Free Press, 1967, p. 217. Copyright by The Free Press, a division of Macmillan Publishing Co., Inc.

6 Plaza Mayor in Pedraza, Spain. Portals made of logs were used around
the plazas of small and poor towns in Spain as well as in the frontier
settlements of New Spain. Compare with figures 29, 30. (Reprinted by
permission from E. Gutkind, *International History of City Development*,
vol. 3, New York: The Free Press, 1967, p. 389. Copyright by The Free
Press, a division of Macmillan Publishing Co., Inc.)

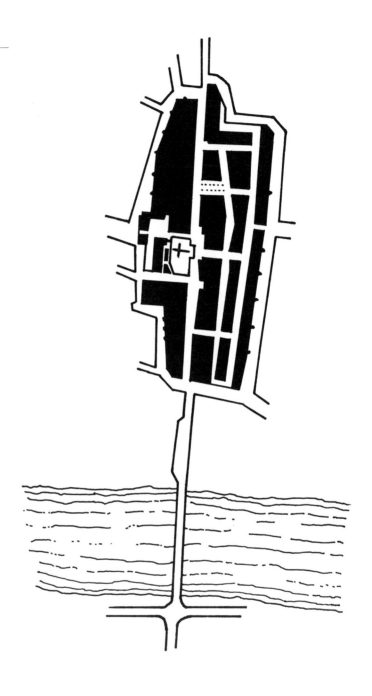

7 Santo Domingo de la Calzada, Spain, a bastide town. Built in the first half of the eleventh century. Military necessity required that the town be built quickly; the regular form is the result of this requirement. Such Spanish and French bastides were another source of Spanish urban ideas, reinforced by Renaissance preference for rational and geometric forms. (Reprinted by permission from G. M. Foster, *Culture and Conquest: The American Spanish Heritage,* New York: Viking Fund Publication Anthropology, Quadrange Books, 1960, plan 1)

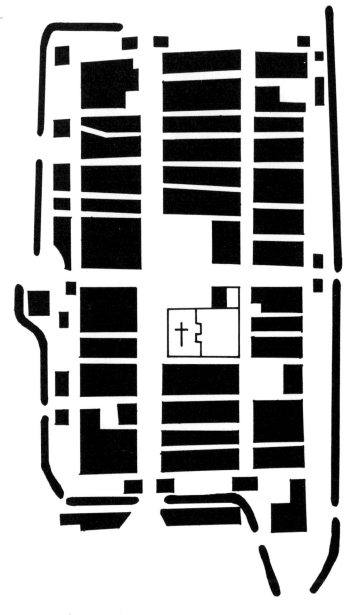

8,9 View of Santa Fe de Granada, Spain. At left, the plan; and at right, an aerial view of the Plaza Mayor and main church. This town was built in 1491 by Isabel and Ferdinand, as a fortress town. Its regular plan and the relation between church and plaza became important models for the new cities of the Spanish colonial period. (Plan from G. M. Foster, *Culture and Conquest*. New York: Viking Funds, 1960, plan 5. View from E. Gutkind, *International History of City Development*, vol. 3, New York: The Free Press, 1967, p. 217. Copyright The Free Press. Both reprinted by permission)

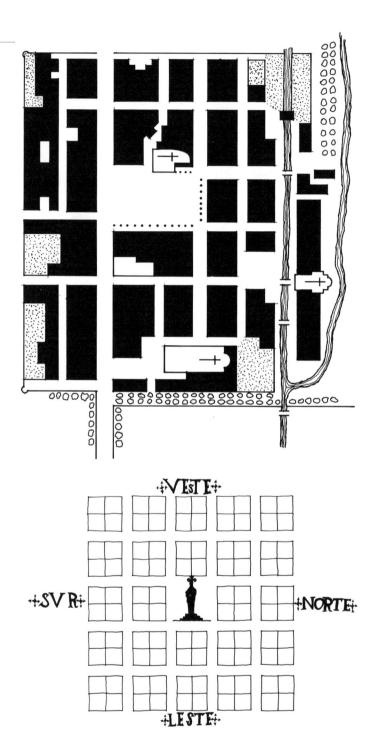

10 Plan of Santiago, Chile. Plan of the city center with porticoed plaza and church flanking the open space. This plan seems to be derived from that of Santa Fe de Granada (see figure 8). The church here is located in a position of honor next to but not "in" the plaza. (Redrawn from G. M. Foster, *Culture and Conquest,* New York: Viking Fund, 1960)

11 Mendoza, Argentina. Plan with statue at the center of the plaza, the kind of emblem that residents could identify with as symbolizing their city. The grid pattern was ubiquitous in Spanish colonial cities; often the names of the owners were written on the houselots (compare figures 44, 48, 56). (Redrawn from G. M. Foster, *Culture and Conquest,* New York: Viking Fund, 1960)

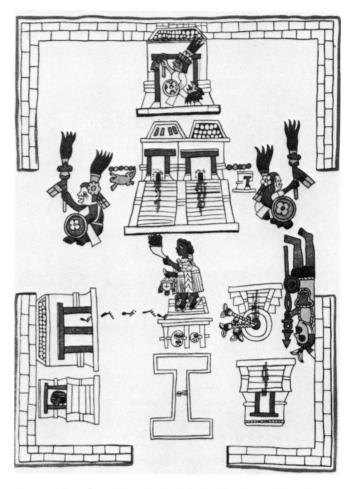

12,13,14 Main plaza at Tenochtitlan/Mexico City. Figure 12 is a fifteenth century drawing by an Indian artist. The artistic brevity and vigor of this plan may be contrasted with the official and probably professional plans of 1562–1566 (figure 13) and of 1596 (figure 14). Kubler (who printed figure 13 in the *Art Bulletin* 24) characterized the plaza of Mexico City as "symmetrical, harmonious and monumental" and asserts that "public plazas of this character do not occur in the medieval towns of Europe." At Tenochtitlan, "four wide boulevards led to the walled temple precinct, with its fortified gateways. The temple enclosure itself was surrounded by monumental palaces and public buildings." R. C. Smith (who printed figure 14 in the *Journal of the Society of Architectural Historians* 14) wrote, "One side was occupied by the cathedral which was in course of construction from 1563 to 1665. Adjacent to it at the east rose the palace of Cortes which took the place of that of Montezuma. The other two sides were filled with buildings having ground-storey colonnades, the *portales* of the merchants. . . . At the four angles of the main plaza of Mexico City appear the eight broad streets that were specified in the Laws." Thus the ideal civic center of the Italian Renaissance was found actually in existence in the Indian capital of Mexico. (Figure 12, D. Angulo, *Historia del arte hispano-americano,* I, Barcelona, 1945, figure 92; figures 13 and 14 courtesy of the Archivo General de Indias, Seville)

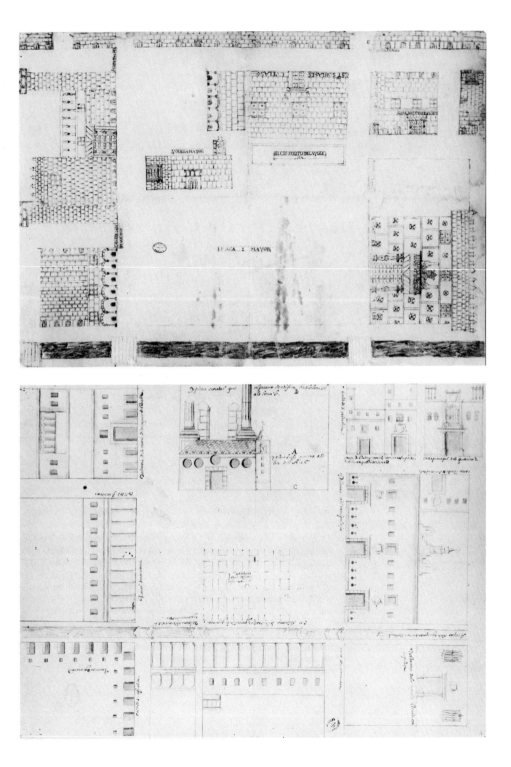

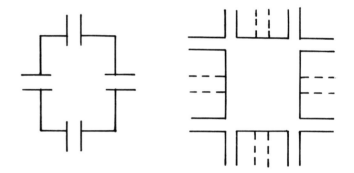

OLD WORLD TYPE   NEW WORLD TYPE

15 Diagram by the authors of Old and New World plazas. In the Old
World plaza, at left, streets would penetrate the middle of the sides; such
plazas had to be carved out of the existing urban fabric, which was
sometimes done in the seventeenth century, or might be added to the
town by being placed outside the walls (compare with figure 5). In the
New World, by contrast, the streets usually branch off from the corners,
at right angles; the ordinances call for important streets to enter at the
center of each side, but this does not occur in any of the provincial
examples we have studied. Note that the corners of the plaza were
supposed to point toward the cardinal directions, so that the winds would
enter the square from northeast, southwest, and so forth, as did the
streets, thus mitigating their harshness.

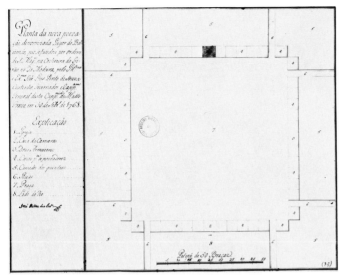

16 Plan of Balsemao, Brazil, 1768. Ordinance 115 requires that "the eight streets running from the plaza at the four corners shall open on the plaza without encountering these portals, which shall be kept back in order that there may be sidewalks even with the streets and plaza". Here in a surprising provincial example from Brazil we see one, extreme way to keep the arcades back, namely, by notching into the surrounding blocks, having then the eight streets enter separately and in fact intersect within the space of the plaza. Common Renaissance tradition works itself out somewhat differently in the northeast of Brazil than the frontier of North America. (Reprinted courtesy of R. Delson, from *New Towns for Colonial Brazil,* University Microfilms Internal, 1979, figure 10)

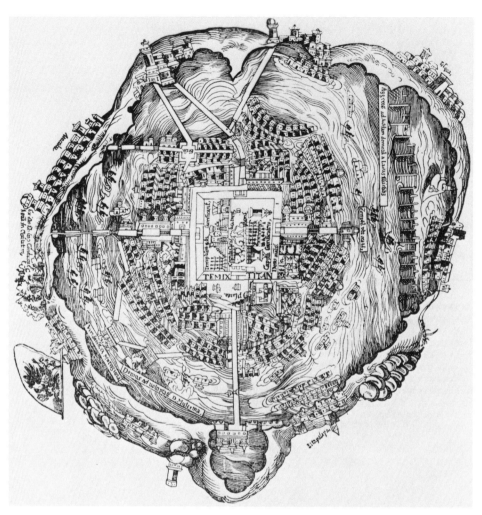

17 Plan of Mexico City, 1524, possibly by Albrecht Durer. Apparently based on the Cortés plan of 1521–1522. The clarity of the Indian city pattern inspired this version, which is embellished, however, with very European late medieval towered castles around the edge. At the center, Durer depicts the great plaza (compare with figures 12, 13, 14), to which roads from the mainland arrive from north, west, and south. The orderly rows of houses described by the conquistadors are plainly visible, as in the dike at right that separated fresh from brackish water. (D. Angulo, *Historia del arte hispano-americano*, I , Barcelona, 1945, figure 542; reprinted from *La Preclada Narratione di Ferdinando Cortese*, 1524)

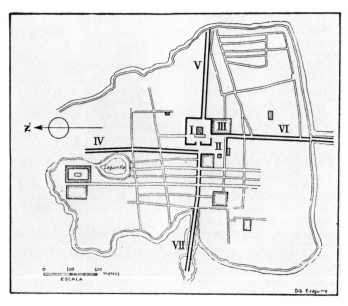

18 Schematic plan of Mexico City. The central plaza is at I, and at II is
the auxillary plaza that hangs like a pendant in the Durer plan. (Reprinted
from F. Violich, *Cities of Latin America*, New York: Reinhold, 1944)

1 Charles V, "Real Cédula de Población otorgada a los que hicieron Descubrimiento en Tierra Firme" Burgos, 1521, *Colección de Documentos Inéditos Relativos al Descubrimiento, Conquista y Organización de las Antiguas Posesiones Españolas de América y Oceanía sacado de los Archivos del Reino*, 42 vols. (Madrid, 1864–1884), XXXI, pp. 13–25.

2 See Ralph Gakenheimer, "The Spanish King and his Continent: A Study of the Importance of the 'Laws of the Indies' for Urban Development in Spanish America" (Master's thesis, Cornell University, 1959); hereafter cited as Gakenheimer. See also part III later in this book.

3 Most of the material on this section comes from the introduction by Juan Manzano Manzano to the *Recopilación de Leyes de los Reynos de las Indias*, 4th ed., 3 vols. (Madrid: Ediciones Cultura Hispanica, 1973), 1, 13–67.

4 See also Daniel J. Garr, "Hispanic Colonial Settlement in California: Planning and Urban Development on the Frontier, 1769–1850" (Ph.D. dissertation, Cornell University, 1971).

5 John Reps, *The Making of Urban America* (Princeton: Princeton University Press, 1965), pp. 26, 36; hereafter cited as Reps, 1965.

6 Glenn H. Beyer, *The Urban Explosion in Latin America* (Ithaca: Cornell University Press, 1967), pp. 58–59; hereafter cited as Beyer.

7 *Ibid.*, p. 39.

8 Walter D. Harris, Jr., *Growth of Latin American Cities* (Athens, Ohio: Ohio University Press, 1971), pp. 14, 205.

9 Francis Violich, *Cities of North America* (New York: Reinhold, 1944), p. 21; hereafter cited as Violich, 1944.

10 Reps, 1965, p. 45.

11 *Ibid.*, p. 36.

12 George Kubler, *Mexican Architecture of the 16th Century* (New Haven: Yale University Press, 1948), p. 76; hereafter cited as Kubler, 1948.

13 Violich, 1944, p. 29.

14 *Ibid.*, p. 170.

15 William H. Prescott, *History of the Conquest of Peru* (New York: Dutton, 1921), p. 330.

16 J.P. Paz-Soldan, *La Ciudad de Lima bajo la Dominacion Espanola* (Lima: Imprenta Gil, 1908), p. 9.

17 "Actas de la Fundacion de la Ciudad de Lima", *Revista de las Españas*, Madrid, Nov.–Dec. 1934), p. 464.

18 Dan Stanislawski, "Early Spanish Town Planning in the New World." *The Geographical Review*, XXXVII, No. 1, January 1947, p. 104. Hereafter cited as Stanislawski, 1947.

19 Francis Violich, "Evolution of the Spanish City: Issues Basic to Planning Today," *Journal of the American Institute of Planners*, Vol. XXVIII, No. 3 (August 1962), p. 170; hereafter cited as Violich 1962.

20 Vitruvius, *Ten Books on Architecture*; Alberti, *Ten Books on Architecture*; Dan Stanislawski, "The Origin and Spread of the Grid Pattern Town," *The Geographical Review*, Vol. 36, No. 1 (January 1946), pp. 105–120, passim; hereafter cited as Stanislawski, 1946.

21 Vitruvius, book I, chapter LV.

22 Kubler, 1948, p. 70.

23 Ignacio Bernal, "Mexico/Tenochtitlan" in *Cities of Destiny*, ed. Arnold Toynbee (New York: McGraw-Hill, 1967),

pp. 204–206, from which this and the following remarks of Bernal Diaz are taken.

24 *Idem.*

25 Richard Morse, "Some characteristics of Latin American Urban History," *American Historical Review,* Vol. LXVII, October 1961–July 1962, p. 336, suggested that it is an oversimplification to treat Spain's conquest of America as an extension of the process of reconquest. The reconquest from the Moors took 700 years and involved 200,000 square miles and the efforts of the whole Spanish people. The conquest of America took only 50 years or so, involved 30 to 40 times as much land, and was accomplished by only a few thousand men. Morse suspects that the difference in scale results in a qualitative difference between the two experiences: "To stress only the similarity of Iberian institutions in these two settings is to run the risk of formalism." (Hereafter, Morse, 1962)

26 *Ibid.,* pp. 319.

27 Stanislawski, 1946, p. 120.

28 Stanislawski, 1947, p. 96.

29 Robert C. Smith, "Colonial Towns of Spanish and Portugese America," *Journal of the Society of Architectural Historians,* Vol XIV, No. 4 (December 1955), p. 3; hereafter cited as Smith, 1955.

30 Violich, 1962, p. 177.

31 Ibid., and Reps, 1965, p. 31.

32 Reps, 1965, p. 31.

33 Stanislawski, 1947, p. 101.

34 Smith, 1955, p. 4.

35 *Idem.*

36 Violich, 1962, p. 172.

37 Reps, 1965, p. 30.

38 *Ibid.,* p. 32.

39 Beyer, pp. 50–56.

40 Smith, 1955, pp. 4–5.

41 Gakenheimer.

42 Morse, 1962, p. 329.

43 *Ibid.,* p. 324.

44 "Descripción Anónima del Perú y de Lima a principios del Siglo XVII, compuesta por un Judio Portugués y dirigida a los Estados de Holanda," *Revista Archivo Nacional,* Lima, Vol. XVII (1944), pp. 3–44.

45 G. M. Foster, *Culture and Conquest: The American Spanish Heritage* (New York: Viking Fund Publications in Anthropology, Quadrangle Books, 1960), p. 47.

46 *Ibid.,* p. 34.

II

THREE AMERICAN CITIES

Although the influence of Spain in the territories north of the Rio Grande was relatively short-lived, several important cities of the area can trace their origins back to a city-planning tradition that is based on ancient Roman practice. The cities themselves are up to 350 years old, having deep and complex historical roots lacking in many other US cities.

These Spanish cities contrast strongly with the settlements of the North Americans in the same southwestern area. The first half of the nineteenth century was a period of free-for-all urban development in the southwestern United States. The vigorous American culture swept before it the preceding Indian and the Spanish cultures and seldom paused for the provision of amenities that could make city life a civilizing experience. Though ideal plans were occasionally promulgated, they frequently lasted just long enough to attract investors and then gave way to piecemeal development, as Reps has shown (1965) "Get something up" was the rallying cry. A grid plan often met the demand for speed, simplicity, and maximum economic return, but this was a utilitarian grid without the humanizing "extras" of plaza, promenade, park, and variation of lot size or street width such as the early Spanish planning ordinances of the Law of the Indies had advocated. In spite of the incredible presistence of the checkerboard block pattern, such American cities can scarcely be said to have had a plan. Indeed, the practice of city planning seemed at this point almost to have disappeared. Until nearly the middle of the twentieth century, North American city plans and planning have had an ad hoc flavor—emergency responses to the crisis of wholesale immigration. The recent shift in national outlook toward reflection and stringent economic evaluation of planning activity at all levels in the society means that planners and their public are taking a new interest in the philosophy of planning. The question of centralized urban planning versus local control is emerging as a basic issue in the latter part of the twentieth century. A revaluation of the role of historical trends in planning

A preliminary version of this part appeared in Dora Crouch and Axel Mundigo, "The City Planning Ordinances of the Laws of the Indies Revisited, II", *Town Planning Review*, vol. 48, Oct. 1977, pp. 397–418. Reprinted by permission.

is taking place as well. This book is an attempt to contribute to this stocktaking by emphasizing the Spanish cultural element in our urban history.

The length and complexity of the historical experience of Spanish cities of the North American Southwest is valuable to an understanding of the planning process and its results. Cities are the arena wherein problems of terrain, economics, politics, social organization, and conflicting cultural psychologies are adjusted to one another in the process of urban development. This adjustment is visible in the resulting fabric of the city.

We shall take three cities of the present-day United States as our examples and examine them on several levels. First, how did each of these settlements correspond to provisions of the ordinances? What variations from the ordinances' prescriptions may be noted in each? What aspects of the planning ideology on which these specific cities are based can we discern? That is, what do these provincial examples tell us about the application of theory and law to the problems of Spanish colonization of the New World? And finally, what can we learn of the perennial tension between centralized and local control of urban development?

The selection of these three cities is based on the fact that each illuminates a different facet of Spanish influence on urban America. Santa Fe is the oldest of the three and the purest in form and adherence over time to the original Spanish plan. St. Louis had the briefest exposure to Spanish planning, but still embodies some traces of forms mandated by the Laws of the Indies. Los Angeles is the last surviving Spanish settlement in the United States (Reps, *The Making of Urban America*, Princeton, 1965, p. 26), too poor and too peripheral to the Spanish Empire to warrant elaborate development according to traditional principles, but yet strongly marked in its self-image as a Spanish city. Certainly the most successful of the three today, Los Angeles shows in its history very clearly how the urban arrangements of the city planning ordinances of the Laws of the Indies were replaced by later North American laws in the second half of the nineteenth century. These three cities of the United States are linked by a common planning heritage: They began as Spanish settlements and still reveal in their physical form the influence of the city planning provisions of the Laws of the Indies. Further, and unlike the sixteen major cities of Latin America mentioned in part I, these three were founded after Philip II's complete codification of city planning ordinances had been issued. At Santa Fe, St. Louis, and Los Angeles, certain requirements of the city planning ordinances of the Laws of the Indies were met, and others were for various reasons ignored. In examining the physical fabric and history of these cities, we come into contact not only with the way our immediate past shapes the theater of our daily lives, but also with an urban tradition nearly 500 years old in this hemisphere and more than 2500 years old in its origin.

The building of Santa Fe, three quarters of a century after the refounding of Mexico City, reveals an amalgamation of Indian and Spanish ideas.[1] The physical form of the city reflects this crucial synthesis between native and imported building customs. The site of Santa Fe, for instance, had been occupied by the Analco pueblo[2] which in turn preserved the site of the Kuapoge pueblo of the early prehistoric period.[3] Still surviving in colonial times near Santa Fe was the Indian pueblo of Quemado, later known as Aqua Fria.[4] Thus, Spanish urban settlements in New Mexico were generally located where preconquest Indian pueblo settlements had been.

The Indian settlements had consisted of groups of cellular, communal houses of stone or adobe (mud brick), made by the repeated linear addition of new rooms, utilizing walls running parallel or perpendicular to one another, and facing onto linear open spaces or courtyards (figures 22 and 23). This system of building was partly determined by the ecology of the region (figure 19) and partly by needs of defense.[5] The area was called New Mexico because the pueblos looked like Aztec dwellings in Mexico.[6] Rows of pueblo houses had two or more storeys. The lower, being used for storage, was completely enclosed and reached by trapdoors. The upper had corridors and balconies of wood, facing in toward the "plaza" and thus forming a sort of citadel.[7]

Just as the Spaniards were willing to learn from the great cities of Mesoamerica, so too at the modest settlements of New Mexico they adopted Indian structures and forms.

Spanish conquerors were little concerned with the climate and soil of New Mexico . . . because neither differed in any remarkable way from that of New Spain. . . . They . . . did not find the country barren. . . . In contrast to the Latins, Anglo-American explorers and surveyors moved into the Southwest from the humid East. (They characterized the region as "barren and uninteresting in the extreme" or "sickening-colored.")[8]

Finding the climate and terrain "normal" and the population "civilized" to the extent that they lived in permanent settlements, the Spanish were ready to come to terms with their new environment and neighbors. These continuing adjustments in some sense parallel the "feedback" system that generated the Laws of the Indies: The Indians accepted the outside influences of these new settlers where these did not affect traditional building forms, and in turn the Spaniards accepted the Indians' age-old communal dwelling, so quickly and easily constructed. Compromise between the Indian town and the needs of Europeans for their particular types of structures became the usual pattern.[9] Indian and Spanish structures alike were "built of mud like Timbuctoo."[10] Common use of materials and common forms meant easy architectural interchangeability between the two cultures.

Like the other Spanish towns of the New World, Santa Fe was established by fiat of a distant government, one highly centralized in theory but with its impact lessened by both distance and the settler's rights of petition, initiative, protest, and delay.[11] For all that the Laws of the Indies might say about the details of land settlement, their administration, at least along the Gulf and in the Southwest, appeared to be tempered with a measure of the freedom that has been characteristic of all frontiers at the edge of permanent settlement."[12] With this degree of freedom possible, then, it is all the more impressive that Santa Fe remains the ultimate expression of the city planning ordinances of the Laws of the Indies on the soil of the United States. Probably this is because of the city's isolation and poverty, which made speculative development and rapid change a minor part of the city's history. "Sluggish fashions and technical conservatism usually characterize the frontier society and peripheral area; in these terms, New Mexico was the provincial outpost in a state of chemical purity."[13] The early seventeenth-century foundation of Santa Fe was the logical outcome of a deliberate policy of pushing the frontier northward, which had been going on in Mexico throughout the previous ninety years. At first, for about forty years, this had been achieved by the sword, but results were unsatisfactory and the cost was high. By 1584, a new procedure had suggested itself, as we see in this letter written by the bishop of Guadalajara to the archbishop of Mexico:

By what I have seen with my own eyes and what I have learned from persons of long experience in this realm of New Galicia (especially from Rodrigo del Rio De Loza, general of the warfare), I would suggest that the king proceed as follows for the pacification of Nueva Galicia and of Nueva Vizcaya:

1. The war as now conducted is very costly and difficult. Although the presidios and soldiers give some protection, they really serve to prolong the war because of the harm they do the natives, capturing their women and children. Thus more nations than ever are now hostile, including many who were formerly at peace and baptized. This past summer all the Indians of Nieves, Rio Grande, the mill of Alonzo Lopez, and of many *estancias* rose up to fight under five or six important chiefs, almost all of them Christian. This uprising was centered at the Pico de Teyre district of Mazapil, but was fortunately stopped, in Christian manner, by Rodrigo del Rio.

2. It is said that these Indians can be subjugated little by little by force of arms; but it is not so, because the costs of such war would end by driving Spaniards out of the land because of heavy taxation. Furthermore, for each nation thus conquered, others nearby, seeing what the Spaniards do and thus fearing them, become hostile and fight, and the process is endless.

3. Cheapest, best, and most Christian remedy is to found six or seven settlements (at Las Charcas, at a point between Mazapil and Saltillo, in the Valley of Las Parras, in the Laguna Grande district, in the Tepeque area, and the mines of Indé), each one of which shall contain two or three Franciscans. At each place there should be erected some modest houses and a church, and the friars should be provisioned for a few years at His Majesty's expense. To protect friars and inhabitants, up to eight soldiers should be stationed in each new settlement, with salary from the crown but receiving orders from the Franciscans. These soldiers would be for defense only, and thus prohibited from making *entradas* without permission of the friars. So that their salary should be small, those soldiers should be married men and be granted the ordinary lands for settlers. To each new settlement should be sent some Mexicans, or Tlaxcalans, or other sedentary Indians, well Christianized, so that they can serve as *fiscales,* song leaders (*cantores*), and in other religious capacities, as well as settlers. Their example, plus the friars' persuasion, will attract the nomads to peaceful settlement. This has been proved on other parts of the frontier. The expense of this will not be great or continuing, such as is the case in the upkeep of the soldiery now. The monasteries can be built for 2,000 pesos each, and the upkeep for two friars in each, with all religious equipment, should be less than 800 pesos; to this should be added 900 pesos for two soldiers (who can be

taken from present presidios and companies, and picked from among married men who would be very desirous of such service). Nor would there be difficulty in getting Indian settlers, excusing them from tribute for ten or twelve years and granting other privileges and aid.

For efficiency all this could and should be entrusted to General Rodrigo del Rio de Loza. He is anxious that this plan be carried out, and he is the only one to whom it should be entrusted. This would not mean immediate suspension of warfare, but within a few years the expense of soldiery could be greatly reduced; and part of this cost could then go into the more desirable activity as above outlined.[14]

By 1609–1610 this procedure had been operating for about twenty years, so that even the details of the beginning of Santa Fe had been worked out at other sites: entrusting the task of conversion to Franciscans, protecting them by a few soldiers, providing supplies for the first few years, and sending a group of already pacified Indians to serve as contacts with and examples for those to be pacified. By this method, it usually took about ten years to pacify a new group of nomadic Indians and turn them into sedentary farmers and dutiful vassals of king and church.[15] Since a great deal of sentimental history has been written deploring the total effect of the Spaniards upon the Indians, it is well to pause here and reflect that so few Spaniards and their civilized Indian partners had so profound an effect upon the tribes they were seeking to domesticate, in large part because they really did have a way of life to offer that the Indians could easily perceive as superior to what they had been living.[16]

The church took a strong interest in urbanization as a corollary of conversion. To show the dominance and prestige of the new religion, Indian sites were frequently reused, as the former Moorish sites in Spain had been reused in the previous century.[17] During the seventeenth and eighteenth centuries, then, control of the Indians in New Mexico rested with the missions.[18] The first mission at the Puarray pueblo was founded in 1581, and by the time Santa Fe was established in 1610,[19] there were already 8,000 Christian converts in the region.[20] This achievement was the result of the work of eight missionary priests.[21] Since San Miguel, the oldest church still in use here, was begun between 1605 and 1608 by Don Juan de Onate,

Bancroft may be right in asserting that all 8,000 converts were at Santa Fe, and we may even infer that the existence of so large a group of converts was a strong motivation for the founding of the new town.[22]

As mission territory, without an indigenous Christian tradition, Santa Fe was placed in the care of Franciscans. The Province of the Holy Gospel of Franciscan Observants of New Spain (headquartered in Mexico City) had in its charge several divisions called *custodies*; the Custody of the Conversion of St. Paul had two branches, a smaller one at El Paso and a larger one in the interior of the Kingdom of New Mexico.[23] Santa Fe remained part of this custody for 177 years, until 1776.[24] Senior religious officer of New Mexico was a *custos* (guardian); there was no bishop until after 1832, and no seminary.[25]

The New Mexican branch of the custody came to include three Spanish villas (towns) and twenty-two Indian *pueblos* (villages), lying along the Rio del Norte. Santa Fe lay farthest from the river, eight leagues away on a branch stream. The whole group lay within forty leagues of each other.[26] In the immediate vicinity of Santa Fe, nine priests cared for eight pueblos and the Villa de la Canada as well as Santa Fe, some 7,480 souls altogether, by the time Dominguez wrote in the late eighteenth century.[27]

The separate settlements of Spaniards in their villas had less influence on the Indians than did the missions, partly because the towns were far fewer, irregularly distributed, and slow to grow. On the other hand, they were centers for the Spanish way of life. In fact, to the invading Anglos of the nineteenth century and their scholarly successors of the twentieth century, there was little to distinguish Mexican and Indian settlements, since both were so different from the Anglo. To cite just one instance, since the Spanish settlement regularly used a grid street pattern, it has been assumed without verification that any regular pattern observable in an Indian settlement must be the result of contact with the Spaniards. On the contrary, excavations have shown the regularity to be an indigenous feature dating to the twelfth and thirteenth centuries, if not earlier[28] (see again figures 1–4).

The site of Santa Fe has been successively an Indian Pueblo before 1609, capital of a province of New Spain 1609–1680, headquarters of rebellious Indians 1680–

1692, capital again of a Spanish province, after 1821 capital of a Mexican province, then center of an American territory from 1846, and finally capital of a US state since 1912.[29] The city under Spanish rule was the seat of political and military authority. As such, it represented the far-off governments of Mexico City (700 leagues, or more than 1,000 miles away) and of even farther Seville—even if it represented them only faintly.[30]

La Villa Real de la Santa Fe was organized during the winter of 1609–10 by Don Pedro de Peralta.[31] From the tradition and law embodied in the 1573 ordinances, Don Pedro could receive instructions about locating his site, founding and laying out his city, and setting up both a government and an economic system.

First, the governor of New Spain would have conferred with him, offering him "honors and advantages," and sending all the paperwork required by Ordinance 2 into the Council of the Indies at Seville. From knowledge gained in earlier exploration, the governor would have assigned him a territory. Then, after an overland trek from Mexico, de Peralta would have "made the selection of the site where the town is to be built" (ordinance 111).

Santa Fe is located at the foot of a *sierra* (mountain range) which rises to the east, later to be called Sangre de Cristo,[32] and on a small river called also Santa Fe (figure 25). These ideas about location conform to ordinance 123 which draws on Alberti, who in turn drew on Vitruvius; by 1573, when the city planning ordinances were codified, the Spaniards had had enough experience in founding cities in the New World to know of the validity of Vitruvius and Alberti's prescriptions. The little river ran across the site, conveniently demarcating the city proper from the settlement for captive Indians whom the Spaniards brought with them. The Spanish settlement lay to the north.

De Peralta then proceeded to lay out the town according to ordinances 110, "dividing it into squares, streets, and building lots, using cord and ruler, beginning with the main square from which streets are to run." The early presidio here answered the demand of ordinance 133 for a "defense or barrier." Don Pedro would also have paid special heed to ordinances 21, 22, 23, 32, and 109. (Trent claims that detailed plans for Santa Fe were sent from Spain,[33] but I have found no evidence of this.)

Thus, the sequence of urban development seems to have been the following:

1. Obtain license to found a town.
2. Recruit settlers, lay in supplies, and so forth.
3. Travel to the site.
4. Arrive at area to be settled.
5. Select precise site.
6. Hold ceremonies of taking possession.
7. Lay out fortified settlement, build it, inhabit it.
8. Lay out fields, plant crops.
9. Build an irrigation system.
10. Subjugate and convert the Indians.
11. Lay out plaza and street of the town.
12. Mark out house lots and build separate houses.

Once the settlement was established, further activities would be

13. Attract more settlers from Mexico.
14. Build large church to replace chapel of original fortress.
15. Lay out subsidiary plazas, streets, and house lots.
16. Build additional churches, monastaries, government buildings, shops, houses.
17. Send reports, illustrated with maps and plans, to Mexico City and Seville.

Spaces of the earliest Santa Fe have survived better than the buildings that edged them, for the settlement suffered some destruction in the Indian uprising of 1680. Considerable building and rebuilding took place after Santa Fe was resettled,[34] but we have no plans from the seventeenth century, and none from the first three quarters of the eighteenth. The earliest plan (figure 25) is from 1766–1768 and was drawn by José de Urrutia.[35]

One reason the river is such a prominent feature on Urrutia's map may be that in October 1767, at the end of the August–October rainy season, there was a great flood in which the river changed its bed and threatened public buildings. By November 7 the water had receded sufficiently that all the city could be called out to work to restore the river to its usual bed.[36] Provision of an irrigation system had been one of the first concerns of de Peralta and his settlers, a system still functioning in the middle of the nineteenth century when Davis described it:[37] There was a major ditch (the *acequia madre*) three to five yards wide and two to six feet deep running on each side of the river. (figure 32) From them, smaller cross ditches led to smaller still, all entering the various plots of land at their highest points. Flow gates were used to control the water. The land was divided into small beds sixty by forty feet, with mounded edges. Since one man could control the flow of water into five acres in one day, most holdings were five acres, though some were ten. Davis commented that territorial law recognized water as a public necessity "like roads in the East." He reported that fifteen to twenty men were hired to repair the system annually, but because of the danger of flash floods, all would rush to repair and prevent damage in the case of a bad storm.

Eventually the river was embanked against flooding, as it ran through Santa Fe. Once established, probably early in the eighteenth century, this irrigation system was used to grow crops of wheat, maize, legumes, green vegetables, melons, and apricots. The water also operated three mills.[38]

As basic as water supply was the defense of the new settlement. An enclosed quadrangle pattern is found generally in Spanish America (figure 63) since defense was a common problem (ordinance 128). The plan of the "presidio" of Santa Fe in 1791 is of the usual pattern; what is today the governor's palace is in the lower right corner of figure 63a. A settlement would outgrow these constraints as soon as it could, since to be "restricted as in a presidio" was something to complain of,[39] but in areas with warlike Indians, there would be continued advantages in having such a refuge. In fact, as late as 1812, Pino describes small semimilitary settlements that were dotted around New Mexico, 102 of them, and were called *plazas* from their form of a rectangle 200 by 500 *varas*, with bastions[40]— just the form of the original presidios of Santa Fe, Santa Barbara, and so on.

A wall that ran northward from the plaza at Santa Fe was described by Pino as "an obstacle to the beauty of the city because it is becoming more dilapidated every day."[41] Since it disintegrated soon after the American occupation, the wall was sold (for materials?), and new private houses were put up in the area. This demise was regretted by some, as the wall had formerly been well kept and "famous for its length and good proportions."[41] This wall probably formed one of the long sides of the original presidio.

Inspection of the early maps of Santa Fe shows that the initial enclosed rectangle was soon amplified by a more open and expansive arrangement, so that the governor's palace, instead of turning inward, opened out onto what became the main plaza of the city. The fortified rectangle was originally nearly 400 feet wide, with the palace occupying half of the southern side. The east and west sides were twice as long, some 800 feet. Located within the perimeter were the barracks, chapel, offices, magazines (storage rooms), and prison of the colony, as mandated by ordinances 121, 124, and 126. From existing plans, however, the dimensions were about 350 by 500 feet; the fort may have been rebuilt to smaller size after the 1680 uprising.

When the Governor's Palace was reoriented to the plaza outside the fortification, the builders of the town were responding to ordinance 112. Plaza size was regulated by ordinance 113. The original plan for the city of Santa Fe called for a large central plaza, much larger than the one that has survived, as shown in the 1766–1768 map (figure 25). By 1800 the main plaza was significantly smaller than it had been, probably because of the usual process of encroachment[42] (figure 28).

All the business of the little settlement of Santa Fe took place at the Plaza Mayor (the usual title for such a square)—commerce, politics, marketing, religious processions, and entertainment (figure 31). At the end of the day, the people would gather here to promenade, see, and be seen. From the plaza, the regular caravans departed for Mexico City or Los Angeles, carrying blankets and buffalo skins, and to the plaza they returned three years later, bearing "ecclestiastical equipment, general supplies, missionaries, and an occasional new governor"[43] (figure 30). Even though this was the center of provincial government, few special buildings were put up here to accommodate these needs. Poverty is reflected at Santa Fe and elsewhere in the slow accumulation of community buildings such as town halls, slaughter houses, jails, and hospitals. Besides poverty, the inefficiency of town government contributed to these delays.[44]

The ordinances called for porticoes around the plaza and along the main streets. At Santa Fe, only along the governor's Palace have the usual colonnades survived to our own time. Quite possibly they once bordered the entire plaza as ordinance 115 dictated (figures 29 and 30). Early photographs show the porticoes that edged the plaza at Santa Fe and formed covered sidewalks along the streets at the center of town. Though these were crudely executed with logs, they were reminiscent of the classical porticoes of the plazas of Spanish cities. Some towns in Spain still today have colonnades made of logs, so in this respect Santa Fe was an image of "home" (figure 6).

In Renaissance urbanism and architectural symbolism, the porticoes signified a civic or public space. Consequently, porticoes would be found at the plaza and along the main streets, whereas residential streets would present blank, planar walls to the passerby (figure 29). In Venice, for example, loggias were added to the Piazza San Marco as a Renaissance (and therefore classical) remodeling of the medieval space. So too, here in a most primitive outpost of Spain in the New World, porticoes of logs arranged around the main plaza of the settlement spoke to inhabitant and visitor alike of that venerable urban tradition, and gave a sense of place as well as a practical focus for many functions in all weathers.

Around the plaza were grouped major buildings (figures 28 and 30). To the north lay the palace and a similarly sized building that together formed the southern edge of the military parade ground farther north, which had formerly been the enclosed courtyard of the presidio. The palace was used for the offices of the governor and for the legislature. Along the east and west sides of the plaza were originally houses, most notable of which was the *ayuntamiento* (city council chamber). By the 1840s most of the structures fronting the plaza had shops in them.[45] Commerce in Spanish towns was at first considered a necessary evil, taking up very little space, and that in modest and often temporary facilities. Later, commerce began to invade the major public spaces, such as the main plaza at Santa Fe and along the main streets.[46]

The south side of the plaza was the location of the military chapel, called Our Lady of Light (*Castrense*); at some time an Oratory of the Holy Trinity stood on the west side of the plaza. The area of the plaza was two to three acres.[47] At the center of the plaza, Governor Don Antonio Narvona (also called Narbona) had built in

1825–1827 an adobe base three *varas* high on which stood a rock sundial.[48] In 1844 a bullring was set up in the plaza.

Elias Brevoort, who came to Santa Fe in 1850, reported that the plaza was used then as a corral: "Nothing there but a great space, people encamped and wagons all about the square. The market consisted of people seated on the northwest corner of the plaza with baskets; later buildings were provided for them on the Rio Chiquito. After the arrival of the California troops and at the close of the rebellion under General Carleton's military adminstration, trees were planted and the plaza and other places improved."[49] It was Major John Ayers who began in 1866 to plant trees in the plaza.[50] At that time there were "many places suitable for parks and already planted with many cottonwood trees."[51] The Plaza Mayor was "improved" in the last half of the nineteenth century with a picket fence and a wooden bandstand adorned with gingerbread carvings—replacing the bullring.[52]

Those whom Brevoort saw selling their wares at the northwest corner of the plaza were taking advantage of the traffic going and coming from the Governor's Palace nearby, utilizing the portico of the palace itself as their marketplace. Davis reports that they sold vegetables, meat, and fruit there, while the hay and grass market was in a narrow street at the southwest corner of the plaza. The plaza was the center, then, of the business life of the town, and was also used for cockfights, especially on Sundays.[53]

Although the pattern for the streets was planned at the beginning, the streets themselves remained unpaved for a long time, and were still unpaved when Davis visited in 1846.[54] The plaza was in a very real sense the thoroughfare of the city. Other streets began at the plaza, and were not as regular here as in other Spanish settlements, as inspection of the plans shows (figure 26). Streets were eight *varas* (twenty-two feet) wide. Only near the plaza were the houses compactly sited and fronted with porticoes, "rough but ornamental and convenient," as Davis describes them.[55] The main street, today called San Francisco Street because it leads to the Cathedral of St. Francis, had porticoes on its south side (figure 29).

In Spanish colonial settlements, the important buildings usually face the plaza—"the buildings of the church and royal house and for city use"—as prescribed by ordinance 126. In spite of the prohition against individual lots lining the plaza, at Santa Fe and later at Los Angeles, homes of important persons also faced onto the plaza. We can imagine the little buildings placed at first in a regular pattern around the plaza, helping to form the boundary of the defensible area, and later straggling away from the center in a more haphazard manner, so that they could be described by Dominguez as separate sets of buildings, like homesteads.[56]

Other details of the layout of Santa Fe correspond to other ordinances, such as ordinance 129, which specified the layout of town commons. The commons at Santa Fe stretched to the north, beyond the presidio grounds; at some periods, the boundaries between them were not clear. The 1846 "Military Map" of the city shows this area being used to grow corn (figure 26).

Although in some settlements the church or cathedral also faces the main plaza, at Santa Fe the laws are followed literally and the main church is located off the east side of the plaza; by ordinance 124, it "shall not be placed on the square but at a distance and shall be separated from any other building." An early description mentions two plazas (as suggested in ordinance 118), the second apparently the small square in front of the principal church. By the 1740s, a house was obstructing the entrance to the church, so the governor bought the house and removed it.[57]

The church at Santa Fe served as the administrative focus of a missionary program that by 1630 had sent twenty-five missions to ninety pueblos of 60,000 Indians, as mandated by ordinances 17, 27, 136, 140, and 141–148, "to bring on to our obedience all the natives of the province" (138). At Santa Fe, the church of San Miguel and its *barrio* on the south bank of the river formed the kind of separate Indian town specified by ordinance 148. At first, the Indians would have been Tlascans or other pacified tribes brought from Mexico to serve as examples to the local Indians. Although local legend holds that San Miguel is the oldest church in the United States,[58] excavation has not been able to substantiate this. The records say that by 1630 a church was completed at Santa Fe to serve the garrison and settlers, some 250 Spaniards.[59] This may refer to San Miguel, but more likely to the predecessor of the Church of St. Francis. The latter was built beginning in 1714, on the site of a pre-Revolt church destroyed in 1680. Although rebuilt again in the nineteenth century as the cathedral, its Conquistadora Chapel, sacristy, and sanctuary behind the rear cathedral wall are all eighteenth century. The church of San Francisco stood in its own block, with a garden and spring (which was shared with the other settlers) to the south of the convent. It was probably the spring that determined the location of the religious complex. A cemetary was located within the wall, next to the church (figure 27).

A third church was the Confraternity and Chapel of Our Lady of Light, already mentioned as fronting on the plaza. This chapel housed a religious society for soldiers, founded in 1760. Its building was completed in 1761 with a week of festivities including masses in the mornings and comedies in the afternoons. The structure seems to have utilized a preexisting building, for excavation shows the probable date of the foundations as 1710. The governor, Don Francisco Marin del Valle, provided the construction funds out of his own purse. He built a cross-shaped building 100 feet long and nearly as wide, with two plain towers with bells, a little taller than the roof. The altar stood at the south end, and the choir at the north was reached by a ladder. The roof was supported by large unpainted pine beams braced by brackets at the wall, and a tin chandelier hung at the crossing. In spite of a distinguished membership of military leaders and the affluent (ordinance 99, "illustrious men of known ancestry"), the society was effectively dead by 1781.[60]

Besides these public religious buildings, there were private chapels at people's homes. Since the clergy levied double the usual fee for a marriage if it were not performed in the principal church, it seems evident that rich and important people liked to be married in their private chapels, a practice that the church tried to discourage by the "fine."[61] Eventually Santa Fe had five churches and two public oratories.[62]

In the seventeenth and eighteenth centuries, erecting churches in any Spanish town was a function of wealth, not of congregational pressure for more space. Churches and priests were supported usually by endowments from the rich or tithes from the congregation, except in mission areas where their support was a government function, at least until the waning days of the Spanish Empire. At Santa Fe, in spite of the fact that the area was in mission status for nearly 200 years, the church was supported by tithes.[63] By contrast, the Spanish crown took advantages of the religious zeal of the Franciscans and had them support the colonization of California from their Pious Fund, so that less capital was required from the royal treasury. (This is discussed more fully in the last part of the book.)

The domestic as well as the monumental buildings of the settlement were the concern of the ordinances (for example, ordinances 128, 132, and 134). Not only are the settlers to "establish their houses and to build them with good foundations and walls" (132) but are "so far as possible to have the buildings all of one type for the sake of the beauty of the town" (134). The architecture was extremely simple, using adobe brick and some stone, with room sizes based on lengths of available logs for ceiling beams. Rooms were grouped around a patio, which might or might not have a portico. Flat roofs were common and contours soft because of the use of adobe plastered over for protection against weather. The architecture was a mixture of Spanish and Indian ideas, suitable to a mixed population and to the climate.[64] Adobe is easy to use, not requiring the sophisticated techniques of masonry (figure 33).

For Anglo visitors or settlers after the 1830s, this architecture did not speak of "home," and they tended to dislike it. For one who reported that the private buildings were low, comfortable, and clean,[65] several said that the unadorned earth houses "lacked everything"[66] and that the blank facades of the houses made the town seem "almost deserted" and gave it a disagreeable aspect.[67] "It has more the appearance of a colony of brick-kilns than a collection of human habitations," wrote Davis when he first arrived, and he commented on the dirty streets and the fact that all building was the same mud color. Not content to comment, he went on to find out why the houses were as they were: The houses of adobe have walls thicker than stone or brick would be, he reports, and are therefore cooler in summer and warmer in winter. The adobe bricks were six times the size of an English brick; originally made by the resident himself, by the 1840s they cost $8–10 per thou-

sand delivered. They were laid in the same mud, and plastered. Because of the local weather, this proved to be a
very permanent construction system. The thick walls also
supported the heavy roof, which had wooden sleepers
(beams) holding wooden boards, and was topped by a
layer of mud "to make it waterproof." A low parapet
surrounded the roof, and the occasional rain water was
carried off by wooden spouts and deposited into the street.
The residents inspected the roof after every rain, and if it
leaked, they added more dirt. With such a system, it is
obvious that houses of only one storey would be the rule,
and at the time of Davis's stay, there were only two two-
storey houses, neither built by Mexicans (figure 34).

The usual form of the house was of a hollow square,
with rooms opening by their doors onto the patio via a
covered portico that ran all around the court. The interior
of the house was finished with a gypsum whitewash (called
vezo by Davis, but more correctly *yeso*), but since this
comes off on one's clothes, the rooms were lined with
calico to the height of four feet, adding a touch of bright
color to the interiors. Twice a year the houses were reno-
vated by putting a new *yeso* surface on the walls—the
women did this using a fleece or their hands—and a new
mud surface on the floor. Wooden floors were rare, but
sometimes a carpet of local manufacture called *gerga*
(again, this is Davis's term; we would say *jerga*) was used.
Ceilings were never plastered, but finished either with exposed beams that (in the houses of the rich) were carved
and painted or, in the main room, arranged in herringbone
pattern of small round sticks painted red, blue, or green
placed between the beams. Another choice was to stretch
bleached muslin along the ceiling. Heat was provided in
the main room by a fireplace in the corner, with a small
horseshore-shaped opening eigtheen to twenty-four inches
high and wider at the bottom. The plan of the fireplace
was also horseshoe shaped, and there was a raised hearth.
Logs were placed upright at the back, and this arrangement
was an efficient heat source. Furniture was simple—folded
mattresses covered with blankets and placed around the
edges of the room, in the Moorish fashion. These would
be unrolled at night, and the sitting room became a bed-
room. Few houses had bedsteads; a low wooden frame
was sometimes used. Trunks and chests held clothes. The

rich would have pine chests and settees. Sometimes guests would be received and entertained on a blanket spread out in the center of the floor. In the kitchen, earthen vessels were used to cook in, though there was no stove that Davis recognized as such.[68] Glass being unavailable, paper was used to cover windows or make blinds.[69]

But a city does not consist only of houses. Public buildings were mandated by ordinance 121, both royal and civic and religious structures. Though larger than the other structures of the town, and containing the first library to be found in the region, the Governor's Palace was made of the same materials and in the same style as the rest of the town. It may have been the special concern of the architect(s) mentioned in ordinance 135. In a symbolic gesture of conquest, the palace was erected in 1610 on the site of the former Indian pueblo.[70] In the 1680 uprising, it was partially destroyed, so that it had to be rebuilt in 1697. An account of 1731 described the new palace as built by Governor Bustamante at his own expense; this probably means that he removed the old roof and tops of walls and renewed them.[71] By 1832 the building was already in bad repair,[72] but the indefatigable Davis inspected it thoroughly in the 1840s and tells us that the structure is 350 feet long or so—"others say 400 feet"—and 20 to 75 feet wide. A portico 15 feet deep ran along the whole plaza length, with a small projection at each end. The projection at the east was being used as a post office; at one time it had been a chapel for the governor, and at least one governor is buried under its floor. The west bastion was at the time used as the jail. The building was "in the style of the 1650s".[73]

When the parish church was built, by 1717, the east and west towers that had flanked the palace were torn down to straighten the plaza. The east one had extended well out into what became the plaza area, as a bastion, as is shown in the 1791 plan (figure 63a). The one at the west had been the military magazine before it became the jail (*calabozo*), and by the 1840s was partly ruined.

Within the presidio were official reception rooms and offices, military barracks, stables, the arsenal, servants' quarters, and a central patio of ten acres, which was used as a vegetable garden. Water was supplied by springs to the east. Among the suites of rooms opening onto the

portico was the Office of the Secretary of the Territory, in
whose inner room the archives, by then nearly 300 years old, were stored. The executive office had bleached muslin tacked up as a ceiling and a calico dado, which also was to be found in the legislature's room, "lest they carry away any whitewash on their clothes, a thing they have no right to do in their capacity as law-makers." Also here in the palace was the library of the territory, fifteen feet square and filled with books, mostly law books, court reports, codes and congressional documents.[74] The palace was restored in 1909–1913.[75]

The palace was the special concern of William G. Ritch, who wrote of it in his *History of New Mexico* (1884)[76]

No, that is the only palace in the United States. In Mexican matters every capital town must have its palace on the plaza, and if it was only a 7 × 9 hut it was all the same a palace. [This one] is more like a rope walk than anything else—it is nevertheless a palace and must be preserved.

Just as Alberti could say, "The house is a little city, the city a great house," so too it was easy for Ritch to follow his remarks on the governor's palace immediately with an observation on the city: "Santa Fe is a great historical capital or place, the greatest in the United States, and should be kept so by every means possible, by preserving all that there is and adding as much as possible. The history of old Santa Fe is the history of the Southwest." As a historian, Ritch felt keenly the loss of the archives of the city and territory that had been burned with the church vestments in the plaza during the Indian uprising of 1680. Another nineteenth-century chronicler, M. S. Watts, reported that

the archives, when I first came there, were just in boxes in the Governor's room in the palace: ordinary dry goods 10-bushel boxes without any arrangement. Some Archives were sold as waste paper in 1866 or so by Governor Pile but about 25% of these were recovered, and by 1878 were placed in the Library, with the land grant papers going to the surveyor general's office in old Santa Fe in 1858. Some of the Archives were taken during the Indian uprising to the county of Rio Arriva and concealed, so that not all were burned.[77]

In addition to the archives of the territory and the law books in the palace library, there was another archive at the Church of St. Francis, called the Library of the Custody. In 1788 it was inventoried as having 384 items, a growth from the earlier count of 256. Its contents were baptismal records, burial and marriage records, patents, and inventories of missions and convents.[78] These records were probably housed at the church or in one of the buildings of its compound. The census of 1860 shows fifteen public and two church libraries in New Mexico, with a total of nearly 11,000 volumes.[79]

Another room of the palace deserves mention, though it was kept as purposely empty as the library was full. This was the Office of Indian Affairs, which was kept as an open space for the Indians to sit in when they came to do official business.[80]

Also part of this complex was the 100-foot-long structure used in the 1840s as the courthouse. It had formerly been the storehouse of the quartermaster. The one-storey building was 25 feet wide. In the 60-foot courtroom, square pillars down the middle helped to support the usual earth roof.[81] This part of the old presidio faced on the street that ran from the northeast corner of the plaza, for Davis says that the US, District, and Supreme Courts faced on this street.[82]

By the 1850s, Santa Fe was equipped with the following buildings:[83]

1 hotel,
1 printing office,
25 stores,
3 shoemakers,
1 apothecary,
1 bakery,
2 blacksmiths.

It also had a public primary school which paid its teacher 500 pesos a year, the highest teacher's salary in New Mexico.[84] This growth in public and quasi-public buildings was due to growth in both population and trade. Let us examine first the history of population at Santa Fe and then turn to trade.

We do not know exactly how many Spaniards came with de Peralta to found Santa Fe, but by 1633 there were 50, a large proportion of the 200 in the province.[85] Most of these were soldiers, needed to protect the priests and civil authorities, and to terrorize and "reduce" the Indians—which meant forcing them to live a settled life according to the Spanish pattern. In 1639 more than 50 persons were making a living growing wheat and maize by irrigation, for the Convent of St. Francis.[86] During the entire seventeenth century, the Spanish presence at Santa Fe relied paradoxically on the presence of Indians from Mexico, and later in the century on other nonlocal Indian servants. Ordinances 136 and 138 required that "persons designated for this purpose" shall try to win the friendship of the Indians who are to be converted, and bring them into obedience to the king of Spain. One assumes that the example of converted, peaceful Indians who had already been through the process was considered salutary. It was also convenient to have their services.

Spanish policy toward the Indians was most carefully conceived and self-consistent. Basic to the Spanish approach was the conviction that they were generously sharing with the natives their culture and civilization—both "totally lacking" in Indian life. The Spaniards did not understand that they were attempting to replace one group of cultural traits with another. To them, civilization was synomous with the Castilian language, adobe and stone houses, trousers, a political organization with the king of Spain at its center, and Roman Catholicism. Later, during the briefer Mexican rule, the cultural package consisted of the Mexican dialect of Castilian, rectangular houses, trousers, individual land holding, representative government and citizenship rights, and elementary schools without religion. Then, in the 1840s, civilization meant North American civilization—Indians were to be sequestered on reservations and Mexicans ignored as much as possible. The North American cultural package was signaled by the American dialect of English, American agricultural technology, elementary schools with religion, and the Protestant religion. Today we would probably specify the criteria of our culture as literacy, specialization of labor leading to different social roles, individual rights (citizenship), and freedom of choice.[87]

The Mexican Indians who lived in Santa Fe were called *genizaro* (a word derived from *janissary*); some were captive, others free, but all were living in the Spanish fashion.[88] As time went on, the term *genizaro* came to be used in New Mexico for all non-Pueblo Indians.

In spite of having brought pacified Indians with them to serve as good examples, the Spaniards ran into trouble with the indigenous population before the seventeenth century was over. Resentful of the denigration of their religion and the disruption of their culture, the Indians organized a revolt and massacred all the isolated Spaniards at the various mesas, driving the larger groups out of the territory to refuge at El Paso. Some of those killed were missionaries, some were retired soldiers. These had formed small farming villages, marrying and otherwise interacting with the Indians. The two groups mutually borrowed crafts, cuisine, agricultural methods, language, and healing methods.[89] It is difficult now to estimate the numbers involved in these outlying villages, but at Santa Fe, Benavide reports that 250 Spaniards and 700 Indians were living there before the revolt, and that the parish church was nearly completed.[90]

After the Indian uprising and mutual slaughter of 1680, the site of Santa Fe was recolonized in 1692 by Don Diego de Vargas and 800 settlers,[91] "without a blow, by words of pardon and peace."[92] When reestablished, the settlement had 127 Spanish families with a few Indians and two priests. The Indians seem to have been 40 families of *genizaro*.

By 1706 there were 100 soldiers with their wives and children at the presidio of Santa Fe, according to the declaration of Fr. Juan Alvarez, who also mentions "settlers" without giving a number. In charge of these people were the governor and a priest who is described as "poorly supplied with vestments, bells, etc."[93] A little later, by 1744, the number of Spanish families was still at 127, and they earned a living raising wheat, sheep, and cattle, and weaving blankets and hosiery.[94]

A census was taken in 1776. It showed 1 governor and family (6 persons), 229 Spanish families (1167 persons), and 42 families of *genizaros* (164 persons).[95] By the 1790s Santa Fe had a population of 2,000 or a little more and was one of four towns this size in the Rio Grande Valley.[96] Yet its population is supposed to have been 3,741 in 1805, growing to 6,000 by 1821, while New Mexico's grew from 19,000 to 30,000 in the same period.[97] Of these, 9,000–10,000 were supposed to be Indian.[98]

Mexican independence came in 1821, formally cele-
brated at Santa Fe on 6 January 1822—"Never did Santa
Fe behold such a splendid display"—but at first there was
little actual change for New Mexico or for this city.[99] At
Santa Fe the effect eventually was to make possible direct
trade with the United States.[100] In 1824 the presidio company was supposed to have 119 soldiers, and a budget of
$35,488, but since the budget existed only on paper, one
wonders about the soldiers. In 1827 Col. Narvona took
the first official census, finding that New Mexico had a
population of 41,458, mostly living along the Rio del
Norte within a distance of sixty to eighty leagues.[101] The
population at Santa Fe was 5,275 in 1831.[102] A second
census was taken in 1838 by Gov. Don Manuel Armijo.[103]

Head of the government of the area from 1823 to 1846
while it was under Mexican rule was a *jefe político* who
lived at Santa Fe. The area was a Mexican province to
1824, then temporarily a state with two other territories,
then a territory; in 1836 it became a department, remaining so until the American take over in 1846. All branches
of the government were controlled by the governor.[104]

As late as 1859, when the area had passed to US control,
the population at Santa Fe was only 4,846,[105] while New
Mexico had 61,547, of whom 25,089 were listed as illiterate. Davis says he thinks at least half were illiterate, as
only 460 were in school, and almost no women could read
and write.[106] The population did not grow in the 1850s
but by 1880 it was 6,635, and by 1889 it was 8,000.[107]

For many years Santa Fe was the only city and cultural
center in New Mexico. The territory was never an economically successful colony because there was almost no
mineral wealth in the area and little agriculture. Santa Fe
was thus an artificial city in the sense that it was only a
center of government and missionary effort and had no
viable economic base.[108]

In 1827 Narvona's census reported that people made
their livings in agriculture and stock raising (sheep and
goats), trade, buffalo hunting, and some mining.[109]

As long as Santa Fe was only a distant and tenuous
dependent of Mexico City, the vast distances and hostile
territory were bound to inhibit trade. A caravan of up to
500 persons would leave annually from Santa Fe for Mex-

ico City, but return was expected only in three years. The caravans at this time consisted of burros since there were no roads and the terrain was rough. Each would carry up to 300 pounds. Up to 1000 burros might form one train.[110] These traders would have to pay as much as a 100-percent tax on their goods at the Customs House located on the east side of the Plaza Mayor. The reason for the size of the tax was that under the Spanish economic system, there were no taxes on land, but there were of course some expenses of government that had to be met.

Biggest items of the trade were cotton goods, especially American made, which would be traded for local blankets. To sell these goods brought in from Mexico City and from the Gulf of Mexico, the New Mexican traders would scatter throughout the territory in October to attend as many fairs as possible.[111]

During the years 1775–1776, there were several attempts to find an overland route to California from Santa Fe, especially a safe one to Monterey.[112] These efforts were eventually successful, for Davis tells us, "Since the settlement of California, a considerable trade in sheep has sprung up between the two countries. Large flocks have been annually driven across the deserts from New Mexico, and which have commanded in California a price that renumerates the owners for the risk, trouble, and expense of driving them thither." Sheep that cost $2–3 in New Mexico brought $6–8 in San Francisco.[113]

But by virtue of its location, Santa Fe came to the attention of the vigorous American culture that had rolled over Spanish St. Louis and was on its way west. As early as 1812, Robert McKnight and a party of nine or ten reached Santa Fe over the plains, attempting to trade. Their goods, however, were confiscated, and the party were arrested and held in Mexico for ten years. In 1815, Auguste F. Chouteau and Julius de Mun came to New Mexico from Missouri and were well received for a while, but in 1817 their goods were confiscated and they were arrested.[114]

Once rule had shifted from Spain to Mexico, there was a loosening of this protectionist policy, so that by the 1830s there were many visitors and American merchants at Santa Fe.[115] Some Americans decided to stay over the winter in the area and hunt beaver, returning with the

skins and not money as the skins were not taxed.[116] As
early as 1821 or 1822, a regular caravan left Independence,
Missouri, for Santa Fe each year, composed of as many as
90 to 100 wagons, for protection against wild Indians.
They would arrive in July and sell the goods wholesale at
prices 80 to 100 percent over St. Louis or Philadelphia
prices—which was considered a great bargain. The cara-
vaneers would leave again in August[117] (figure 30). By
1849 caravans of 20 to 40 wagons were arriving "contin-
ually," at least in May, according to the report of William
R. Goulding, who accompanied the Knickerbocker Exploring Co. in that year.[118] By the 1850s trade along the
Santa Fe Trail amounted to $1 million per year,[119] a flood
that would greatly dilute the Spanish component of life at
Santa Fe.

Founded a scant 100 years after the discovery and occupation of Darien in the Isthmus of Panama, Santa Fe
marked the culmination of northward expansion of the
Spanish into hostile territory.[120] Though the Indians were
considered at first to be "so barbaric as to be not even
worth exploiting",[121] the ideas of God and Empire proved
strong enough to maintain the settlement and give it a
form that typified Spanish urbanism in the New World, a
form that persists in the central part of the city to this day.
At Santa Fe as elsewhere in Spanish America, Italian Renaissance ideas of city layout, expressed as early as 1554
in the rebuilt urban fabric of Mexico City, were imposed
upon an "Indian civic armature which was found to be
highly suitable," and in fact more easily adaptable to these
ideals than contemporary European models.[122]

The fact that Santa Fe was peripheral to the Spanish
(later Mexican) territory gave it more freedom than other
more centrally located sites. When American culture overran it, Santa Fe was again peripheral and so developed its
own unique blend of Spanish and American cultures.

Santa Fe, for instance, was the first place where persons
of Anglo-American and Mexican-Spanish culture sat together on law courts and in the legislature, as Davis, who
was the US attorney in Santa Fe reported.[123] While they
were trying the cases or making the laws, their Indian
counterparts were waiting in that bare room of the governor's palace to be noticed. Indian culture has continued

to be a largely unacknowledged substratum of Spanish city life in the New World. A paradigm of the city form mandated by the Laws of the Indies,[124] Santa Fe is also to some extent an embodiment of the compromises between Renaissance and Indian ideas of urban form, generated by the particular conditions of colonization in the New World.

19 Native American planning for solar heating. Part of the perceivable regularity of Indian settlements in the Southwest may be due to traditional manipulation of solar heating. Since this region is sparsely wooded, with forests often at great distance from inhabited pueblos, every possible conservation of human energy and of wood for fires is essential. The orderly spacing of these row houses maximized exposure to the winter sun. (Reprinted, by permission, from R. Knowles, *Energy and Form,* Cambridge, Mass.: MIT Press, 1978, figure 28)

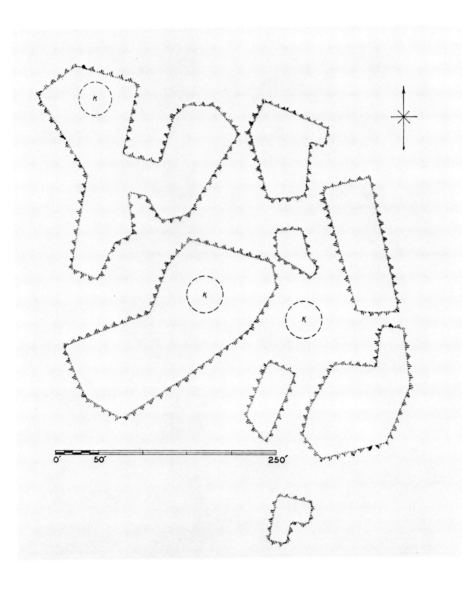

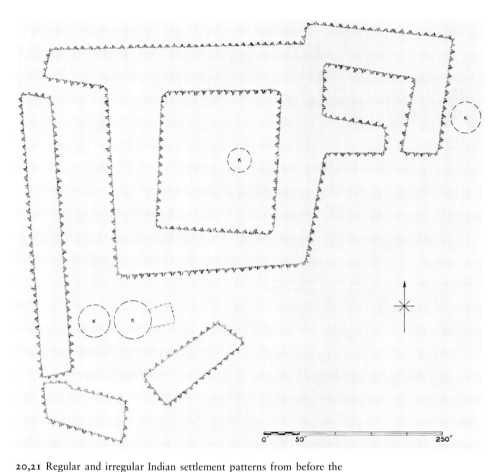

20,21 Regular and irregular Indian settlement patterns from before the Spanish rule in New Mexico. Although some precontact Indian sites were irregularly arranged, others, like the site on the right from north central New Mexico, show not only a regular pattern but also arrangement around open courtyards. This pattern is not, then, the product of inter-action with the Spanish conquerors, but rather an indigenous cultural feature that could be easily assimilated by the invaders since it matched their own native settlement patterns. At left, the irregular layout of a prehistoric site at the juncture of the Rito de la Olia and the Rio Grande del Rancho, about seven miles south of Taos, from the thirteenth century. At right, a prehistoric site on the west bank of Ojo Caliente Creek, north central New Mexico from the fourteenth century. (Reprinted by permis-sion from Stanley A. Stubbs, *Bird's-Eye View of the Pueblos*, Norman University of Oklahoma Press, 1950, figures 1, 2)

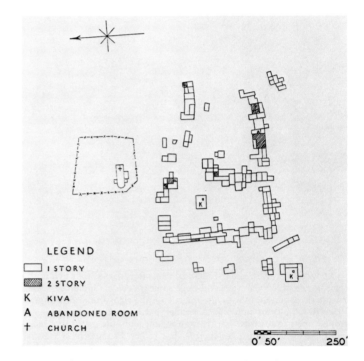

LEGEND

☐ I STORY
▨ 2 STORY
K KIVA
A ABANDONED ROOM
† CHURCH

0' 50'   250'

22 Plan of Santa Clara Pueblo, New Mexico. Shows the pre-Conquest pattern of dwellings with party walls, arranged around two courtyards. This pattern has persisted in spite of the additions of a church and of a few outlying dwellings. (Reprinted, by permission, from S. A. Stubbs, *Bird's-Eye View of the Pueblos,* Norman: University of Oklahoma Press, 1950)

23 Aerial view of Isleta Pueblo, New Mexico. In 1680, 2000 people lived here; by 1963 the population had recovered to 1974 persons after an earlier decline. In this photograph, newer construction follows the roads at upper right, while the traditional plaza-centered, fairly regular settlement is at lower left. Scholars are agreed that Hopi culture is unusually tenacious in retention of traditional forms, and this includes settlement patterns. (By permission from *Population, Contact, and Climate in the New Mexican Pueblos,* by Ezra B. W. Zubrow, Anthropological Papers of the University of Arizona, 24, Tucson: U. of Arizona Press, copyright 1974, figure 9, p. 33)

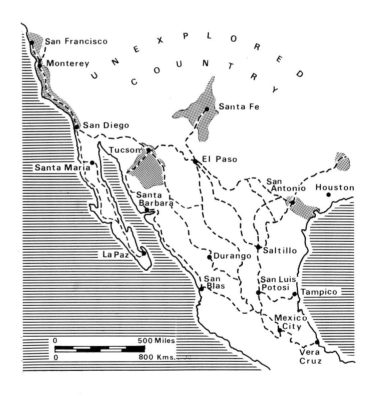

24 Trails from Mexico into the Southwest. Trails from Mexico City northward into our provincial area are shown in dashed lines, and the mission fields as grey areas. The distance from Mexico City to Santa Fe was about 1,000 miles, much of it through the driest desert. Climatically and topographically the area shown here forms a single region with some internal variation, at least as far north as Santa Fe. The indigenous population, extending the similarity with conditions in Mexico, included tribes like the Hopi, who had already been living in settled villages, and the peaceful California Indians, who took readily to domestication at the missions, but also some warlike groups such as the Apache, who were nomadic and intractable. (Plan originally published in C. Hollenbeck, *Spanish Missions of the Old Southwest,* New York: Doubleday, Page & Co., 1926, figure 1; redrawn by John Harvey for our articles "The Laws of the Indies Revisited", *Town Planning Review,* vol. 48 #4, Oct. 1977, reprinted by permission)

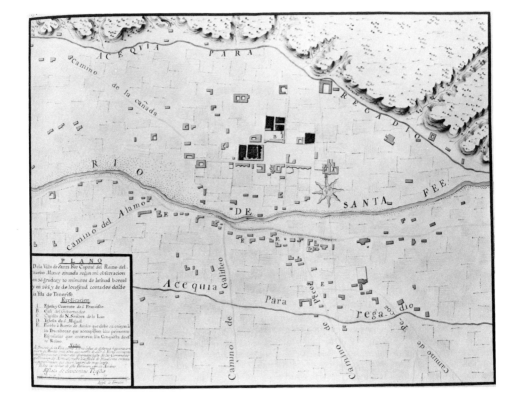

PLANO
De la Villa de Santa Fee Capital del Reino del
nuebo Mexico situada segun mi observacion
en 36 grados y 10 minutos de latitud boreal
y en 262 y de de longitud contados desde
la Isla de Tenerife.
Explicacion
A. Ygelsia y Convento de S. Francisco.
B. Cafa del Governador
C. Capilla de N. Señora de la Luz
D. Iglesia de S. Miguel
E. Puerto ô Barrio de Analco que debe su origen à
los Tlascaltecas que acompañaron à los primeros
Españoles que entraron à la Conquista de este
to Reino
Nota

25 Urrutia's map of Santa Fe. This is the earliest known. Its Spanish caption has been translated by Adams and Chavez in their *The Missions of New Mexico, 1776. A Description by Fray Francisco Atanasio Dominquez with Other Contemporary Documents*: "Plan of the Villa of Santa Fe, Capital of the Kingdom of New Mexico, situated according to my observation at 36 degrees and 10 minutes north latitude and 262° and 40' longitude, reckoned from the Island of Tenerife. Legend: A. Church and Convent of St. Francis. B. House of the Governor. C. Chapel of Our Lady of Light. D. Church of St. Michael. E. Pueblo or Suburb of Analco which owes its origin to the Tlascans who accompanied the first Spaniards who entered in the Conquest of this Kingdom. Note: To the east of the Villa, about a league distant, there is a chain of very high forested mountains which reach so far from south to north that its limits are unknown even to the Comanches, who came from the north, ever along the base of said sierra during their entire migration, which they say was very long. All the buildings of this place are of adobes. Scale of two hundred toises. Joseph de Urrutia."
Comments: The church and convent of St. Francis (A) are the present cathedral, several times rebuilt on this site, originally headquarters of the Franciscan missionaries to New Mexico. The house of the governor, today the Governor's Palace (B) was begun in 1610 as the major structure of the early presidio, rebuilt in 1692 and thereafter; it faces the main plaza of the city. The Chapel of our Lady of Light (C), called Military Chapel on other maps, is a structure of the eighteenth century and later, originally built as a religious confraternity for the officers stationed here. The Church of St. Michael (San Miguel; D), on the other hand, was always for the Indians and claims to be the oldest church in continuous use in the United States; it is supposed to date from before the foundation of Santa Fe by five or six years. This church stood at one end of the separate Pueblo of Analco (E), where the captive Indians whom the Spaniards brought with them from Mexico lived; legend has it that they were Tlascans—no other proof has been found. At the center of the map lies the Rio de Santa Fee, given prominence here probably because of a great flood that occurred in 1767. Lying to the north and south of it, and roughly parallel to it, are the irrigation ditches called "Acequia para regadio." To the west and south of the built-up area are the fields, laid out orthogonally, and among them the routes to other settlements are indicated by their names: Camino de la Canada, Camino del Alamo, Camino de Galifteo, and Camino de Pecos. The town lies at the foot of a sierra shown here as a series of bluffs to the north and northeast. Even in this plan the difference in scale between the Spanish area north of the river and the Indian area to the south is evident, a difference encouraged by the Laws of the Indies. (Courtesy of the British Library, by whose permission this map is printed from the original)

26 Map of Santa Fe in 1846 by Emory and Gilmer. The so-called Military Map, drawn incident to occupation of the city by American forces. Note that they use both Spanish and English to label the map. Among the interesting features: The Chapel and Park of the Rosary at upper left is one of several new religious buildings since Urrutia's days. The sierra appears at upper right, and the channel of the irrigation system seems to lead into the top of the corn fields at center, directly west from the sierra. What had been the enclosure of the presidio is still partially enclosed by buildings but apparently used for agriculture and not military exercises, for it is labeled Corn Fields. The Governor's Palace shows as a dark rectangle below this, facing onto the plaza with its clearly demarcated colonnades. Opposite the palace stands the military chapel. To the east, the Church of San Francisco has an enclosed courtyard in front, marked by a cross. At the center of the city runs the Rio de Santa Fe, with the Chapel of Guadalupe at the west end of the built-up area. Major roads lead off to the northwest, southwest, and southeast, with the Church of San Miguel at the intersection of one of these and the only long east-west street parallel to the river and south of it. This street has houses along both sides, presumably of the original captive Indian families and later comers. At bottom right one segment of the irrigation canal is shown. (Courtesy of the National Archives: Record Group 77: Fortification File, Dr. 142)

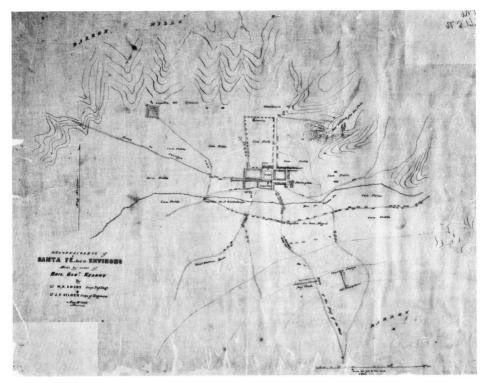

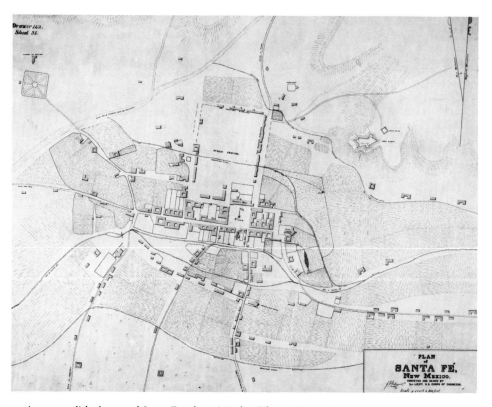

27 A more polished map of Santa Fe, also 1846, by Gilmer. Figure 26
seems to be an early version of this plan by Lt. Gilman, also probably
1846. The church of the Rosary and its formal park are at upper left,
while the newly built Fort Marcy stands on the bluff at upper right; this
fort was erected at the time of the American occupation, but used only
briefly before being allowed to crumble away. The irrigation canals have
their direction of flow shown by arrows. The Rio do Santa Fe is blue, as
is the water from the spring near the Church of San Francisco. All these
water channels flow to the west, where they join the (dry) river bed
shown at upper left. One channel flows through the public grounds, the
former presidio enclosure, formed by the old military barracks, the hospital, and the Governor's Palace. Colonnades shown as dots edge the
plaza, the main streets, the conventual buildings at the Church of San
Francisco, and a quasi-governmental building at the end of the street that
runs westward from in front of the Palace. Diagonally across the street
from the latter, a building has encroached into the north-south street.
Many of the houses are arranged around courtyards; others, especially
in the Indian village south of the river, are U-shaped. The street leading
to San Miguel in an east-west direction is shown to terminate at the
church, which, like the cathedral, is set off in its own walled plaza. Fields
close to the settlement are shaped as fairly regular quadrilaterals. Roads
leading out of Santa Fe usually have their places of destination marked
on them; the one to the south "to Independence Mo." is the terminus of
the Santa Fe Trail. (Courtesy of the National Archives: Record Group
77: Fortification File, Dr. 142; brought to my attention by John Reps)

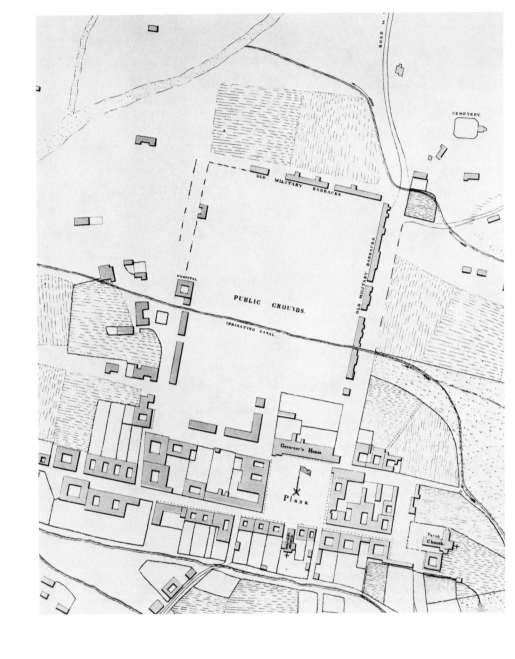

28 Detail of figure 27, showing the central business district of Santa Fe. The quintessential Spanish colonial city center is here dominated by an outsized American flag, which may also be seen in the view of Santa Fe in 1848 (figure 34). From the columns to the structures behind them, roofs would have spanned to protect pedestrians from sun and occasional rain. By the 1840s, most of these structures were occupied by stores, while the informal market was still held in the plaza. Besides the Governor's Palace, which was the administrative and legislative center of the territory, other government functions such as court (northeast corner) and customs house (east side) faced onto the plaza. Here the caravans to Mexico City, Los Angeles, or Independence were assembled, and here the promenade at the end of the day took place. The colonnaded street to the right led to the cathedral; one side of this street was residential, and therefore not colonnaded (see figure 29).

29 View along San Francisco Street, Santa Fe, from the plaza to the cathedral. Though made a cathedral, with a bishop, only in the 1830s, this church was from its founding in the seventeenth century the center of the missionary effort in New Mexico. Often rebuilt, only a few rooms are even as old as the eighteenth century. A low wall encloses the open space in front of, and beside, the church. This street leads directly to the gate in that wall from the plaza, seat of secular power. Houses to the north of the street face directly onto the street, a custom of the Greco-Roman world passed on to the Spanish by their Moorish conquerors. Here, however, the south side of the street had porticoes; we see the roofs of those in the foreground, and the columns themselves of the buildings nearer the church. (Courtesy of the Museum of New Mexico, Santa Fe)

30 Caravan on San Francisco Street just south of the plaza. The westward extension of San Francisco Street, as it edges the plaza, is shown here, with the cathedral in the distance. The military chapel is just off the picture to the right. A caravan, probably from Missouri because of the oxen, which were not used in trips to either Mexico City or Los Angeles, rests in the street. One corner of the plaza appears at left. The crude quality of the log porticoes is evident, as is the renovation of the plaza with trees and a picket fence, both added after the American occupation. (Courtesy of the Museum of New Mexico, Santa Fe)

31 Scene from the market at Tenochtitlan/Mexico City (previously published with Bernal's article on Tenochtitlan in *Cities of Destiny*). In every Spanish colonial city, Indian vendors sold their wares in the plazas. Here at Santa Fe, these were stationed along the north side of the plaza, and even in the porches of the Governor's Palace. (Courtesy of the Bibliotica Mediceo-Laurenziana; from the Codex Fiorentino)

32 Drawing of a reconstruction of the great irrigation ditch of Santa Fe. The irrigation system, which was the first communal building activity at Los Angeles, was at Santa Fe the means of existence in the desert. It began from the spring near the Church of San Francisco, which was probably located there to utilize the spring; very early the waters were led to the presidio; eventually a whole series of major and minor channels made a network through the fields and houses. This recent drawing shows one such channel at Santa Fe. (Courtesy of the City Planning Dept., Santa Fe; Kate Krasin, artist)

33 Earliest surviving house at Santa Fe. Houses at Santa Fe were from
the beginning made of easily available local materials: stone, adobe mud,
wooden roof beams. The oldest house now standing there is the Juan
Rodriguez House, from 1844 and later; though relatively late, it is in the
same style as those earlier ones that have disappeared. The same kind of
house would have stood at Los Angeles, but not at St. Louis, where the
early French influence and the dampness of the climate made adobe both
unfashionable and impractical. (Courtesy of the City Planning Dept.,
Santa Fe)

34 View of Santa Fe in 1848. The artist placed himself south of the city, between two of the major roads, along which traffic is moving. The wide spacing of the houses, seen here, is still common in desert areas. At center is the huge American flag in the plaza, echoed by another at Fort Marcy on the hill to the right. Between them a tiny cross marks the Church of San Francisco. At the top of the plaza lie the old barracks, which form the northern edge of the old presidio. The regularity of city blocks near the plaza is noteable. (Courtesy of the Map Collection at the Library of Congress; brought to our attention by John Reps)

NOTES

1 Mexico City was refounded 1541; Santa Fe was founded 1609.

2 E. R. Forrest, *Pueblos and Missions of the Old Southwest* (Cleveland: 1929), p. 41; hereafter cited as Forrest.

3 J. G. Meem, *Old Santa Fe Today* (Albuquerque: n.d.), preface.

4 A. Dominquez, *The Missions of New Mexico, 1776*, trans. and annotated E. B. Adams and A. Chavez (Albuquerque: 1956), p. 41, n. 69; hereafter cited as Dominquez.

5 Ralph K. Knowles, *Energy and Form* (Cambridge, Mass.: 1978), fig. 28; George Kubler, *The Religious Architecture of New Mexico*, 4th ed. (Albuquerque: 1972), p. 15; hereafter cited as Kubler, 1972.

6 Herbert E. Bolton, *The Spanish Borderlands: A Chronology of Old Florida and the Southwest* (New Haven: 1921), p. 165; hereafter cited as Bolton, 1921.

7 Don Pedro Bautista Pino, the *Exposición*, 1812, quoted in Lic. Antonio Barreiro, the *Ojeada*, 1832, p. 29, and in Don José Agustin de Escudero's additions, p. 32; all are in *Three New Mexico Chronicles*, trans. and annotated by H. Bailey Carroll and J. Villasana Haggard (Albuquerque, 1942); hereafter each reference will be by author and page only. For further information on the arrangement of pueblos, see S. A. Stubbs, *Bird's-Eye View of the Pueblos* (Norman, OK: 1950) and Ezra B. W. Zubrow, *Population, Contact, and Climate in the New Mexico Pueblos*, Anthropological Papers of the University of Arizona, No. 24, both amply illustrated.

8 Ye-Fu Tuan, *Topophilia* (Englewood Cliffs, NJ: 1974), p. 66 quoting J. R. Bartlett of the United States and Mexico Boundary Commission and Lt. J. H. Simpson.

9 Kubler, 1972, pp. 15–17.

10 William Heath Davis, *El Gringo, or New Mexico and Her People* (Santa Fe: 1938), p. 39; hereafter cited as Davis.

11 Herbert E. Bolton, *Texas in the Middle 18th Century: Studies in Spanish Colonial History* (Berkeley: 1915), pp. 9–10; hereafter cited as Bolton, 1915.

12 Violich, F., "Evolution of the Spanish City: Issues Basic to Planning Today," *Journal of the American Institute of Planners*, vol. 28, No. 3 (August 1962), p. 171.

13 Kubler, 1972, p. 131.

14 As quoted in Philip Wayne Powell, *Soldiers, Indians and Silver* (Berkeley and Los Angeles: 1952).

15 *Ibid.*, p. 213.

16 L. B. Simpson, *The Encomienda in New Spain* (Berkeley: 1929), *passim*.

17 Kubler, 1948, p. 64.

18 Bolton, 1921, pp. 164–166, 190.

19 Most authors, e.g., Sanford Trent, *Architecture of the Southwest* (New York: 1950), p. 90, give 1610 as the date, but Herbert E. Bolton and T. M. Marshall, *The Colonization of North America* (New York: 1930), p. 72, prefer 1609.

20 Forrest, p. 17.

21 *Ibid.*, p. 41.

22 Hubert Howe Bancroft, *History of Arizona and New Mexico 1530–1888* (1889; reprint ed. Albuquerque: 1962); hereafter cited as Bancroft, 1889.

23 Dominguez, p. xv.

24 *Ibid.*, p. 6.

25 *Ibid.*, p. xviii; Pino, pp. 50, 55.

26 Dominguez, p. 6

27 *Ibid.*, p. 127. In Bancroft, 1889, p. 176, there is a good map of the locations of pueblos in the region of Sante Fe.

28 E. H. Spicer, *Cycles of Conquest* (Tucson: 1962), pp. 298–300; Stubbs, p. 14.

29 Reps, 1965, p. 43; Violich, 1962, p. 43.

30 Dominguez, p. 12

31 The phrase "de San Francisco" seems to have been added to the name of the city no earlier than the nineteenth century, referring to the saint after whom the principal church was named, the great patron of the Franciscan missionaries. Dominguez, p. 13, no. 3.

32 Dominguez, p. 12.

33 Trent, p. 91.

34 Bancroft, 1889, p. 203, says the site was retaken by the Spanish on December 16, 1692, but other authors disagree.

35 I have used Dominguez's translation of the caption of this map.

36 Bancroft, 1889, p. 259. n. 13.

37 Davis, pp. 67–69.

38 Dominguez, p. 40.

39 Possibly this complaint was a pun on the meaning of *presidio* as prison. Petition of Fray Francisco de Ayeta, May 10, 1679, as quoted in Hackett (see note 86).

40 Pino, p. 27.

41 *Ibid.*, pp. 80, 84–85, 186, n. 25.

42 Violich, 1962, p. 43.

43 Trent, p. 94.

44 Beyer, p. 55.

45 Davis, p. 41.

46 Beyer, p. 51.

47 Pino, p. 85; Dominguez, p. 40; Davis, pp. 39, 41.

48 Pino, p. 85.

49 Elias Brevoort, "Santa Fe Trail 1884," Manuscript, P-E8, Bancroft Library, University of California, Berkeley.

50 Bancroft, 1889, p. 791, n. 7.

51 Pino, pp. 85–86.

52 Davis, p. 44.

53 Davis, pp. 46–47.

54 *Ibid.*, p. 39.

55 *Ibid.*, p. 41.

56 Dominguez, p. 39.

57 Meem, preface.

58 Forrest, p. 41, claims that San Miguel was built 1605–1608 by Don Juan Oñate.

59 Bancroft, 1889, p. 162.

60 Davis, p. 49; Dominguez, pp. 32–33, 246, n. 52.

61 Dominguez, p. 244.

62 Pino, p. 85.

63 *Idem.*

64 Trent, p. 91; Violich, 1962, pp. 195–197.

65 Pino, pp. 85–86.

66 Dominguez, p. 39.

67 Pino, p. 85.

68 Davis, pp. 40–41, 50–53, 100.

69 Dominguez, p. 278, quoting a letter to Provincial Fray Isidro Murillo, of June 10, 1776.

70 Hugh Morrison, *Early American Architecture* (Oxford: 1952), p. 183. Pino, p. 187, n. 260 (by editors).

71 Dominguez, p. 22.

72 Pino. n. 260.

73 Davis, p. 44, where he does not, however, say that a governor was buried under the floor; unfortunately I have lost the source of this notion.

74 *Ibid.*, pp. 44–45.

75 Trent, p. 91; Pino, n. 260. See also P. A. F. Walter, "El Palacio Real" in *Old Santa Fe*, pp. 333–334.

76 William G. Ritch, "History of New Mexico 1884," unpaginated manuscript, Bancroft Library, University of California, Berkeley.

77 J. Watts, "Santa Fe Affairs," Manuscript, Bancroft Library, University of California, Berkeley, p. 10.

78 Doninguez, pp. 22ff.

79 Bancroft, 1889, p. 641.

80 Davis, pp. 46–47.

81 *Ibid.*, p. 43.

82 *Ibid.*, p. 41.

83 *Ibid.*, p. 42.

84 Pino, p. 96.

85 Davis, p. 39.

86 C. W. Hackett, *Historical Documents Relating to New Mexico Nueva Vizcaya and Approaches Thereto, to 1773* (Washington, D.C.: 1923), pp. 108, 119.

87 Spicer, pp. 5, 7.

88 Dominguez, p. 42, n. 72; Spicer, p. 300.

89 Spicer, P. 300.

90 Bancroft, 1889, p. 163, n. 43; Bolton and Marshall, p. 243, where the figure is 750 Indians. Hackett, pp. 108–119, says Santa Fe had 50 of the 200 Spaniards and Mestizos in the province in 1638; these supported themselves by growing wheat and maize by irrigation.

91 Rexford Newcomb, *Spanish-Colonial Architecture in the United States* (New York: 1937), p. 30.

92 Bancroft, 1889, pp. 197–198; Hackett, however, on pp. 108, 299, quotes Fr. Miguel de Monchero, writing in 1744, as giving the date 1682.

93 Hackett, p. 373.

94 *Ibid.*, p. 24.

95 Dominguez, pp. 42–43. These population figures do not correlate well with Zubrow, *Population, Contact, and Climate in the New Mexican Pueblos*, who gives, in figure 4, a population for the pueblos in 1800 of about 10,000 with the total New Mexico population as about 25,000 for that year.

96 Spicer, p. 100.

97 Bancroft, 1889, pp. 299–300.

98 *Ibid.*, pp. 311–313.

99 *Ibid.*, p. 309.

100 *Ibid.*, p. 299.

101 *Ibid.*, pp. 311, 313.

102 Pino, p. 84.

103 *Ibid.*, pp. 88–89.

104 Bancroft, 1889, pp. 310–311.

105 *Compendium of the 7th United States Census*, p. 381.

106 Davis, p. 64.

107 *Ibid.*, p. 39; Bancroft, 1889, p. 790.

108 Trent, pp. 94–95.

109 Pino, pp. 89–90.

110 Davis, pp. 76–77. Caravans with wagons drawn by oxen became typical of the Santa Fe Trail to Missouri as it developed into a real road.

111 Pino, pp. 109, 119, 120.

112 Dominguez, p. xv.

113 Davis, p. 75.

114 Bancroft, 1889, p. 297.

115 Eleanor Lawrence, "Mexican Trade between Santa Fe and Los Angeles, 1830–1848," *California Historical Quarterly* (1931), pp. 27–39.

116 Pino, p. 108.

117 *Ibid.*, p. 106.

118 Quoted in Oliver LaFarge, *Santa Fe* (Norman, OK: 1970), p. viii.

119 Davis, introduction by Fergusson.

120 Bolton and Marshall, p. 73.

121 *Ibid.*, p. 235.

122 Kubler, 1972, p. 102.

123 Davis, introduction by Fegusson.

124 Kubler, 1972, p. 18.

2

ST. LOUIS

St. Louis, that quintessentially American middle western city, is appropriately diverse in its ethnic origins and diplomatic chronology. Founded as a de facto French outpost, the site actually belonged to Spain after 1762. Then, as an aftermath of the Napoleonic Wars, St. Louis and its territory were handed back to France in 1800, but they did not take possession until 1804. Then France sold the territory to the United States as part of the Louisiana Purchase.

It has usually been assumed that Spanish impact on St. Louis was negligible, but we shall see that this assumption needs to be reassessed. We are not claiming that St. Louis was a Spanish city in the same sense that Vera Cruz was, or even Santa Fe. St. Louis was far from the centers of Spanish power. It was under Spanish control for only a few years, at a time when the empire was in very weakened condition. Under these circumstances, it is thought provoking to find here any traces at all of Spanish urban thinking. The traces are faint, but we do find them, and they speak to the strength and richness of an urban tradition that even in its death throes could manifest itself over such distances. It has been an interesting site to us precisely because of its unusual cultural layering and the challenge it poses of trying to discern the traces of Spanish rule.

From New Orleans, the French governor of Upper and Lower Louisiana had granted the site of St. Louis to the firm of Maxent, Laclede, and Company in 1763. Probably the governor and the fur company were unaware that the area had been ceded to Spain in 1762. One of the partners of the firm, Pierre Laclede Liguest, traveled to the site in the fall of 1763, selected the precise location of the post, and sent a group of workmen there in February 1764, to begin clearing the site and erecting temporary shelters.[1]

Many of the city planning ordinances of the Laws of the Indies mandated decisions that founders of settlements might well have come to by common sense or flashes of insight. By having these ideas incorporated into the laws, however, the founders could be lacking in both and still succeed. One way, for example, to select a site was to look for a place already "populated by Indians and natives" (ordinance 36) if they seemed to be healthy, then the presumption was that Europeans could live in the same areas.

The common sense of this idea seems to have guided the French in choosing the site of St. Louis, a place just to the north of a village of Peoria Indians, separated from them by a little river. Rather than reduce these Indians to serfdom, as was the Spanish pattern at Santa Fe, Laclede's company wished to use them to expedite the fur trade, the reason for which the post was set up.

The site chosen was on a plateau above the junction of the rivers. Limestone ridges separated the village from the Mississippi River; high water came to the foot of the limestone bluff, but low water left a sand flat that served as a beach where small river craft could be pulled out of the water (figure 49). On the plateau, the village site sloped gently, having good drainage and no ravines. Both timber from the heavy forest cover and outcrops of durable stone could be used as building materials.[2]

"A commercial place with money behind it," St. Louis flourished from the very beginning. Although to the east the territory from the Mississippi River to the Allegheny Mountains was vaguely under English control, to the west the hitherto untapped fur trade could bypass the English and funnel through the new settlement and down the Mississippi to New Orleans. The French-Canadian residents of Illinois were apprehensive about what the new English rule would mean for them, and so it was not difficult to persuade them to emigrate across the river to Laclede's new town, especially when they were promised that the land-use traditions of the older French villages would be continued.[3] Clearing was begun at St. Louis on 15 February 1764, and by June there were two or three huts and many six- or seven-foot platforms on which people could sleep without fear of animals. The workers were led by Auguste Chouteau, then only 14 years of age! Under his direction, work began on a headquarters of stone for the company. (This is probably the hip-roofed building at the center of figure 49.) By August 1766, there were fifty families living in forty houses.[4] The village occupied the area now dedicated as the Jefferson Memorial Arch (compare figures 38 and 46). The river served as chief water supply, and the village was strung out along it.[5] As Wade points out, the village came first, and agriculture developed later.[6]

Laclede had planned St. Louis along the lines of Montreal, Mobile, and New Orleans.[7] Several of the early maps of St. Louis seem to refer to this earliest version of the town. Curiously, they do not agree as to its configuration. A map of 1780, which was recopied in 1841 (figure 39), claims to agree with Chouteau's 1764 map, now lost. These show one large block inland from the river side of the town, at the center, and a second square block still farther inland, in line with the first. Figures 38 and 39 also included a fully developed wall with bastions and towers, which certainly did not exist in 1764. Therefore we must be cautious in accepting every detail of these maps as literally true; they seem to include official hopes as well as actual arrangements.

Unlike most of the other maps, the Dufossat map of 1767 (figure 35) seems to be based on observation rather than hope. The setting of St. Louis, overlooking the Mississippi River and bracketed by two little rivers, is clear, as is its relation to the Indian village to the south and the "French village under the domination of the English," immediately across the Mississippi. Both villages are laid out according to a simple grid, but the one on the east bank seems to have an open plaza at the center, formed by leaving empty the space of two city blocks. If this arrangement had already been in existence at St. Louis, Dufossat could as easily have shown it there. One other extremely interesting fact about this map is that in spite of being made by a Frenchman, and in French, the map now is kept at the *Biblioteca nacional* in Madrid,[8] perhaps in response to ordinances 21, 22, 23, which required keeping the governors and the Council of the Indies informed.

Dufossat had been a French army officer. When he came to St. Louis he was an officer in the Spanish army, taking part in an expedition from New Orleans that was to design and build a presidio at the mouth of the Missouri River. He was one of two engineers that accompanied this expedition.[9] Probably the Spanish governor of Louisiana had instructed Dufossat to send him an accurate plan of the new settlement, soon to come officially under Spanish control. This plan would have been then sent on to the Council of the Indies in Spain.

Collot's 1796 map (figure 40) has not only a preoccupation with defense, but also a block-and-street layout that agrees substantially with Dufossat, in spite of the nearly twenty-year passage of time. Only by noting the location of the church on the seventh inland block from the north can we find correspondence with the 1780 map. But instead of the blocks between the church and the river being left vacant for the plaza, they are as much occupied by the small black rectangles that I take to be houses as any other block. Collot's maps are "unrealistic" in that they show all the streets perpendicular to the river as running straight down the bank to the water, a feature unknown to any other map, even the 1822 one (figure 45). Yet a different engineer (St. Lys), in the same year (1796), shows a very large, square plaza at almost the exact center of his plan (figure 41). This plaza, however, is one block north and east of the church—instead of due east. (Perhaps this was an area politically and economically easier to clear for the proposed plaza.) The discrepancies between these maps leave doubt that a formal plaza existed at this time.

The Soulard map of 1804 (figure 42) was drawn by the Surveyor of Upper Louisiana for presentation to the US Army at the time of the Louisiana Purchase. Like the Dufossat map, it has an air of verisimilitude. The topography of the site is clear, as are the towers and bastions that form the inland defense of the city. The town itself is shown schematically and is like the Chouteau maps in its configuration. At center, two square blocks are noticeably larger than the others, and one has a church on it. Diagonally across one square block from the church is another building, probably the company headquarters turned government center.

While the general configuration of the St. Louis plan, stretched out along the river and fortified on the land sides, resembles New Orleans quite strongly, in detail there are differences. Consider the street width: At New Orleans, they are thirty-two feet, but at St. Louis streets were supposed to be twelve *varas* or thirty-four feet wide. At St. Louis there were three major streets parallel to the river, each actually thirty-six French feet wide. The first, at the edge of the plaza was called La Rue Principale, or La Grande Rue, or La Rue Royale; this is now Main or First Street. The second was called La Rue de l'Eglise or La Deuxieme Grande Rue, and is now Second Street. The third was called either La Rue des Granges, because it ran up to a hill with the community barns on it, or La Rue Barrère after a baker who lived on the street; it is now Third Street. Perpendicular to the river, the streets were thirty feet wide. Most important of them were La Rue de la Place, also called La Rue Bonhomme, and now Market Street, La Rue Missouri now Chestnut Street, and La Rue Quicapou (Kiakapoo) now Pine Street. Of these, only the first went down to the towpath and the river.[10]

At both New Orleans and St. Louis, the large central block was 300 feet square. Other Spanish sites in Missouri also used a 300-foot-square block;[11] it seems to have been a popular late-eighteenth-century size and shape, even though it was not exactly what was called for in ordinance 113. Studies of St. Louis have frequently assumed that this 300-foot-square block was the plaza. In fact, however, this block belonged to Laclede and then to Chouteau. The plaza was the oblong block to the east of it, shown in the maps (figures 38 and 39) as a gap at the center of the row of blocks along the river. To the north and south of the 300-foot-wide central blocks, the usual block size was 240 feet by 300 feet, easily divided into four house lots of 120 feet by 150 feet. This neat regularity gradually faded after 1766 when deeds began to be recorded, for as the lots were subdivided they became smaller and less uniform.[12] The need for a professional surveyor was soon felt, and Chouteau's amateur plan of 1764 was superseded in 1770 when Martin Duralde was appointed by Lieutenant Governor Piernas to do the first official survey for the Spanish government.[13]

Both a prudent regard for possible flood damage, and a desire to preserve for community use the pleasant promenade along the bluffs insured that in early French and Spanish St. Louis a wide public space was left at the east edge of the settlement. This promenade provided "sufficient space where the people may go to for recreation" (ordinance 129).

At the lower level there was a boat landing, visible in figure 49. One street, La Rue de la Place, led up from the river and boat landing to the esplanade, and on to the central plaza, today's Market Street (figure 39). On this point, the French and Spanish documents agree on the existence and persistence of this plaza in the town.

The St. Louis *Place* was maintained for the most part intact during the colonial period. An exception was the granting of a section 60' × 150' to Benito Vasquez in 1713 (Livres Terreins III: Fo. 4). Buenaventura Colle also came to own some of it but the petition of Madams Loisel, the village Midwife, for another section was turned down. The tract became the "Market Place" of the American period; the first market house was built on it in 1811. The last section owned by the public was sold off in 1856.[14]

In addition to the market, the unimproved plaza was used for drilling the militia and for public gatherings, as its names reflect: La Place Publique, La Place des Armes, or simply La Place.

In 1765 Laclede's grant was withdrawn, but the post continued under French control. The first troops under Captain St. Ange arrived in the same year. St. Ange continued as provisional governor for five years.[15] In addition to maintaining whatever form Laclede's workmen had managed to impress on this site in the wilderness, St. Ange was the first of many governors to take the defense of the settlement as a major concern.

Although Spain had legal claim to Upper Louisiana from 1762, the process of taking possession was slow, hampered by the same problems of distance and lack of money then facing Spain in California. At St. Louis, Spanish claim to the area was established by 1770, under the rule of Captain Pedro Piernas, Lieutenant Governor of Upper Louisiana. He arrived in May, to relieve St. Ange, and quartered his troops in a house rented from Laclede.[16]

For the next ten years, Captain Piernas and his troops were the active presence of Spain in these northern reaches. They defended the town, with the passive assistance of palisades around the house lots and the great fence around the commons east of town. Within the village, greater security was made possible by having the buildings and lots contiguous, and encircled by fences. The local custom was to have pickets or stockades eight or ten feet tall, made of mulberry, cedar, or oak, completely encircling each lot; big houses, such as the Chouteau mansions, had stone walls. A decree of Governor Gayoso de Lemos at New Orleans, dated September 1797, stated,

It shall not be permitted to any new settler to form an establishment at a distance from the other settlers. The grants of land must be so made as to not to have pieces of vacant ground between one and another, since this would offer a greater exposure to the attacks of the Indians and render more difficult the administration of justice and the regulation of the police so necessary in all societies and more particularly in new settlements.[17]

These fences guarded against Indians. The advantage of enclosing all the private lots is obvious; by just barricading the ends of the streets in an emergency, it would be possible to have a continuous enclosure around the village for defense.[18] But a mere stockade would not be effective in a real war.

In the summer of 1779, war between Spain and England seemed likely to affect even remote St. Louis. The Mississippi River was one place where Spain and England had a common border. The British were stirring up the Indian tribes all along the western frontier as part of their effort to crush the American Revolution. It is not surprising therefore that the Spanish officers at St. Louis began to give careful thought to the defense of the site. They were concerned not only about Indian attacks but also about the possibility of a major offensive launched from either Detroit or New Orleans, along the rivers which were the easiest contacts between St. Louis and the wider world.

The governor decided to have four stone towers or forts constructed around the village. The one on the west was built first, to dominate the town and its approaches from an elevated gun platform; it was named after San Carlos. When this one was nearly finished, a second was begun at the north. Between the two, and arching around to the south, a trench was dug to double the barrier already formed by the commons fence.[19] Concurrently, correspondence between Patrick Henry in Virginia and Governor Bernardo de Galvez in Louisiana had worked out an agreement assuring common action against their common enemy, Britain. The troops of George Rogers Clark were to be given supplies, and Clark was to cooperate with the new lieutenant governor, de Leyba. On 26 May 1780 an attack by England's Indian allies against the settlement resulted in the massacre of those outside the stockade wall. Altogether, 22 were killed (15 whites and 7 slaves), 7 wounded, and 71 captured.[20] Some 29 Spanish soldiers with artillery, aided by 281 residents, fought off the attacks with the help of Clark's men, who distracted the Indians.[21]

Encouraged by the success of these defenses, the next Spanish governor, François Cruzat, planned to augment them by building a stockade eighteen feet high and six inches thick. By December 1780, $2,000 per month was being spent on the stockade, much of which went to pay for the demilune (semicircular tower) of stone on the buff at the north end of the settlement. As actually built, the palisadoes were nine feet (not eighteen) high, connected the demilune with the San Carlos tower, and then ran south to the Little River below the town. Bastions at the two western angles covered the flanks of the curtain. In this fence, over a mile length, there were four main gates.[22] By the summer of 1781 the work was finished, and St. Louis was ready for the next attack. By 1785, however, the whole stockade was in ruins; it had been built hastily of uncured wood, with no paint to preserve it, in the same way as the settlers' common fences against animals. The Canadian military engineer Chaussegros de Lery commented, "In peacetime such forts are not built in the colonies because they rot quickly and are useless by the time war is declared."[23]

The next lieutenant governor, Manuel Perez, decided in 1788 to build the northwest bastion in stone. It was never quite finished, but the structure did have walls thirteen to fifteen feet thick, gun embrasures, a guard room, and a powder magazine.[24] For many years this tower stood at the corner of Franklin Avenue and Third Street.

The next lieutenant governor, Zenon Trudeau, planned elaborate defenses in the best European mode, with space for refugees, stone buildings, and so on. His scheme is shown in the map "Plan de la Ville de St. Louis des Illinois sur le Mississippi avec les Differents Projects de la Fortifier par George de Bois St. Lys Ancien Offr. Francais 1796," shown in figure 41. Since, however, this project was to cost 10,000 pesos, it was not completed, and the ten-foot stone walls around the mansions of Auguste and Pierre Chouteau continued to be the basic fortifications of the village. Military experts apparently were called in frequently, and made their suggestions to the authorities, but little was done. We know of the following military engineers who studied the questions of defense at St. Louis: Dufossat, Varela, Warin, Vanden Bemden, de Finiels, [Callott,] and Soulard.[25]

Yet another Spanish lieutenant governor, an Irish officer named Charles Howard, arrived in St. Louis in late April 1797, bringing with him the engineer Louis Vanden Bemden; they were joined in June by another engineer, Nicolas de Finiels, who mapped the Mississippi from St. Louis south to New Madrid. The 1788 accomplishment of clearing the river of pirates had done much to increase trade with New Orleans, which in turn increased the size and importance of St. Louis and made a map of the river useful and necessary. Vanden Bemden analyzed the military situation at St. Louis and came up with three different plans at three different budgets; the third, and least expensive, called for repairing the existing defenses and was the one selected. The old fort around San Carlos tower was repaired, and one new tower nearly completed, when it was decided to build four new stone towers. By May of 1798 these were nearly finished. Two stood on a hill and two along the Petite Rivière, where there was also a blockhouse at what is now Fourth and Chouteau. The towers stood at Third and Olive, to cover a deep ravine; at Third and Washington near the road to St. Charles; at Fifth and Gratiot; and at Second and LaSalle, on the old road to Carondelet.[26] The new towers formed a rough semicircle around St. Louis, along the west side, from which Indian attack might come. A curtain and earthworks to connect the towers were planned but never built; instead, the defenders relied on the fact that the towers were all placed within gunshot of each other. Vanden Bemden's plans are not published here, but see Callott's of the same period (figure 40), and Soulard's (figure 42); Soulard had been Vanden Bemden's assistant.

Owing partly to their hasty construction, and partly to the weather, these defenses were in constant need of repair.[27] Already by 1799, most of the defenses were either incomplete or ruined. The San Carlos tower was being used as a jail, the barracks as the court house; the bastion became a garden; the blockhouse became an abbatoir, and the beams from the demilune eventually (1819) became part of a printer's press.[28] Repairs in 1800 were supervised by Antoine Soulard, who had come to St. Louis in February 1795 as Surveyor General of Upper Louisiana; he may have been a refugee from the French Revolution. In 1797, working under Howard and Vanden Bemden, he had made plans for the fortifications. Under later US rule, he continued as territorial surveyor; his is the 1804 (?) map published here (figure 42). Destruction of the fortifications was hastened by a fierce hurricane on 3 April 1803, which took the roofs off the barracks and the armory. Indian scares in the fall and winter of 1804 led to hasty repair of the old fortifications.[29] These were the last repairs to the defenses of St. Louis, which for over thirty years of Spanish rule had been the constant preoccupation of the governors and of the military engineers they hired.

In addition to ordinance 133 and to the 250 years of practice that had elapsed between the founding of the first Spanish colony in the New World and the founding of St. Louis, Spanish ideas about fortifications and defense owe much to a group of treatises published in Italy in the sixteenth century. Notable are Machiavelli, *Arte della Guerra*, published in 1521, Polybius's book on Roman warfare, published in 1530, and Guillaume du Choul's 1555 treatise on Roman encampments, published in Spain in 1579.[30] All of these treatises demanded a grid plan with an open square at the center as part of the defensive system. We have seen that the Spanish were not slow to employ trained military engineers even on these farthest outreaches of empire. They were hired for their expertise, not their nationality; those who worked at St. Louis were Dutch, French, Irish, and Spanish. Because of unsettled conditions in Europe—the French Revolution, followed by the Napoleonic Wars—and the opportunities that the frontier represented, and probably also a long tradition of adventurism in the Spanish army, even the lieutenant governors were often other than Spanish, though serving the Spanish crown.

Thirty-four years after the first Spanish lieutenant governor took office in St. Louis, he was replaced by an American. In 1800 Louisiana had been returned by Spain to France as part of the Bourbon Family Pact, but effective control of Upper Louisiana remained with the Spanish. After Napoleon came to power, he sold the territory to the new United States of America in 1803. The Louisiana

Purchase was perhaps the most daring act of Jefferson's presidency, causing a flurry of comment at the time. Captain Amos Stoddard of the US Army took possession of St. Louis as representative of the French on 9 March 1804, and on 10 March 1804 assumed American control[31] (figures 43 and 44).

The forces under Stoddard's command were sixty soldiers, a galley with twenty-four oarsmen, and a military hospital with a surgeon but few patients. The Spaniards informed him that there were few patients because of the healthy climate.[32] Despite the healthfulness of the site, St. Louis did not long remain the Missouri stronghold for the frontier already was moving westward. In 1806 Cantonment Bellefontaine on the Missouri River became the frontier, being farther west. There was some talk of rehabilitating the fortifications of St. Louis for the War of 1812, but the westward movement of the frontier had made this unnecessary.[33]

By the middle of the twentieth century, of the US cities with populations exceeding 50,000, only eleven had begun with defensive walls.[34] According to Nelson, St. Augustine and Pensacola, Florida; Provo, Spanish Fork, Fillmore, Cedar City, Salt Lake City, and Ogden, Utah; Boston, Massachusetts: Charleston, South Carolina; Savannah, Georgia; Nieu Amsterdam, Albany, and Schenectady, New York; Detroit, Michigan; New Orleans, Louisiana; and St. Louis, Missouri, had such walls, but it is obvious that not all of these had a population exceeding 50,000 in 1950. His study also assessed Montreal and Halifax in Canada. Each of these cities began as a civil settlement and then was fortified, unlike Monterey, for instance, which began as a fort and grew into a civil settlement. St. Louis is an important member of this small class of cities. Moreover, its Spanish qualities are seen most clearly in its defensive system.

A feature of early St. Louis that developed from both French and Spanish concepts of urban living was the commons (*ejido* in Spanish). Common lands were used by the French settlers for grazing, hunting of small game, and gathering firewood and cutting building timber. As the number of settlers, and therefore the number of cattle, increased, it was necessary to set aside more land for this commons; eventually all the shore line and the entire west-

ern outskirts of the village were included. The western
commons was fenced immediately after the founding of
the village, being enclosed at least by 1775. The fences ran
from natural or man-made features such as the Indian
mound (at the foot of Wyandotte Street in today's South
St. Louis) to the Petite Rivière and from the demilune at
the north.

Spanish law recognized the value of the commons (see
ordinance 129). Maintenance of the fence was governed
by town ordinances and had to be completed by sowing
day, April 15, each year. Individual farmers worked on
stretches of the fence, and their work was checked by
umpires; if their cattle broke through into the fields beyond, they were fined. The system of common grazing
grew until 1786. At the height of the commons system,
one fence ran all the way around *Prairie des Noyers* and
Grandes Prairies (see figure 40). Then the system of commons grazing declined. By 1796 the Great Fence was abandoned except for large sections that became private
property. Although the Great Fence was the basis of the
outer line of defense of the settlement, Governor Trudeau
reported in 1798 that since there were relatively few farmers, much energy was wasted in keeping up this stockade
annually. Growing scarcity of fencing material was an
additional reason for abandoning the stockade. Another
was the attraction of the Anglo-American farming system
of self-sufficient compact farms. Unlike the French or
Spanish system of village communality, the Anglos lived
separately and "fenced and cultivated when they pleased."
The Commonfields of St. Louis and Her Neighbors" (figure 47) shows the French system of laying out fields in
long narrow configurations, usually 6 to 8 *arpents* wide
and 40 deep. (An *arpent* was 180 French feet = 192½
English feet.) Farmers would live in town and go out to
till, a sensible system during the years of danger from
Indian attack. As early as 1779, however, the governor
received a perition for an Engish-style farmstead, and by
1789 farms south of St. Louis were being enclosed in four-
or five-acre lots "after the English fashion"—thus neces-
sitating the ruling by the Governor Gayoso de Lemos
against this non-Spanish land division.[35]

It should be noted that the map of the commonfields
calls two kinds of land by this name: the grazing and

woodlot, called here "Commons of St. Louis," and the meadows that had been divided into strip fields, called here "Prairie des Noyers Common Field," and other prairies. In ordinary speech, these fields were called *terres de champs* by the French and outlots by the Anglos.[36] If the commonfields of St. Louis are compared with the plan of either Santa Fe (figure 27) or of Sonoma (figure 48), the square or nearly square lots of the Spanish contrast with the long narrow lots of the French. On the other hand, the division of land at St. Louis was not precisely according to the French or French-Canadian custom, for in those areas the long narrow strips of farm land began in each case at a river, which most of the prairies of St. Louis do not do. It seems possible that here the pragmatism of the Spanish rule, which could adapt cultural features from the Indians of the Southwest, compromised with the French traditional land pattern, expanding it for use away from river edges. Even after St. Louis became American, the laws of the Missouri Territory recognized the concept of commons. Firewood for St. Louis was still being provided from common lands seven or eight miles down the river as late as 1820. The last fragment of commons in St. Louis is Lafayette Park in South St. Louis.[37]

How much land would one family receive for farming in these prairies? Spanish law as quoted in documents of 1806 alloted land for settlers based on family size: 100 arpents for the settler, 100 for his wife, 50 for each child, 20 for each slave, to a maximum of 800 arpents per family. Title was confirmed after raising three crops; once title was established, land could be bought, sold, and mortgaged. This is quite different from land policy in the Southwest and, I think, must be due to French custom. By 1797, Spanish law allowed only Catholic farmers and artisans to own property. However, "Most of the land in what is now St. Louis county was taken up by Anglo-Americans before the end of the Spanish period, when names like Abbot, Adams, and Allen join older names like Alvarez, Aubin, and Aubuchon in the annals of St. Louis."[38]

Under the French, St. Louis had five major field areas: One immediately to the west of the village, the Champs de St. Louis, was laid out before 1766 with fields 1½ mile by 192½ English feet (that is, a Paris acre), crossed by a public road 36 feet wide that led to St. Charles village. In

1765 or 1766, the second Grande Prairie was established 2 miles northwest of the village, at the place where Laclede had a large country house (on which the Indian attack of 1780 was focused). In 1766, the third, the Petite Prairie, was laid out adjacent to the Peoria Indian village, which is seen on the earliest map. The fourth, farther out, was a relatively small field called Cul de Sac and dates from 1768 or before. The fifth, the large Praire des Noyers (walnut trees) south of Cul de Sac, was 1½ miles wide and 6 miles long.[39] Groups of fields were scattered like this to give each farmer a variety of soil and microclimatic conditions. Farmers who lived in the village of St. Louis went out together to work on their fields, a much more community-oriented system than the Anglo-American one that superseded it.

According to the Spanish census of 1791 (taken, as at Santa Fe, to inform the Council of the Indies), these fields produced 6,575 bushels of wheat, 8,606 bushels of maize, and 4,870 pounds of tobacco, making the settlement self-sufficient, except in wartime; in 1797 food had to be imported.[40]

Within the village, house lots were divided into a garden and a court—what we would call a farmyard. Some included also vineyards and orchards. The houses were widely spaced, assuring privacy and preventing the spread of fire, already a problem at Detroit and New Orleans. Some houses had barns, but most people used the communal barns on the Coteau des Granges to the west of town, where horses, cattle, hay, and grain were housed. Earliest St. Louis had no stores, no warehouses, no inns, and no industrial buildings, but by 1770 there were 115 houses holding 500 persons. Thomas Hutchins, who visited St. Louis in 1776, reported 800 whites and 150 negroes, of whom he classified 415 and 40, respectively, as gunmen; they were living in 120 houses.[41] Another visitor in 1791 reported 500 militia, a strong castle, and a "tolerable wall nearly all around the town," but also thought he saw 300 good houses.[42]

By 1800 the population had grown to 1,039, with house size increasing as the village grew.[43] By 1804 there were 180 houses. At first they were built after the Louisiana pattern and had no basement or attic, but were square, which made it easier to heat them. These French houses were surrounded by a porch on three or four sides, as seen in the upper left of figure 49. An anonymous description from 1807 waxed poetic about the place:

> You would almost believe the houses were united and that the roofs upheld and supported one another, so gradually and so beautifully has nature bent her brow for the reception of this village. From the opposite shore it has a majestic appearance which borrows from its elevated site and from a range of Spanish towers that crown the summit of the hill and lend their Gothic rudeness to complete a picture that scarcely has a parallel.[44]

In its second generation, St. Louis developed industry. Mills were the earliest nondomestic buildings. The first was owned by Laclede and built by Joseph Taillon before 1770, on the Petite Rivière; it was rebuilt several times at Chouteau's Pond, now at Poplar and Eighth Streets, until 1853.[45] Other early industries were shoemaking, coopering, gunsmithing, and lumber milling (which might be water, wind, or horse operated). In 1795, a Pennsylvania German opened a pottery, and as early as 1768 there were salt works and maple sugar works.[46] Spanish regulation of trade, which encouraged monopolies, ended in 1804 when the Americans took over.[47]

Under American rule, the district of Louisiana was set up, with St. Louis as district headquarters. In 1805 these became, respectively, territory and territorial capital. In 1812, the Missouri Territory was carved out of the larger whole, and St. Louis naturally became capital of Missouri, having already been incorporated as a town in 1809.

In physical as well as in legal terms, St. Louis felt the impact of Anglo culture. Already by 1810 the promenade along the river was gone, sold off as building lots.[48] In the 1822 map (figure 43), a new street along the river, Front Street, marks the eastern side of these new lots. Even so, the lots did not go down to the water's edge, for a drawing of 1858 (figure 51) shows the shore as a wide sandy band between water and buildings, teeming with commercial activity. Many ships are being loaded and unloaded, and the freight is being carried off by horses, carts, and men. An early commentator, Henry Marie Brakenridge, who tells us about the river front, reflects a typical Anglo impatience with the old form of St. Louis. He was so disturbed by the layout of the city that he wished "that as happened to Detroit, a conflagration would seize it and burn it to the ground," so that a new design could be adopted.[49]

Early population figures for St. Louis are, as Morse pointed out,[50] unsatisfactory because so many of the putative inhabitants spent much of their time away at the mines or fur trading. The population, only 2,600 in 1815, had increased sufficiently by 1821 that Missouri could be admitted to the Union. Although St. Louis had by now 621 buildings and a population of 5,600, the capital was transferred to Springfield, reflecting the common American preference for situating a state capital elsewhere than the state's principal city. In 1822 St. Louis was incorporated as a city, and for the next thirty or forty years was unquestionably the most important inland city of the United States[51] (figure 50).

"The remarkable growth of western urban life did not come without pain. Burgeoning populations and expanding economies strained municipal institutions, intensifying old issues and creating new ones."[52] We see this process in all three of the cities examined in this part, a process intensified by the clash of cultures: at Los Angles, Spanish and Anglo; at Santa Fe, Anglo, Spanish, and Indian; and at St. Louis, Anglo, Spanish, and French, William Carr Lane, mayor of St. Louis in 1825, put the situation succinctly:

A few years since this place was the encamping ground of the solitary Indian trader. Soon it became the depot and reservoir of many traders under the organization of a village, and now you can see it nearing its crest in the attitude of an inspiring city. . . . The Regulations adopted in the first stage did not suit the second, and those of the second, are in their turn out of date.[53]

Like French rule by traders but unlike Spanish rule by military officers, the government of St. Louis rested in the hands of merchants when Lane was mayor. The city had a five-man board, which derived its authority from the Louisiana Territorial Government. Three of the five were wealthy traders; one was a newspaper editor; all of the board were well educated—even to the university level.[54] Lane, for example, had trained as a doctor in Philadelphia, a city with a plan that influenced his ideas about the growth of St. Louis; Lane was mayor five times. Editor

Joseph Charles had lived in New York, Philadelphia, Lexington, and Louisville before coming to St. Louis and used what he knew of these cities as a standard for St. Louis.[55]

Because of this socioeconomic background, the new rulers of the city embodied the new American approach to urban problems and opportunities. Though the market and the market square remained the heart of the city, and the streets and highways persisted as urban arteries,[56] nearly every other aspect of the town was changed. Examples of specific changes in St. Louis will show the difference it made to the city that it was no longer Spanish. Whereas under Spanish rule the land had been the patrimony of each family and the common wealth of the municipality, now it became a commodity to speculate in, and the price per acre rose from $30 in 1815 to $2,000 in 1819.[57] The energetic new city government undertook to get the streets paved (between 1827 and 1830) and accomplished this by a tax rebate to property owners.[58] Under the Spanish, there had been no land taxes, hence no possibility of rebate, and little interest in paving. The only early public work we know of is a drainage ditch along La Rue Missouri in 1778.[59] As early as 1810, the idea of building a water system was being discussed, and in the 1820s St. Louis prepared to build it.[60] A board of health was set up in 1822.[61] St. Louis was a pioneer in the movement to save urban greenery, led by Mayor Lane in the 1820s. Perhaps some residents missed their promenade along the river. It was not until the urban renewal projects of the midtwentieth century that this promenade was restored, however (figure 46).

Although the least Spanish of the three cities considered here, St. Louis is perhaps the most interesting subject for tracing the impact of the city planning ordinances of the Laws of the Indies. Both Santa Fe and Los Angeles had native Indian populations. But neither site had the challenge to Spanish urban ideas of a small but vocal and sophisticated French population. Urban development in St. Louis was a unique interaction between Spanish law and French custom.

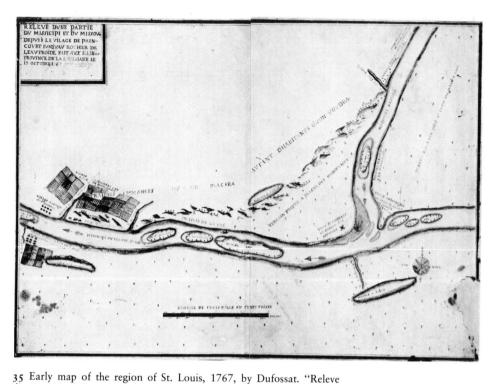

35 Early map of the region of St. Louis, 1767, by Dufossat. "Releve
d'une partie du Missicipi et du Missouri depuis le vilage de Pain-Court
jusquau rocher de leav·froide fait aux Illinois province de la Louisiane de
15 Octobre 1767—Guido Dufossat": map of the juncture of the Mississippi and Missouri Rivers and the sites of St. Louis (under its nickname
Pain-Court, Short of Bread) and the French village across the river in
Illinois, recently come under English rule. The Spanish governor of Louisiana sent an expedition to survey and evaluate this site for its strategic
potential. Dufossat's map was part of their report; it was sent on to
Spain, where it is now in the National Library at Madrid. Dufossat was
a French officer who served in the Spanish army, as did many refugees
from the French Revolution. He shows the village as consisting of only
two houses and a church, whereas the records indicate at least half a
dozen structures by this time. (From a facsimile; courtesy of the Map
Collection of the Library of Congress)

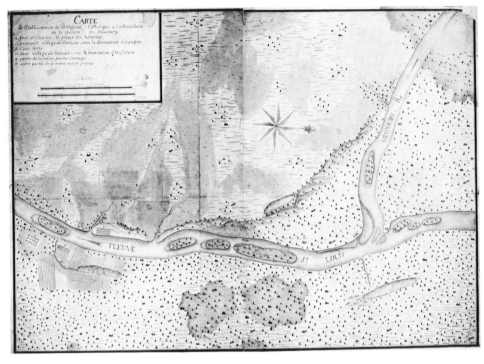

36 Second very early map of St. Louis, probably by Dufossat. The original
is in the Madrid National Library at Madrid. Internal evidence, such as
the way the trees are drawn, the lettering, the border of the cartouche,
and the definition of Pain-Court as under the domination of the Spanish
and its neighbor as under the domination of the English, point to Dufossat
as the cartographer.

The form and size of the village of St. Louis have increased greatly in
complexity, but it is hard to tell whether this is a function of the scale of
the map or of the passage of time. Fields of the villagers, on all three
maps, are shown as striated areas, corresponding well to the French
custom of laying out long narrow strips, grouped closely together. (From
a facsimile; courtesy of the Map Collection of the Library of Congress)

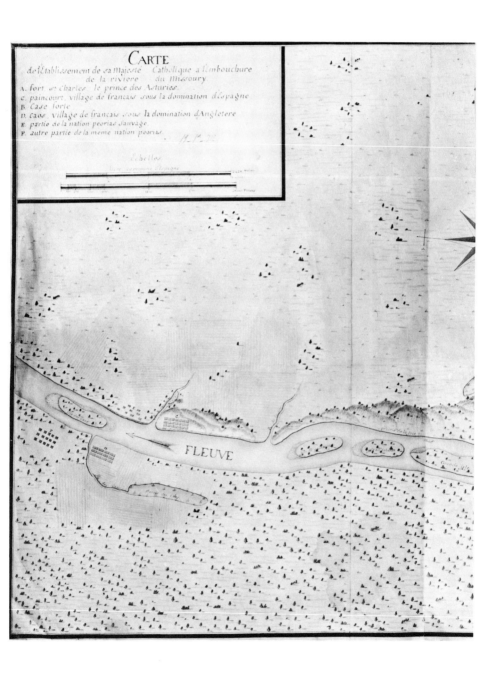

CARTE
de l'Établissement de sa majesté Catholique a l'embouchure
de la rivière du Missoury.
A. fort st charles le prince des Asturies.
c. paincourt, village de francais sous la domination d'espagne
B. Case forte
D. caos village de francais sous la domination d'Angletere
E. partie de la nation peorias sauvage.
F. autre partie de la meme nation peorias.

Echelles

FLEUVE

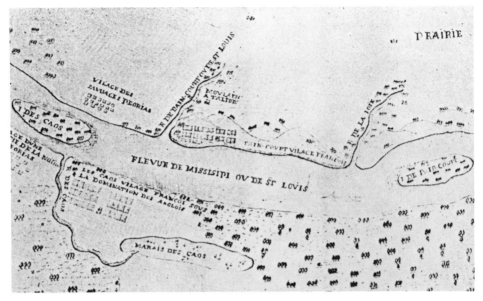

37 Third early map of St. Louis, possibly derived from the Dufossat map.
In Peterson's monograph *Colonial St. Louis*, this is called the Soulard
map (caption) or the Dufossat map (description of map) and is said to
be in the Lowry Collection of the Library of Congress. Diligent search
has failed to find it there. The internal evidence of the map suggests a
source close to Dufossat, but perhaps not his own hand. For instance,
the trees no longer have shadows. Some of the names have interesting
differences from the first two maps: the Vilage Sauvage des Peorias has
become the Vilage des Sauvages Peorias, and the village across the river
likewise has its words rearranged. Both the "English" village and Pain-
Court have grown larger, with the Illinois town exhibiting a central plaza
while St. Louis does not. The site of St. Louis is shown as flanked by
small rivers; the one at the left powered early mills, but is long since
covered over. The islands shown on all three of these maps still appear
on the 1796 maps. The river itself is now Missisipi rather than the
Missicipi of the signed Dufossat map. (C. E. Peterson, *Colonial Saint
Louis,* St. Louis: Missouri Historical Society, 1949, figure 2)

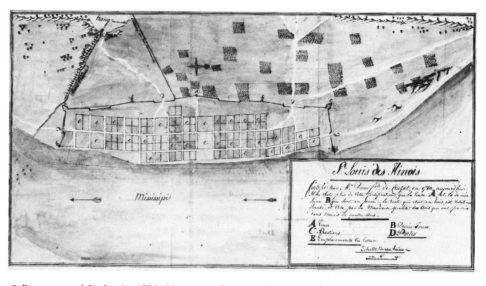

38 Perez map of St. Louis, 1788. Lieutenant Governor Perez sent this
map to Governor Miro of Louisiana in 1788. Governor Miro sent it on
to the Archives of the Indies in Seville, as part of a report about the St.
Louis area. According to the caption, the map shows the fortifications of
St. Louis built by Lieutenant Governor Cruzat in 1780, with a tower at
A, rounded bastions (demilunes) at B, large pointed bastions at C, gates
at D, and buildings at E. Note that the two large square blocks at the
center both have buildings (shown on other maps to be the church and
Chouteau's house). The plaza is the rectangular space between the square
blocks and the river. Outside the town, the striated fields of the early
maps seem more scattered in this one. One road enters from the west,
and the little river flows to the south. This map was captioned in French,
therefore presumably drawn by a French surveyor. A copy of this map
is in the Map Collection of the Library of Congress. (Reprinted from the
original, courtesy of the Archivo General de Indias)

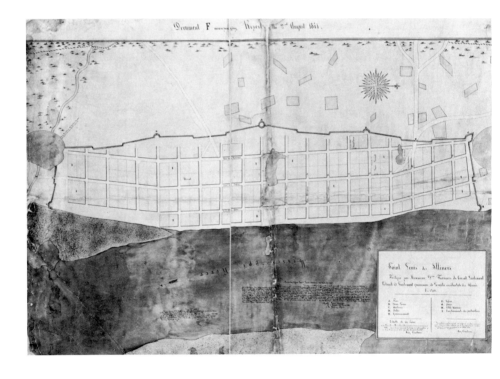

39 So-called Chouteau map of St. Louis, 1825. According to the super-scription, this map was redrawn in 1841 after a map of 1825 that had been certified by Auguste Chouteau to correspond to the way he laid out the town in 1764, serving as first surveyor here when he was only 14 years old. Comparison with figure 38 shows, however, that the form of the map is based on the 1780 version and not on the reality of the settlement's arrangement in 1764. Cruzat's 1780 fortifications are repeated, though the caption says 1870 by mistake; actually, Cruzat's fortifications consisted of one tower (at A) and a mile-long stockade, so that these maps depict rather what he wanted to build than what he did build.

Chouteau laid out a wide space along the edge of the bluff, then a single row of house lots, a street, a double row, a street, a second double row, a third street, and then two isolated house lots. Sets of four house lots formed a block. Narrower streets ran east-west between the blocks. North and south of the center of the town, the groups of blocks are adjusted to the terrain, running backward at a slight angle from the river. There are eighteen rows of blocks from south to north, whereas the 1796 St. Lys plan (figure 41) shows only eleven sets of blocks. The fields of the village, schematically shown as parallelograms, lie to the west. Two major roads enter the city from the west, the right one being joined just outside the stockade wall by a third from the north.

Later inscriptions on the map refer to its use in 1841 and 1846. (Courtesy of the Missouri Historical Society)

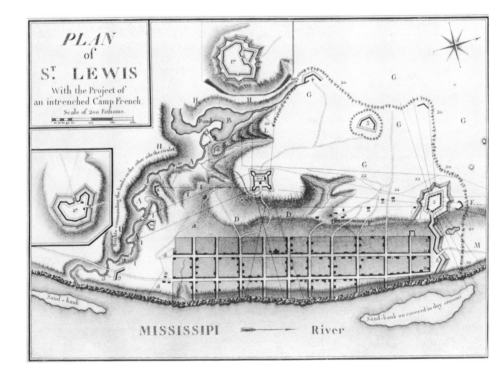

40 Callot's plans to fortify St. Louis, 1796. Both the realities and the dreams of 1796 are shown on this plan for fortification projects at St. Louis, taken from a copy of Callot, *Voyage dans l'Amerique Septentrionale*, 1826, in the Library of Congress. Georges Callot, later general and governor of Guadalupe, was brought to St. Louis to plan the latest Baroque defenses for the western edge of the town. The Indian mound at the north of the site was to become a diamond-star bastion, marked 2, with a short run of zigzag earthworks down to the Mississippi at the east. A tower was indeed built at this spot, called the Demi-Lune. A much smaller bastion was to overlook the Little River to the south. The high ground west of the city was to be defended by redoubts, of which the large one to the south is shown in two versions, each more elaborate than the actual round tower with square outworks and small bastions, which actually was built in 1780. The wooden stockade that ran from the Little River around the west and north of the plateau and town was to be utilized as part of the defenses.

As interesting as this imaginative fortification system is the information Callot gives us of the state of the town: There are $10\frac{1}{2}$ or 11 sets of blocks from south to north and $2\frac{1}{2}$ running inland from the river. Almost all seem to have houses on them, indicated by 170 small black rectangles at the edges of the blocks. In the 1796 version of this plan, even the plaza has three structures on it, while the 1826 version shown here has been altered, these black rectangles removed from the plaza but others added to the east side of the church block. The pattern in blocks, in fact, looks strikingly like the supposedly schematic layout of the Dufossat map twenty-nine years earlier. The high banks of the river are clearly shown.

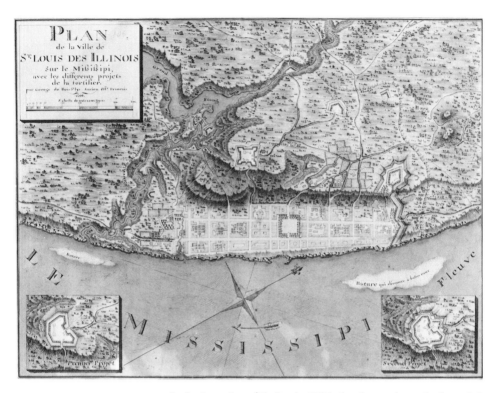

41 St. Lys's version of St. Louis, 1796. Another engineer, St. Lys, tried his hand at the defenses of St. Louis in 1796. Somewhat more realistic about the site and its prospects, he shows only one actual stretch of wall, again running from the diamond-star bastion to the Mississippi, but repeats it in a dotted line south of the city, to block off the approaches through the low-lying land there. From the diamond-star, he also flings a loop of two open, west-pointing bastions and then amplifies the great tower. His main plan gives the tower pointed bastions at the four corners, and two supplementary projects ("floating" in the river) show variations on the irregular ten-sided polygon of Callot's plan. St. Lys also has a small bastion guarding the Little River, outside the dotted line that may represent a future wall or existing earthwork. The line of existing stockade seems to show as the same kind of prickly curve that Callot uses. Within the town, however, St. Lys seems to have been much more observant than his predecessors. He gives St. Louis a large square plaza, possibly planted with two rows of trees, in the best Baroque fashion. To achieve this square shape, he has had to slice into the house lots immediately to its west. One block south, a cross-shaped and marked building is probably the oldest church. Several blocks of houses, especially those nearest the plaza, seem to have interior courtyards, just as we have seen at Santa Fe. In other blocks either he is showing many outbuildings or else the first spaciousness of St. Louis is giving way to the demand for centrally located space and being sold off in smaller parcels. St. Lys's plan again has $10\frac{1}{2}$ sets of blocks from south to north, with the plaza inserted between the fifth and sixth; the town is still $2\frac{1}{2}$ blocks wide. The Indian village at the south has completely disappeared. (Courtesy of the Missouri Historical Society)

42 Map of St. Louis, probably done by Soulard in 1804. With this map we are back with a settlement of nineteen sets of blocks. Antoine Soulard was the official surveyor at the end of the Spanish period, and after the American purchase went to work (at reduced salary) for the new government. It seems likely that this map was drawn to inform the new officials about the site. It appears to embody the same reality as the Chouteau and Perez-Miro maps, except that greater correspondence to reality is shown in the round and pointed towers and bastions, with no connecting wall (which by this time had rotted away). An interesting feature that seems to tie the map directly to Soulard is the large farm lying south of the town, across the little river; in later maps of St. Louis, this is identified as the Soulard farm. Soulard seems to have taken possession of the site of the Peoria Indian village, indicating their displacement or extermination.

This map was reprinted by Peterson in his *Colonial St. Louis*, where the attribution and date are given. The original is now in the National Archives. It is part of the US Army Corps of Engineers collection, and seems to have reached Washington after being given by Soulard to Major J. Bruff of the US Army, just after the transfer of control. (Courtesy of the National Archives, by whose permission this map is printed from the original)

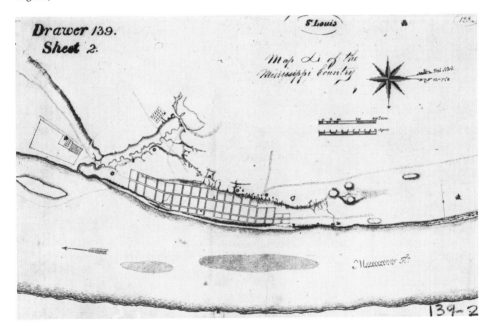

43 Stoddard map of St. Louis, perhaps 1805. Called the Stoddard map after the new American military governor. It was probably drawn by an army surveyor. Although very close in time to figure 42, this map depicts a new row of eight blocks on the west edge of the city, and doubling of one block to the north, which do not exist on Soulard's map. This version is also much more precise about the fortifications, including details about the fortress around the great round tower at the center of the western edge of the site. (Map courtesy of the National Archives; caption courtesy of the Map Collection of the Library of Congress)

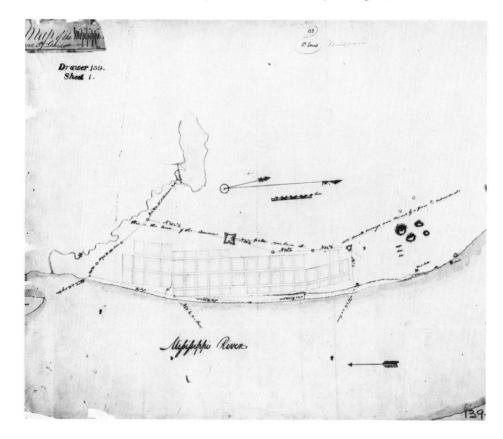

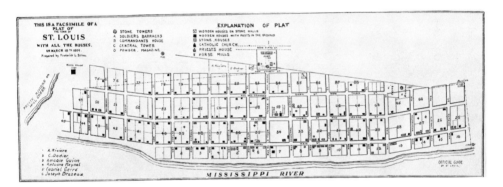

44 Billon's plan of St. Louis, showing ownership of houses as of 1804 (printed in his *Annals of St. Louis 1804–1821*). At the center of the plan, block 59 has the church and rectory; 34 is the company block (originally Laclede's but later Chouteau's); and 7 is the public plaza. The fortress with its round tower called San Carlos is at the top of the plan between 4th and 5th Streets. At the lower left of the map begins a list of landowners; the rest of the list is missing, but it has been copied onto an ozlid print of the plan, now at the Library of Congress. According to Dr. Lewis C. Beck's *Gazetteer of Illinois and Missouri* (Albany, NY, 1823) there were, in 1770, 100 wood and 15 stone buildings; his study draws heavily on wills and other legal documents. (From a facsimile; Courtesy of the Map Collection of the Library of Congress)

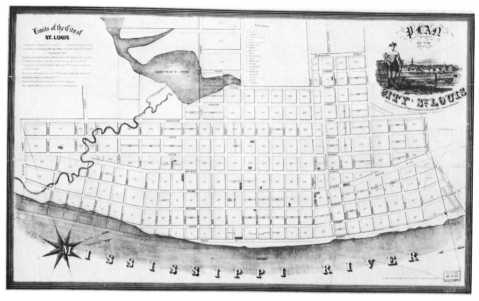

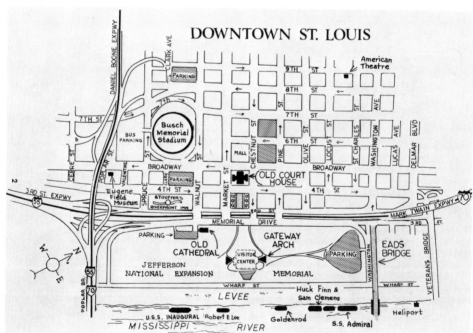

45 Official city plan of newly-incorporated St. Louis, 1822–1823. By 1822, when this map was drawn up by City Surveyor and Commissioner R. Paul, St. Louis had doubled in size and was well on its way to becoming the gateway to the West, most important inland city of the country. The 300-foot strip along the top of the bluff had been sold off as building lots, including the open space between the plaza and the river, and was now edged by a new Front Street. Many of the streets had changed their names to English ones. The block with the cathedral on it had been divided. A new courthouse to the northwest signaled the northward shift of the civic center. Compare with figures 46, 47. (Courtesy of the Library of Congress; brought to our attention by John Reps)

46 Downtown St. Louis in 1975. The site of almost all of earliest St. Louis is included within the super block bounded by Poplar, the 3rd Street Expressway, and the Eads bridge. Only the Old Cathedral stands in its accustomed place. (Reprinted by permission, from R. M. Goodson, *Guide Listing Attractions Places of Interest in and near St. Louis Missouri*, 1975, p. 2)

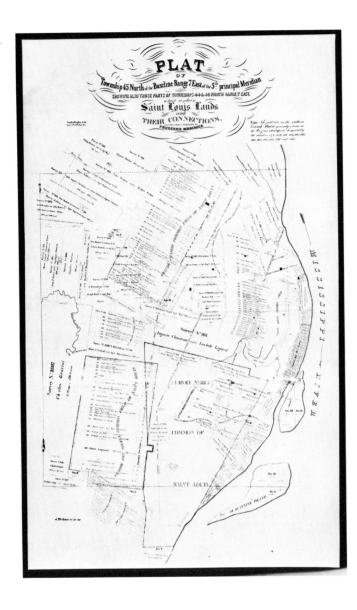

47 Lithograph map of the commonfields of St. Louis, probably the 1830s. Since lithography was unknown at St. Louis until the 1830s, the map is not likely to be earlier than that. The early site of the village is shown at the water's edge, with block 7 the early plaza; 34, Chouteau's lot; and 59, the church lot. By now a fifth row of blocks is beginning to take shape on the west edge, and other new ones crowd up against the little river to the south. The pattern of ownership of farm land in long narrow strips is shown by the inscription of names. The open area marked Common of St. Louis was used by the original settlers collectively, to graze their cattle and to collect fire wood. Variations in the angular position of the groups of names indicates their grouping into Prairies, which would be fenced as a unit. The farmers would receive the number of strips (one or two *arpents* wide and forty *arpents* long) depending on their status and family size; they lived close together in the village and traveled out daily to work. This system persisted until the very end of the eighteenth century. At that time, the Indian threat abated and the Anglo-American practice of individual farmsteads gradually superseded the old French system. Certain streets in modern St. Louis owe their configuration to the old prairie boundaries, for example, Jefferson Avenue, once the west edge of Prairie des Noyers. This land system was already developed when the Spanish took over Louisiana, and they did not attempt to displace it. Compare with figure 48 for Spanish land division in California. (Courtesy of National Archives)

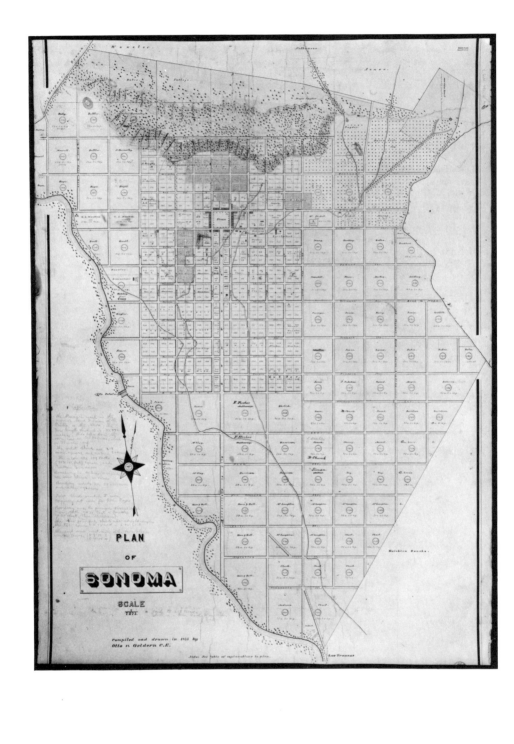

PLAN

OF

SONOMA

SCALE

compiled and drawn in 1855 by
Otto v. Geldern C.E.

48 Allotment of fields around Sonoma, California, 1875. The plan of
Sonoma, California, northernmost California settlement of the Spanish,
is published here for comparison with figure 47. Around the plaza at the
center, what seem to be porticoes run along the fronts of the buildings
facing the open space. Typical late-nineteenth-century trees line the plaza
in the 1875 plan. Names of the owners of the house lots and field lots
are written on their land. Just as at St. Louis, the house lots are arranged
in groups of four to make city blocks. Unlike St. Louis, the fields are also
square, much more like those at Santa Fe, in appearance. Drainage
channels are shown and would have been utilized for irrigation, but do
not affect the plan of the town as does the great river at St. Louis. Part
of the urban area seems to be given over to gardens. This plan is by Otto
van Gleden, the original of which is in the Bancroft Library at the
University of California at Berkeley. (Reprinted, by permission; brought
to our attention by John Reps)

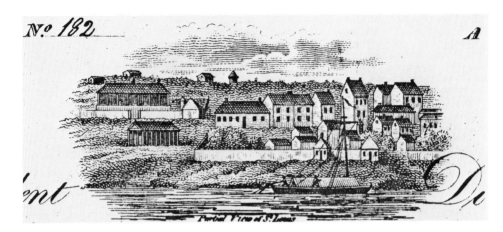

49 View of St. Louis from the river, 1817. "A St. Louis banknote, engraved by Leney and Rollison of New York . . . The earliest known . . . The most familiar buildings are the Laclede-Chouteau house in the Louisiana style with a great veranda (upper left) and the round stone tower fort (built 1780) on the skyline," writes Charles Peterson in *Colonial St. Louis*. The banknote is in the collection of Eric P. Newman of St. Louis. (Reprinted with Mr. Newman's permission)

50 View of St. Louis about 1840. Shows marked urban growth. It was "painted from nature by J. C. Wilk. Drawn on stone by J. C. Wilk Lithographic Establishment of E. Dupre St. Louis Mo. 26 × 16 10/16. Lithography, colored," as the caption tells us. Seen from across the Mississippi, with the river and boats in the middle ground, St. Louis seems to have doubled since 1822. (Reprinted from Daniel C. Haskell, "American Historical Prints, Early Views of American Cities, Etc.", 1932, by permission of the publisher, New York Public Library)

51 St. Louis waterfront, 1858. In the foreground, river steamboats are pulled up to the sand bar. In the next strip, men and carts and horses hurry to unload and load the boats. The upper half of the picture is filled with commercial buildings. Front Street is nearest to us, though scarcely formalized by paving or even a visible edge. After a double row of buildings, Main Street is labeled, and then Second. Where Main and Market intersect, Chouteau's block is almost completely filled with structures, and the only vestige of the former open plaza is the designation City Hall in front of one of the buildings in the group bounded by Front, Market, and Main. (Courtesy of the Missouri Historical Society, from the Palmatary lithograph of the city)

NOTES

1 Much factual material on St. Louis is from Charles E. Peterson, "Colonial St. Louis," published first in the *Missouri Historical Society Bulletin* (April, July, and October 1947) and then revised as *Colonial St. Louis: Building a Creole Capital* (Missouri Historical Society, 1949); hereafter cited as CSL. Mr. Peterson drew my attention to this booklet, and I am grateful; interpretation of the material is my own.

2 CSL, pp. 97, 100.

3 CSL, pp. 97–98.

4 CSL, p. 97 n. 10.

5 CSL, p. 95.

6 R. C. Wade, *The Urban Frontier: The Rise of Western Cities, 1790–1830* (Cambridge, Mass.: 1959), introduction; hereafter cited as Wade.

7 Reps, 1965, p. 75.

8 CSL, figure 1.

9 CSL, p. 21, n. 69.

10 CSL, p. 100.

11 CSL, p. 99, n. 15.

12 CSL, p. 101, n. 28.

13 CSL, pp. 101, 109–110.

14 CSL, p. 99, n. 16; Vasquez, a retired Spanish soldier not only received a grant of part of the plaza on September 3, 1773 (CSL, p. 100, n. 17) but also had a pig farm in the countryside. See G. Victor Davis, "Notes on Block Seven, the Disappearance of St. Louis' Place Publique," National Park Service, St. Louis, February 1939.

15 CSL, p. 14.

16 CSL, pp. 20–21, citing James B. Musick, *St. Louis as a Fortified Town* (St. Louis: 1941), based in turn on the Houck documents from the colonial archives and on engineer Vanden Bemden's reports of 1797 in the Nasatir archives.

17 CSL, p. 102, quoting ASP: Public Lands (PL), Vol. IV, p. 4.

18 CSL, p. 102.

19 CSL, p. 21.

20 CSL, p. 23, n. 76.

21 *Encyclopedia Britannica*, 14th ed., s.v. "St. Louis"; CSL, p. 67 citing L. Kinnaird, *American Historical Review*, Vol. 4, No. 1 (October 1935).

22 These gates are shown on the Perez map of 1788 (figure 38) and are referred to in the Council minutes of July 9, 1782; the minutes are in the Bancroft Library, University of California, Berkeley; CSL, p. 24.

23 CSL, p. 24.

24 CSL, p. 25, n. 85, where the plan is said to be in Houck, *History* I, p. 312.

25 CSL, pp. 11, 26.

26 CSL, p. 29.

27 CSL, p. 69.

28 CSL, p. 30, n. 111.

29 Wade, p. 4.

30 All are cited in Reps, 1965, p. 32.

31 CSL, p. 30, n. 112.

32 CSL, p. 68.

33 CSL, p. 30, n. 111.

34 H. J. Nelson, "Walled Cities of the United States," *Annals* of American Association of Geographers, Vol. 51 (1961), p. 2.

35 CSL, pp. 64, 106, 104, 103, 107, 108.

36 CSL, p. 63, from a document of 1806.

37 CSL, p. 106.

38 CSL, pp. 101, 106, n. 72, 63.

39 CSL, pp. 107–108.

40 *Ibid.*

41 CSL, p. 62.

42 CSL, p. 62; cf. George McBride, *The Land Systems of Mexico* (1923; reprint ed., Octagon Press, 1971).

43 Wade, pp. 4, 9, says the population in 1800 was 925, of whom 268 were slaves.

44 CSL, p. 30, n. 113, quoting Musick, p. 107, who found the quotation in the 1807 *Literary Gazette* of Cincinnati.

45 CSL, p. 138, n. 42.

46 CSL, pp. 138–140.

47 CSL, p. 60.

48 Wade, p. 19.

49 Published in the *Missouri Gazette*, October 11, 1810; quoted by Wade, p. 28.

50 Morse, 1962, p. 337.

51 *Encyclopedia Britannica*, 14th ed., s.v. "St. Louis."

52 Wade, p. 270.

53 *Ibid.*, p. 27.

54 *Ibid.*, pp. 73–74.

55 *Ibid.*, p. 320.

56 *Ibid.*, p. 83.

57 *Ibid.*, p. 164.

58 *Ibid.*, pp. 183–184.

59 CSL, p. 100.

60 Wade, p. 294.

61 *Ibid.*, p. 299.

3

LOS ANGELES

Because there is a larger body of specific data about early Spanish Los Angeles than there is about Spanish St. Louis, we will be able to examine here the application of specific city planning ordinances from the Laws of the Indies in the development of the fabric of the settlement.

To begin with, Los Angeles obeys the siting provisions of the ordinances: The site should be healthful for people (34), within fertile ground (35), with an indigenous population (36), with access by land (37), with water and building materials, preferably from existing settlements nearby (39), and not on the coast (41). As Harry Kelsey has pointed out, the founders of Los Angeles obeyed these provisions with perhaps more zeal than was entirely necessary, locating their settlement at the very site of an Indian village, Yabit.[1] The founders thus ignored ordinance 38. But no objections from the "very docile and friendly"[2] Indians at the Los Angeles site have been recorded.

In April 1781 Felipe de Neve, governor of California, moved from his capital, Monterey, to the mission of San Gabriel, to prepare for the arrival of settlers and soldiers for the new pueblo of Nuestra Senora La Reina de Los Angeles de Porciuncula that he proposed to found. On 26 August he issued instructions about the new settlement. These instructions show his response to a royal request of 1777 to update settlement legislation in California, incorporating the presidio-oriented Regulations of 10 September 1772. de Neve had been given unusual independence and authority by the king. After a tour of the province in 1777, De Neve decided to found a new kind of settlement, to be located at inland river sites and to be agricultural rather than military or missionary. His aim was to make California less dependent on Mexico for supplies. De Neve selected the sites of San Jose and Los Angeles and sent to Mexico for settlers. (figure 53) They began to arrive at Los Angeles by June of 1781. By 4 September 1781, de Neve certified to Commandant General Croix that the establishment of Los Angeles had taken place and, since financial records of the colony began to be kept also in September, we may take it that 4 September marks the official if not

This chapter draws on Daniel Garr, "Hispanic Colonial Settlement in California: Planning and Urban Development on the Frontier, 1769–1850", Cornell U. dissertation, 1971.

the actual date of settlement.[3] The royal proclamation of 11 September 1772, which de Neve was obeying by this foundation, had regulations and instructions for establishing royal presidios along the northern frontier of the empire[4] (figure 52). This decree was based on the earlier city planning ordinances, especially ordinances 2–5, 34, 38, and 41. However, de Neve's instructions, dated 1 January 1781, were "calculated in part to bring about a radical change in the mission system and, perhaps, a reduction in the temporal power of the padres." Until this time, colonization in California was left to the Franciscans, but now the state took a direct part, even paying the settlers a salary, and also encouraging the Indians to continue living in their own villages, away from the missions.[5] (This shift would culminate in secularization of the missions about fifty years later.) De Neve's instructions were approved in a royal order dated 24 October 1781.[6]

The settlers that de Neve called to found Los Angeles were typical of the northern frontier of New Spain in being mixtures of Spanish and Negro, Spanish and Indian, or all three. Eleven families, forty-four individuals, completed the journey to Los Angeles and took part in the first establishment of the pueblo.[7] These numbers represented an approximation of the requirements of the Laws of the Indies (ordinances 89 and 101). By ordinance 90, each family received a house lot and some fields and their own branding iron. Neither the early maps nor the documents indicate that the division of land into four parts required by this was carried out at Los Angeles. However, Richman states that there were here four classes of land: house lots, fields, commons, and municipal land whose income went for public purposes.[8]

Ordinance 103 stipulated that no settler was to receive more than five *peonias* and three *caballerias*.[9] A *caballeria* was a plot of 100 feet in width and 200 feet in depth on which to build a house (ordinance 105). Lot sizes at Los Angeles were smaller, perhaps reflecting the greater need for security or perhaps showing the evolution of the rules of settlement 200 years after the first promulgation of the Laws of the Indies. A common size for lots here was twenty *varas* by forty *varas*, a *vara* being about thirty-three inches; a house lot was then 55 feet by 110 feet. The fields assigned to Los Angeles settlers were about 550 square feet, and each settler received two dry and two irrigable fields.[10] Assignments of both house and field lots (*suerte*) was made by lottery (ordinances 127 and 130).

Two maps, reproduced in Bancroft, show the early layout of Los Angeles. The one entitled "Pueblo of Los Angeles" is probably the earlier of the two. (figure 55) Both give some indication of the distribution of land at the settlement, and the arrangement of public and private buildings is shown in the somewhat later map, "Los Angeles in 1786," which also shows the assignment of lots. (figure 56) One must note that the parts of the map are not drawn to the same scale, for actually the farm lots were five times the size of the house lots.[11] (figures 55 and 56). No specific site for a church is shown in this later map, though the earlier one has a cross that may indicate the presence of at least a chapel. The plan as shown is again an approximation of that sort of plan mandated by the Laws of the Indies, as we have seen in discussing Santa Fe. Ordinance 110 tells how to divide the land into plaza, streets, and house lots, relating the plaza, streets, and gates, and leaving room for future growth. From ordinance 112, the plaza is to be square or rectangular; from ordinance 113, the plaza should be large enough even if the town grows, with 200 feet by 300 feet a minimum size. In De Neve's original plan for Los Angeles, the plaza had been 75 *varas* by 100 *varas*, about 206 feet by 275 feet, a little smaller than the laws required.[12] Guard house, public granary, government house, chapel, and other official buildings were placed along the edges of the plaza. Los Angeles had only three main streets rather than four beginning from the plaza, according to these maps. Perhaps the defensive provisions of ordinances 128 and 133 took precedence in this case over ordinance 114, which demands that four principal streets begin at the plaza, one from the middle of each side and two streets from each corner of the plaza. Ordinance 115 calls for covered sidewalks, plainly visible in an early view of Los Angeles (figure 61), where not only the plaza but also the parts of the principal streets near the plaza are colonnaded. "These are of considerable convenience to the merchants who generally gather there," ordinance 115 reminds those who are to lay out cities.

The plan for Los Angeles, a public square with meeting house and town houses, home lots, field lots, and common pasture, is a combination of private and common property that has such social advantage that it has recommended itself to settlers for over 2,000 years, being used in the Aryan village, the German *Mark*, the Roman *presidium*, the Puritan village of New England, as well as in the New World colonies of the Spanish. Among all these settlers, the town comes first, as a concept and an entity, a whole subdivided into its parts. With the Anglos, the town was an afterthought, a mere center point for the convenience of trade, the result of agglomeration of private houses and businesses.[13] In both systems, there was an advantage to being among the first settlers, as far as allotment of land was concerned, but Spanish law required that some of the lands of the original platting be retained by the crown for assignment to later settlers (ordinance 127) and some for permanent public use (ordinances 129 and 112).

Unlike St. Louis, which for the past thirty years had been undergoing rapid change at the hands of American settlers, as late as the 1830s at Los Angeles the old Spanish system of land tenure still prevailed. According to the usual Spanish system, all unoccupied land belonged to the municipality; a person who wanted or needed land would petition the city for an empty lot (ordinances 127 and 130). The original land grants of 1781 had been formalized to some extent in 1786 when the titles were confirmed[14] (ordinances 102 and 103). Under these rules, land could be willed to heirs, but not sold or mortgaged.[15] There was some infirmity in these titles since they were not kept in a written record but awarded verbally. Thus the land boom of 1835 rather fizzled out because of the lack of proper maps of the city and clear titles. One wonders whether the flood of 1815, which we know moved the location of the plaza and the main church and caused something of a redistribution of parcels of land, may be blamed for also muddying these titles.

For fifty-five years Los Angeles had been a pueblo with the status of a civil settlement (ordinance 43), and then in 1835 the Mexican government raised it to the status of a city, and the capital city of California at that. The provincial capital of California had been Monterey, ever since its founding in 1770, only one year after Spanish extension into Alta California. Both general administration of the territory and the customs house were located there. However, from 1825 to 1831, Governor José María de Echeandía shifted the customs house (legally) and the capital (informally) to San Diego, a port even better than Monterey, and a great deal closer to Mexico. Although Los Angeles could not hope at that time to function as a deep-water port, it could aim to monopolize the governmental functions of the capital. As the British ambassador wrote in the early 1830s, "The Spaniards have in their colonies always chosen an inland situation for their capital towns."[16] By dint of some intrigue in Mexico City, Jose Carrillo, native of Los Angeles and California's congressional delegate to the Mexican capital, succeeded in shifting the capital of Alta California to his home city.

The *angelenos*, however, were unable to capitalize on the masterful political stroke perpetuated by Carrillo. Los Angeles lacked both proper buildings for a capital and sufficient public spirit to furnish a rent-free structure for the governor's residence. One man offered to rent a hall for $400 and contribute $75 of that sum, but that is as close as anyone came to demonstrating the necessary civic zeal.[17] As early as 1836, Governor Juan Alvarado was able to proclaim that the capital would be restored to his native Monterey, though he did have to make some political consessions to the southern Californians.

These 1835 events created a brisk demand for building lots in Los Angeles, but there were no maps from which grants could be made. In response to the demand for land and the vagueness of existing titles, the town council (*ayuntamiento*) appointed a commission to study the matter. It was unanimously agreed that a uniform procedure for the acquisition of land had to be established. As one councilman stressed in January 1836, "Questions frequently arise with respect to the ownership of houselots and agricultural lands because of the lack of titles." On 8 March the commission reported,

We consulted some of the founders and old *Alcaldes*, (mayors) and learned that since the founding of the pueblo of Los Angeles, the concessions of houselots and land for cultivation has been made, first by military constables and then by the town council *verbally* and without other formality than indicating to the grantees the site and the extent they were to occupy.

The commission had examined an instruction signed by Don Jose Francisco de Ortega, made at San Gabriel on 2 February 1782; they noted that articles 3, 4, and 17 of this document "required that the government provide the grantees with written titles. . . . But there is not a single proprietor who has a written title to his possession."[18] The town council was able to describe the problem of land titles in Los Angeles, but it could not solve the problem, largely because trained surveyors were unavailable. However, by 1841 some steps were taken to mark off the four square leagues of land that constituted the limits of the pueblo grant. Bancroft believed that nothing was done initially in this matter, but by January 1842 Arguello could rule that grants "may not be situated outside the City, and interested parties must solicit houselots within the limits," which certainly implies some consensus on what the limits were. Questions of land ownership continued to occupy the town council through the 1840s. In March 1844 the council declared that all agricultural lands must be cultivated each year or else be forfeited by their owners; we have seen that such land could not be sold.[19] In May of that year the city attorney proposed that all who possessed house lots, developed or not, and all those who claimed *tierras de labor* (land of cultivation) or who had harvested on communal lands were to present themselves within fifteen days in order to solicit the documents for title to that real estate. It was also stipulated that thereafter no land might be occupied without an appropriate written description.[20] Tentative action was also beginning about the formation, closing, and straightening of streets;[21] a commission was proposed in July 1845, and by July 1846 it had permanent status with the police, water, and vacant lands commissions.[22]

During the Mexican War, 1846–1848, California became American territory, and the old system of land tenure did not long survive. Like the Spaniards who established the settlements of Los Angeles in a river valley previously occupied exclusively by Indian *rancherios* and who were at pains to embody their own culture in the fabric of their town, the American conquerors began immediately to impose their own values and arrangements on the place. These new attitudes show in their decisions about matters of political structure and control, as expressed in the tax system especially; about the manipulation, division, and economic viability of the site, as expressed in new surveys and land distribution patterns; and about human welfare, as expressed, for example, in continuing concern for the water supply of the town and in the newcomers' unconcern about open space for community activities. Of major importance was the remedy offered by the presence of the American army to the long-standing problem of the absence of a competent surveyor. Although the imposition of American order was one of the primary tasks of the new authorities, it was not the prevailing visual chaos in Los Angeles that was their chief concern. Rather, it was recognized that "the permanent prosperity of any new country is identified with the perfect security of its land titles." A map that accurately identified land holdings was a prerequisite for future land distribution.[23]

When the Mexican war ended and California came under American control, the new governor, Bennett Riley, sent Lieutenant Edward O. C. Ord in May 1846 to survey Los Angeles,[24] to make a plan that would enable the new city administration to understand what they were governing, and, equally important, to sell lots and thereby fill the empty coffers of the city treasury. Lieutenant Ord mapped all the lands of the area under cultivation, about sixteen square leagues. His map, in Spanish and English, became the new plan for the city. (figure 57) With reference to the dimensions for the new map, Ord was instructed to begin by "measuring the commons (*ejidos*) taking two leagues for each wind of the four cardinal points. Said measurement was suspended and is now recommenced."[25]

His instructions were to

determine the four points of the compass and taking the Parish Church for a center, measure two leagues in each cardinal direction. These lines will bisect the four sides of a square within which the lands of this Municipality will be contained, the area being sixteen square leagues and each side of the square measuring four leagues.[26]

So the very instructions Ord received incorporated confusion about the legal size of the town! If the two leagues had been measured in each direction, the area encompassed by Los Angeles would have been sixteen square leagues, four times that to which the city was really entitled. This confused notion of the extent of Los Angeles was compounded when Yankee immigrants failed to distinguish between leagues and miles. Either the city council in 1846 specifically planned to expropriate a land grant far in excess of the traditional four square leagues (that is, one in each cardinal direction), or it misunderstood the legislation in question, or it perceived the advantages of confusion and took no drastic steps to resolve the question. In any case, this municipal grant claim was later to cause complications in the confirmation of Los Angeles's title by the US Land Commission.

A land auction was held in December 1849 in order to raise the $3,000 in coin for Ord's fee.[27] That sum had initially been advanced to him by the local merchants, "after a good deal of haggling." The merchants, however, could see that the survey was to their advantage. Ord had been told to map potential city blocks and streets: "Lay out streets and blocks where there are no buildings . . . the streets to the southwest of seventy-five feet in width, and to each one (block) 212 yards, and the streets which run from the vineyards to the hills of 60 feet width and to each one (block) 200 yards".[28] Fifty-four lots measuring 40 *varas* by 56 *varas* were sold at the auction for a total of $2,490; subsequent sales were to follow until the full amount of Ord's fee had been secured.[29] Although the Los Angeles lots were perhaps half the size of similar parcels auctioned in San Francisco that year, land in the northern city fetched prices of upward of ten times as much per unit of land, and frequently much more than that. Proximity to the gold fields may account for some of the differential; San Francisco quickly became the commercial emporium and banking center of the West Coast.

A few months after the completion of his survey, Ord described Los Angeles as consisting of "an old adobe church, and about a hundred adobe houses scattered around a dusty plaza and along three or four broad streets leading thereto."[30] Perhaps his description indicated that some streets had been straightened but not narrowed. In an attempt to adapt old property lines in the city to the new plan, in 1854 the council passed an ordinance allowing property owners to claim frontages on the nearest street.[31] A gradual process of "beautification" was apparently under way, for Ord observed in 1850 that Los Angeles "has improved in appearance though not in morals."[32]

Beginning in 1851, the new American government imposed the first taxes on land, unknown during Mexican and Spanish rules. Before 1851, expenses of government were met by tariffs, fines, and licenses.[33] Some 30 million acres in the county that were not public domain were affected. The tallow and hides economy of the Mexican ranchos could not support this taxation, which became an instrument for the destruction of this way of life. With the landed Mexican families becoming poor and powerless, the entire flavor of life in Los Angeles shifted rapidly from Spanish to Anglo. The drought and resulting famine of 1863–1864 destroyed two thirds of the cattle and horses of the area, thus two thirds of the landed wealth,[34] but the new taxes were collected anyway. Within five years of the drought, nearly all the ranchos had changed hands from the old Spanish aristocracy to the new Anglo businessmen who began to subdivide them, thus ending the *latifundia* system, whereby a few landowners held most of the territory and most farm workers were landless.

Pueblo land beyond Ord's survey was surveyed in 1853 by Henry Hancock (figure 58).

Eight blocks of thirty-five acres each were mapped, lying south and west of the plaza three and two miles, respectively.[35] In the 1850s considered separate from the city, this area was annexed to Los Angeles in 1896 and later. To the north and northeast, the four or sixteen square leagues of the city area were encroached upon by the Los Feliz and Verdugo ranchoes, which refused to be surveyed into the city[36] (figure 53).

The Americans sought to incorporate as much land as possible into the city so that it could be sold at city prices. These successive surveys indicate that the land of the city and of its surrounding territory was thought of as disposable wealth and not as a patrimony to be handed on to later generations. What a contrast to the older attitude! Ordinances 117, 127, and 129 had instructed the founders of a settlement to retain land for easy expansion of the town and dispensation to later settlers, a principle of municipal ownership quite uncommon among the Americans.

The new council passed an ordinance granting the thirty-five-acre lots of Hancock's survey to anyone who would cultivate them and make $100 worth of improvements to the land. They reasoned that the city would gain increased tax revenue. This scheme cost the city some of its best lots. Pueblo lands were "frittered away" without regard to the long-term good of the citizens, selling during the 1850s and 1860s for $2.50 to $7.50 per acre.[37] Lots were sold along Main Street and on Fort or Hill Street between First and Fifth Streets; the average size was 120 feet by 165 feet and the average price $50 per lot or forty cents per front foot.[38] The greatest waste was the land between Seventh and Ninth Streets, from Main to Figueroa Streets (the Huber tract of 100 acres), which was given away to those who built an irrigation ditch, which ran openly through the area until 1885. By 1915, the value of this 100 acres was equal to the cost of the Panama Canal![39]

Only a few tracts of land escaped this giveaway, and that because they were "useless." These became, later, the sites of parks: Westlake, Central, Elysian, and Echo Parks. Lot 1, block 25, of Hancock's survey, for example, thirty-five acres in area, which could not be sold even at twenty-five cents an acre, was considered refuse land until in 1886–1887 it began to be made into Westlake Park (now MacArthur Park). Central Park was Block 15 of Ord's survey of 1849; since it was located in the flood plain of the Los Angeles River, it was not suitable for building. The empty land was made a park in 1866. Another parcel of 532 acres could not be sold because it was waterless to the east and had a gully to the west. Perhaps in irony, in 1886 it began to be called Elysian Park, and finally in 1896 began to be improved through a public-works program. Another piece of "refuse land" was provided with an irrigation ditch in 1868, which made industrial development possible. Echo Lake was the only reservoir built in this latter area; the slopes of the reservoir eventually became a park and playground, Echo Park.[40]

It must be noted that under both Mexican and American rule, there was a policy of giving land away to settlers. The chief difference in the two systems was that the earlier one, based on Spanish Renaissance tradition and law, insisted on the retention of some land that was centrally located and convenient for the permanent benefit of the community, while the later system, based on laissez-faire capitalism, allocated for community use only those parcels of land that could not be sold or given away, wherever these might be located.

Whereas under the Spanish, the city and its countryside were a symbiotic unit, under the new American rule they were different legal entities, subject to separate jurisdictions and incurring taxes at different rates. The legal limitations of the city were one of the problems the land surveys tried to settle. In the 1830s Los Angeles had been 111.1 square miles.[41] At conquest it was still the largest city in America, ten miles from east to west and ten from north to south. Reflecting this understanding of "Los Angeles," Ord had included sixteen square leagues in his plan.[42]

With the 1855 survey by Hansen (sometimes confused with the Hancock survey of 1853), the city line was set two leagues from the center of the plaza. This made a total area of 50 square miles. However, in 1856 the US Land Commission confirmed to Los Angeles title to only four square leagues, or about 28 square miles, just 1 square mile more than the minimum size of the town in 1781 at its founding. This size was confirmed again in 1875 by a US patent granted to the mayor and council.[43] The growth of Los Angeles in the twentieth century has, of course, exceeded the wildest dreams of its founders or even the extended area of Ord's survey, for the city is now 459 square miles, nearly as big as Rhode Island!

Perhaps the change from Latin to Anglo is best shown in the new demographic composition of the town and its growth pattern. This growth was slow in the period before the American conquest. Within a generation, between 1791 and 1800, the population went from thirty to seventy families, with the non-Indian population going from 140 to 315. This population, though small, was feisty, as evidenced by the "speedy completion of a jail,"[44] a jail that visiting ranchers, Indians, and sailors no doubt patronized. The Hudson Bay Company's Sir George Simpson observed that Los Angeles was situated "in one of the loveliest and most fertile districts of California; and being, therefore, one of the best marts in the province for hides and tallow, it induces vessels to brave all the inconveniences and dangers of the open and exposed bay of San Pedro."[45] The waterfront drew an international clientele, including Richard Henry Dana of Boston, whose *Two Years Before the*

Mast remains the best popular account of Mexican California and of that trade in bovine raw materials. In addition, overland commerce from New Mexico brought blankets and *serapes* to Los Angeles, to be exchanged for mules and horses at a customary rate of two blankets for each animal.[46]

Los Angeles was not, during our period, an ethnically diverse community. Hastings estimated its population in 1843 at 1,500, mostly Mexicans and Indians. He noted, "Although this town is the largest found in the country, yet from the fact of its being situated in the interior, it is of much less importance."[47] The foreign merchant community was quite small, with much of its activity focused on the port of San Pedro, twenty-five miles away, while Los Angeles retained a distinct Hispanic character.

Besides the sailors, a further challenge to the municipal authorities was the sizable Indian population, which lived in misery and squalor. For the most part, this landless group had settled at Los Angeles in the early 1830s, after the secularization and despoiling of the southern group of Franciscan missions. In 1833 Father Narciso Durán called attention to their plight:

I have seen . . . that in and about said town there are two or three hundred Indian squatters. Beyond comparison they live far more wretched and oppressed lives than those in the missions. There is not one who has a garden of his own, or a yoke of oxen, a horse, or a house fit for a rational being. . . . All in reality are *slaves*, or servants of white men who know well the manner of securing their services by binding them for a whole year for an advanced trifle.[48]

Conditions had only improved a little by 1841; in that year, Duflot de Mofras commented,

All the Pueblo's cultivation is done by Indians who live in a little village planted at the brink of a rivulet at the edge of the houses of the town. These unfortunate ones are often badly mistreated, and do not always receive exactly the price of a day's work which is fixed at one *real* in silver and one in merchandise.[49]

The city council decided to take action against Indian squatters in March 1847. Citing the "frequent complaints which have been made against the huts of Indians situated in the pueblo and principally the scandalous reunions which occur every Saturday," the council required all individuals with Indian servants to house them within the limits of their property, "keeping them subject and sleeping in the house in which they serve in order to check their excesses." Those Indians who were not regularly employed were to be granted lots on the edge of the city, "where they will be given ownership with their respective titles and separate house-lots in such a manner as to avoid scandalous meetings." [50] The care for the native population expressed in these council resolutions is an echo of that mandated by the Laws of the Indies, but the actual condition of the Indians is evidence for the breakdown of that cultural system.

We have seen how Los Angeles began with 46 persons: Population did not fluctuate like area, but showed a steady growth.

1781	46	1850	1,610
1800	315[51]	1860	4,400
1820	650	1870	5,614
1830–1840	770–1,500[52]	1880	11,183[53]

In November of 1844 the city council optimistically resolved to divide the city into election districts of 500 voters. As the figures above indicate, this action was premature, and in fact the elections scheduled for 16 December of that year were not held because of insufficient voter registration.[54]

Few cities of the world have ever grown at the rate of Los Angeles, from 28 to 459 square miles and from 11,000 to nearly 3 million people in a mere 100 years! (In fact, this figure underplays the size of Los Angeles, now the center of a metropolis as big as New England and numbering 8 million people.) The pueblo of Nuestra Señora La Reina de Los Angeles de Porciuncula, the mission of San Gabriel, the port of San Pedro together have become nuclei of a new kind of expanded city.

The center of this growing area was the plaza, set out with its angles at the cardinal points;[55] whether this orientation was true of the preflood plaza is unknown, but it is certainly true of the plaza as shown on Ord's 1849 map (see figure 57). In the beginning, narrow streets ran perpendicular to the sides of the symmetrical plaza, and houses faced inward toward the plaza. As the town grew, however, it wandered away from the plaza by crooked streets, and houses were sometimes placed *in* the intersections. Over the years since the foundation of the settlement, various structures, mainly houses, encroached on the open space of the plaza. Originally a chapel was provided on the south side of the plaza, but by 1814 the foundations of a larger church were set out on the north side, fronting on the plaza.[56] However, the great flood of 1815 changed the river channel from the east side of the valley to the west. At least half of the little town was swept away or badly damaged, and water came right up to the foundations of the new church. This meant that the church had to be moved to higher ground (its present site). At that time a new plaza was formed from common land and by tearing down houses.[57] The necessity of moving the plaza after the 1815 flood explains both how the actual location of the center of earliest Los Angeles could be "lost" and how the present plaza came to be so irregular. Though its size and shape were altered, the plaza remains one of the few pieces of municipal land never sold or given away,[58] and in this Los Angeles contrasts with St. Louis but resembles Santa Fe. Growth around the new plaza came first at the north and then at the south after the new church site was chosen. Houses of the aristocrats (*hijos-dalgo*; see ordinance 99) were built fronting on the new plaza, which was much less symmetrical than the old. The irregular setback line that resulted from this ad hoc solution was "fixed" and regularized by reducing the area of the plaza from the ideal prescribed by the Laws of the Indies.[59] The difficulty that the city council had in reforming the plaza is evidenced by the fact that one of the aristocrats living near the plaza was so obdurate about relocating his house that the main street had to detour around this property north of the church.[60]

The flood, then, compounded the already existing vagueness over land titles and the imprecision of lot boundaries. The ensuing confusion about public rights of way was addressed by a commission appointed in 1836 to study the arrangement of streets, alleys, and plazas. They were to "report a plan for repairing the monstrous irregularity of the streets brought about by ceding house-lots and erecting houses in this city"[61] (figure 60). The commission recommended the drawing of "a topographical plan of the city as it actually exists, on which shall be marked the names of the streets, alleys and plazas; also the house lots and common lands of the pueblo."[62] Though the commission reported itself "amazed, seeing the disorder and manner how the streets run, more particularly the street which leads to the cemetery whose width is out of proportion to its length, and whose aspects offend the sense of the beautiful which should prevail in the city"[63]— pious thoughts well within the tradition of urban form represented by the Laws of the Indies—no competent surveyor could be found to do the work, and as we have seen, it had to wait over ten years for the American conquest.

Even though this initial effort to restore the orderly intents of the original plan did not succeed, some progress was made. In one case, in October 1840, Santiago Arguello granted fifty square *varas* to Antonio Alvitre and stressed the importance of "keeping the order and harmony necessary in the formation of alleys."[64]

The Commission on the Arrangement of Streets, reactivated in 1846, tendered its report in July 1847. It found that the streets were too wide and did not "present the vista required for the beauty of the city."[65] The commission determined that each street should be fifteen *varas* wide (about forty-five feet), quoting book IV, title 7, law 10 of the *Recopilacion*.[66] On a more comprehensive level, it recommended proceeding effectively, to avoid disorder, and more specifically it resolved to narrow the streets and eliminate alleys.[67] In the mid-1840s, then, the town presented a modest appearance (figure 59). Its few hundred buildings were, according to Hastings, "small and otherwise inferior, the walls of which are generally constructed of adobies which are large dried brick, and the roofs chiefly of tiles; they are but one story high, though many of them are very convenient."[68] In this humble setting, the first "city beautiful" movement in California was launched by Alderman (*Regidor*) Leonardo Cota in April of 1845. In a dramatic address before the city council, he argued,

It appears that the time has come in which the City of Los Angeles has begun to figure in the political sphere of things . . . and with appreciable elements of progress; what is now required in order to finish the work? Although this small city is beginning to show its astral magnificence and brilliance in a manner that when a traveler comes to the

City of Los Angeles . . . everybody tells him that it will be the Mexican paradise; but not as it finds itself today, with the majority of buildings presenting an appearance so melancholy, somber, sad, and dreadful that the hecatombs of ancient Rome made a better impression than the buildings of a free people.[69]

Inspired by this oratory, the city council passed five ordinances that had been drafted by Pio Pico and Juan Bandini.[70] These incorporated what we would today call development incentives: First, owners of house must shingle or whitewash their dwelling within three months or sustain a fine of from five to fifteen pesos. Second, owners of buildings under construction on main streets who failed to complete them would be fined according to the value of what had been built, and the land would then be subject to confiscation.[71] Third, lots on which only ruined walls stood would be confiscated if, after two months following the ordinance's publication, they continued in the same abandoned condition. Fourth, those persons who, because of poverty, illness, or other circumstances, could not comply with the preceding were allowed to present their cases to the city council for consideration. And fifth, revenue from fines could be applied to the municipal fund for purposes of improving and beautifying the city. All in all, these new ordinances were within the aesthetic tradition of ordinances 134 and 137.

The municipal authorities once again, however, failed to carry through on this approved policy. Perhaps in this case the political turmoil prior to the assertion of American sovereignty precluded any concerted effort at correcting the chaos that had resulted from previous indifference to matters of urban form. By 1847, Los Angeles was the largest town in California, the focus of Hispanic population and wealth.[72] In January of that year, Edwin Bryant reported[73] on this indifference to matters of form: "Its streets are laid out without any regard to regularity. The buildings are generally constructed of *adobes* and are two stories high, with flat roofs. The public buildings are a church, quartel, and government house. Some of the dwellinghouses are frames, and large."

Los Angeles's first of many spectacular booms took place in the early 1850s, a boom based on cattle, which had previously sold for two dollars for the hide and tallow, and now sold for thirty to forty dollars for the beef. This new affluence made possible the importation of ready-made houses from New York and Boston, which began to alter the appearance of the pueblo quite drastically. These wooden prefabricated houses were joined by others of burnt brick and corrugated iron; the old adobe brick was used no more. After a drought-induced recession in 1856–1857, prosperity returned in 1858–1861, and the first business block was built, the Arcadia at the corner of Arcadia and Los Angeles Streets, followed by the court house and thirty-one other brick buildings in 1859.[74]

The American occupation of Los Angeles changed the city from an inactive collection of adobes, inhabited by a group of people who shared Latin attitudes about work, public and private property, and the role of city government, to a predominantly Anglo body politic, whose highest values were working hard, making money, and having adventure, in that order. The Anglos brought with them not only new ideas about city government and especially its ownership and stewardship of land but also, and more specifically, new—for the place—ideas of what houses are made of, what a downtown looks like and how it works, and even new ideas of what the plaza should be. The older Spanish culture was not strong enough to resist this aggressive new culture and gave way rapidly. Perhaps because it was a relatively more sophisticated culture, however, it left considerably more traces on the life of Southern California than had its Indian predecessor.

When the Anglos took over the government, they did not have the Spanish tradition of the evening promenade in the plaza; nor by tradition did they value urban centrality. They perceived the plaza to be like any other piece of real estate, something to be put to practical use. The decision in 1857 to use the plaza as site for a reservoir and distribution system for water may reflect the demise, by then, of Spanish influence in the life of the community. Although the plaza was "improved" in 1859 by the addition of a picket fence, walls, and shrubs, it soon became dilapidated because it was not maintained. After a dispute about the plaza in 1870, its shape was changed from rectangular to circular; at this time, also, a fence and a fountain were built and walks laid.[75] The plaza was no longer the center of urban life. By 1881 the mainstream of commercial activity had shifted to First Street some four blocks away.[76] As Reps has said, "Only Olvera Street (at the edge of the 1815 church) with its synthetic Mexican bazaar, suggests the humble but carefully planned origins of America's most disorderly metropolis."[77]

The later (post-1850) history of the plaza is bound up with the history of the water supply of the city.[78] Under Spanish law, the city had the right to use the water of the river on which it was located. The first community work after the founding of the settlement had been the building of a water distribution system, beginning with a dam. Then an irrigation ditch was dug for the fields and houses. As the population grew, more ditches were built, but these were rarely supplemented with pipes to private houses. After the American takeover in 1846, the old system was kept for several years, supplemented by water barrels and water carts rather than the Indian carriers of the old days. During the 1850s and 1860s, there were various attempts to build a pipe system for supplying the city with water that utilized the plaza as a storage place. But water rights were a continual source of litigation. From as early as 1810, under the Spanish, there had been litigation between the Pueblo and the Mission over water rights, and again in 1833 under the Mexican government the same contest was renewed. With US occupation, title to water rights became clouded. Some of the municipal water rights were lost by default, and had to be repurchased. The history of Los Angeles could be written in terms of its water supply, and an aggressive history it is! Wits describe Los Angeles as "a desert with hose bibs."[79]

In the transition from Spanish-Mexican to American rule, much was wasted and lost. It is our contention that this would not have happened under the Spanish to whom the municipality's function was to safeguard the public good for not only the generation of settlers but also generations to come. There were, of course, some shortcomings of the Spanish rule, but many of them were economic and not philosophical.

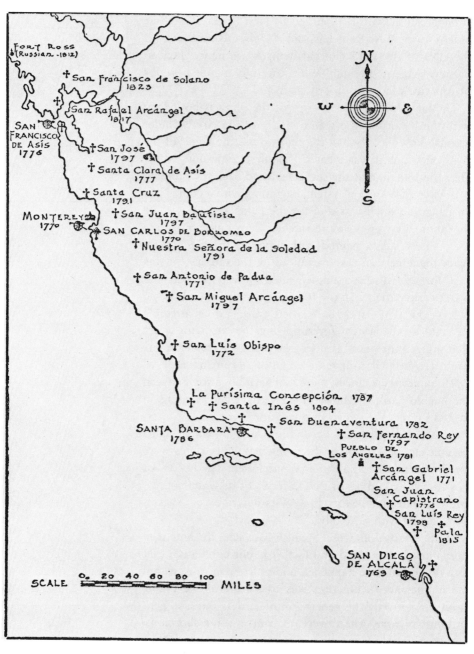

52 Map of Spanish settlements in California, (reprinted from Hollenbeck, *Spanish Missions of the Old Southwest*). The cross symbol denotes missions, and the cannon is used for presidios. San Carlos de Borromeo at Carmel has a decorated cross, as it was head of the mission chain. The pueblo of Los Angeles has its own symbol, neither cross nor cannon. At upper left is the Russian outpost at Fort Ross. The chain of settlements extends a little over halfway northward from San Diego to the Oregon border, perhaps 550 miles, about 20 miles separating each pair of settlements.

53 Map of Los Angeles region in 1800 (reprinted from a copy of Bancroft, *History of California,* at the University of California at Berkeley). Mission San Gabriel is slightly east of Los Angeles, and the Felix and Verdugas ranches are treated as separate settlements. The Porciuncula River is today known as the Los Angeles River; San Pedro is actually closer to its mouth, as befits a nascent port city. Palos Verdes and Santa Monica are already noted as settlements, and the Mission of San Fernando is ready to give its name to its valley.

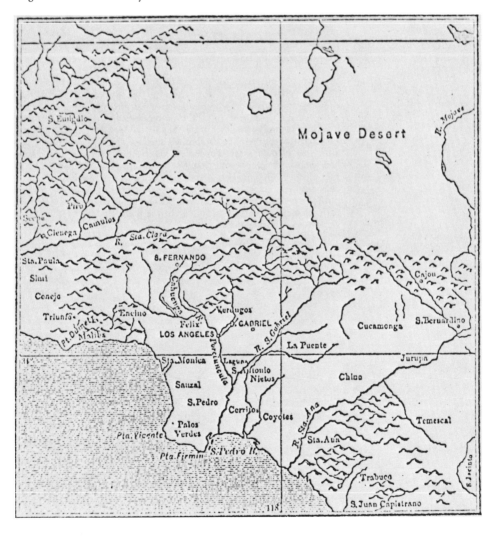

54 Mission San Gabriel, founded 1771 from a sketch by H. Miller, 1856. The large church, the modest but comfortable houses, the neat gardens epitomize the missionary accomplishment on the northwest frontier of the Spanish New World. In California the Indians were not accustomed to urban living, but neither were they as wild as, say, the Apaches of Arizona; rather, they had established sites to which they returned year after year in their seasonal wanderings. By the 1770s, the Franciscans had almost 300 years of missionary effort in the New World to draw on for guidance. The prosperous Indian settlements they established were a constant temptation, considering the moral caliber of the Spaniards sent out to man these remote posts and the increasingly secular spirit of the early nineteenth century. (Courtesy of the Bancroft Library at the University of California at Berkeley)

55 Earliest plan of Los Angeles, before 1786. Entitled "Pueblo de la Reina de los Angeles," purportedly for Governor Felipe de Neve. Bancroft dates it before 1786. The pueblo is enclosed in a rectangle, and is laid out to the points of the compass (as the ordinances require for the plaza). This rectangle encloses a cross. Next to the pueblo lies the aqueduct that brings water from the river to both the village and the fields. This aqueduct taps the river that runs along the far side of the map, beyond the square and rectangular fields of the residents. A ford is noted where the river crosses the road; like most desert rivers, this one would be dry for many months of the year, and thus easily fordable. (Courtesy of the Bancroft Library at the University of California at Berkeley; reprinted from *Provincial State Papers,* vol. 3, p. 55)

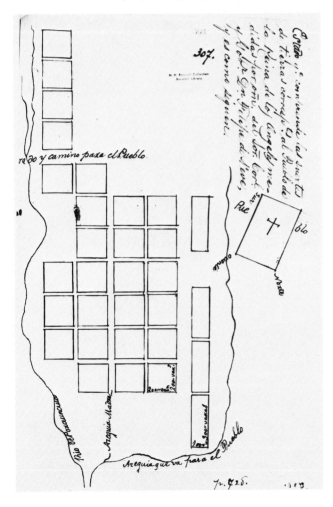

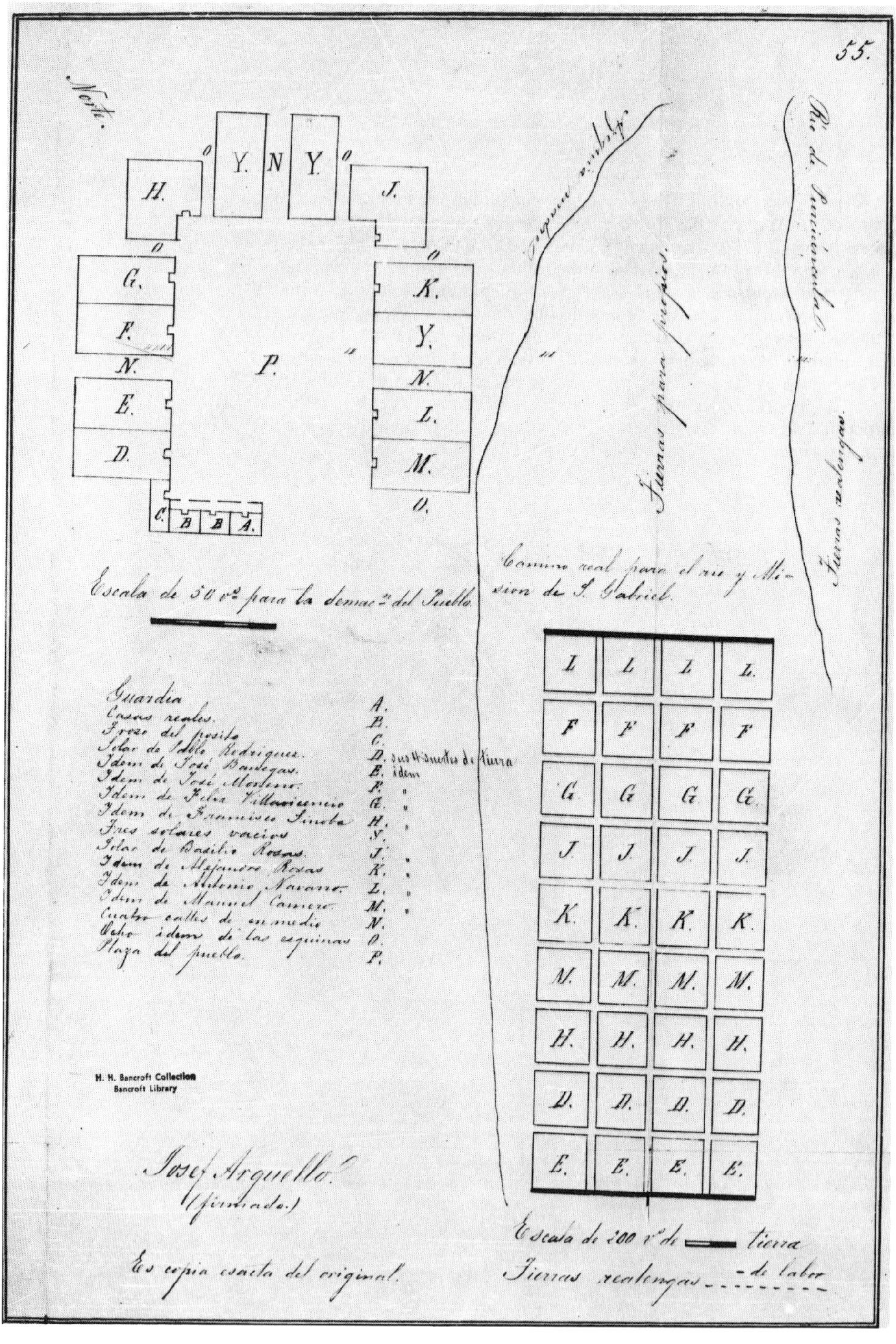
55.
Norte.
Y. N Y.
H.
J.
G.
F.
N.
P.
K.
Y.
N.
L.
M.
O.
E.
D.
C. B B A.
Acequia madre
Tierras para propios.
Rio de Porciuncula
Tierras realengas
Escala de 50 v.s para la demac.n del Pueblo.
Camino real para el rio y Mision de S. Gabriel.
Guardia A.
Casas reales. B.
Troze del posito C.
Solar de Pablo Rodriguez. D. sus 4 suertes de tierra
Idem de José Banegas. E. idem
Idem de José Moreno. F. "
Idem de Felix Villavicencio G. "
Idem de Francisco Sinova H. "
Tres solares vacios Y.
Solar de Basilio Rosas. J. "
Idem de Alejandro Rosas K. "
Idem de Antonio Navarro. L. "
Idem de Manuel Camero. M. "
Cuatro calles de en medio N.
Ocho idem de las esquinas O.
Plaza del pueblo. P.
L L L L.
F F F F
G. G G G.
J. J. J. J.
K. K. K. K.
M. M. M. M.
H. H. H. H.
D. D. D. D.
E. E. E. E.
H. H. Bancroft Collection
Bancroft Library
Josef Arguello.
(firmado.)
Es copia esacta del original.
Escala de 200 v.s de tierra
Tierras realengas - de labor

56 Second map of Los Angeles, 1786 (Arguello's "exact copy"). In Bancroft's *History of California* this appears as "Los Angeles in 1786." Norman Neuerberg drew this version of the plan to my attention, pointing out especially the two different scales that the house lots and field lots are drawn to. The settlement shown in figure 55 is at upper left here. In addition to the earliest agricultural area within the curve of the river and irrigation ditch east of the houses, now a set of formal fields is laid out to the southeast. According to the legend, *A* is the guard house; *B*, the government buildings (*casas real*); *C*, the *trozo del posito* (granary); *D–M*, the individual dwellings. These house lots are in turn keyed to the field lots whose owners are designated by the same letters. In contrast to St. Louis, where the first few years of French control had set up a pattern of individual ownership and the rights to buy and sell real property, in Spanish colonies lots were distributed to the first settlers by lottery; they could be willed but not mortgaged or sold. On this plan, the Porciuncula River (later the Los Angeles) is at right; the chief irrigation ditch ("mother aqueduct") branches from it toward the town and then along the fields. (Courtesy of Bancroft Library, University of California at Berkeley, reprinted from *State Papers. Missions and Colonization*, vol. 1, p. 307.)

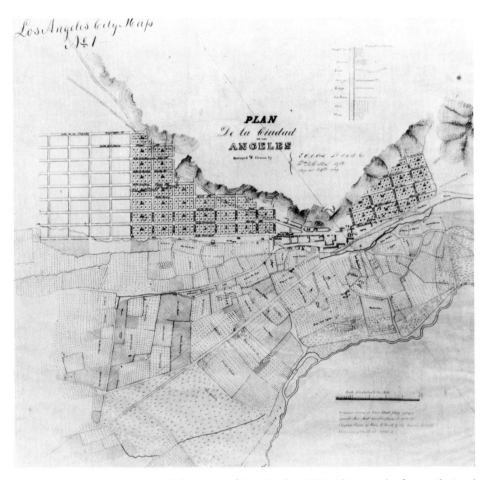

57 Ord's survey of Los Angeles, 1849. This was the first professional survey of the town. The old town is at center, where Ord's base lines meet; its old buildings are drawn with heavy black lines. Even in this late version of the Spanish city, the plaza has its corners to the winds, as the Laws of the Indies recommend. The street pattern, however, is more adapted to the terrain than would have been true in a less provincial site. Fields curve around the community from northeast to southwest, limited by the river channel to the east. Ord's new lots extend the town to the north and to the southwest, with up to ten instead of the traditional four house lots to the block. Some of the new blocks seem already to houses on them. I suggest that the church is the building set into the angle of Ord's base lines. (Courtesy of the California Historical Society, Los Angeles, which now incorporates the collection of historical photographs of the Title Insurance and Trust Co.)

58 Hancock's survey of Los Angeles, 1858. This is not to be confused
with the Hansen survey of 1855. Eight blocks of thirty-five acres each
were mapped, lying south and west of the plaza, extending three and two
miles, respectively. During the 1850s this area was considered separate
from the city; it was annexed in 1896 and later. (Courtesy of National
Archives and Records Service. Record Group 49; Old Map File, California 10; reprinted in R. Banham, *Los Angeles*)

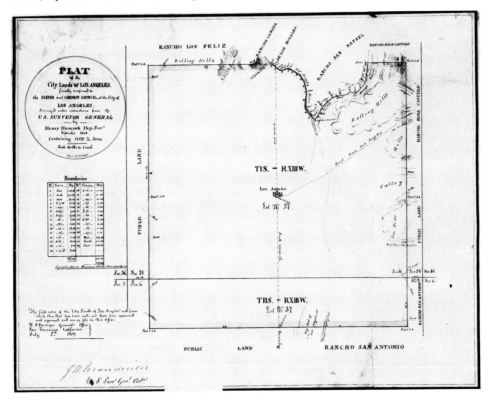

59 Los Angeles in 1846, watercolor by Hutton. This picture must have been done in early spring, when the hills briefly take on an intense green. The figure of a horse further emphasizes the buccolic quality of this early view. (Courtesy of the Huntington Library, San Marino, Cal.)

60 Los Angeles, view in 1853. The artist seems to have been standing on a rise northwest of the town. In the left foreground is the 1818 church with its tall facade. Beyond it stretches the irregular plaza that dates from after the 1815 flood. To the right, across the center of the town, stretches one of the "too wide" streets that Ord complained of, with a two-storey building, possibly one of the new business structures (Pico House?) at the corner. The river and fields extend behind the town, over toward the hills. The original was by Charles Koppel and was printed in US War Dept., *Report of Explorations and Surveys to Ascertain the Most Practicable and Economic Route for a Railroad from the Mississippi River to the Pacific Ocean.* (Courtesy of the Print Collection of the Library of Congress; brought to our attention by John Reps)

61 Los Angeles in 1857. This view seems to be taken from the southeast. Most of the picture is taken up with typical Spanish colonial houses, made of mud brick, with usable flat roofs, and with courtyards large enough to serve as corrals for animals, as we see in the lower right and as the ordinances mandated. (Such fenced, private yards are still the rule in California.) At the end of the street at left, one can make out the church. Part of that street and all of the street to the right are colonnaded. Probably this means that the street at right was the principal one of the town, and led into the plaza; we would expect to find shops located along this street. By this time, Los Angeles has been for ten years the largest center of Hispanic settlement in California. (Courtesy of the Bancroft Library at the University of California at Berkeley)

NOTES

1 Harry Kelsey, "A New Look at the Founding of Old Los Angeles," *California Historical Quarterly*, Vol. LV, No. 4 (Winter, 1976), p. 335.

2 Father Juan Crespi, as quoted by Kelsey, p. 328.

3 Kelsey, pp. 333, 336. We are grateful to Norman Neuerburg for bringing this article to our attention.

4 Hubert Howe Bancroft, *History of California*, 7 vols. (San Francisco, 1884–1890), I, p. 206.

5 Kelsey, p. 328.

6 J. A. Guinn, *History of California and an Extended History of Los Angeles and Environs*, 2 vols. (Los Angeles: 1916), Vol. I, p. 75.

7 Kelsey, p. 331, who effectively disproves Bancroft (9 families) and partially agrees with Richman (11 families, 46 persons).

8 Richman, p. 127.

9 Lt. Edward O. Ord, "Diary 1850–1856," Manuscript, Bancroft Library, University of California, Berkeley, pp. 101–108.

10 Richman, p. 126.

11 Reps, 1965, p. 51 and figure 28; we are grateful to N. Neuerburg who drew this point to our attention.

12 Guinn, I, p. 264.

13 *Ibid.*, p. 73.

14 Bancroft, *California*, I, p. 347.

15 Richman, p. 126.

16 Alexander Forbes, *A History of Upper and Lower California* (San Francisco: 1937), p. 130; ordinance 42 simply calls for the selection of the site of the capital, but more specific directions are given in *Recopilación* IV: 7: 4, II, p. 20 of the 1791 edition.

17 Bancroft, *California*, III, pp. 416–417.

18 Los Angeles Comisión de Policia, March 8, 1836, *California Archives* (hereafter cited as CA), *Los Angeles Archives*, I, pp. 77–78; Requenia to Gefe Politico, Los Angeles, April 22, 1836, CA, *Legislative Records*, III, p. 4. The only written title granted in Los Angeles before 1836 was conceded on June 22, 1821, CA, *Los Angeles Archives*, I, p. 2. All other titles were, or should have been, written entries in the *libro de población*.

19 Los Angeles *Ayuntamiento* (City Council) session of March 8, 1844, CA, *Los Angeles Archives, Ayuntamiento Records*, II, pp. 127–130.

20 *Ibid.*, session of May 11, 1844, pp. 131–133.

21 Bancroft, *California*, IV, p. 628.

22 Los Angeles *Ayuntamiento* session of July 26, 1845, pp. 281, 367–385.

23 Secretary of State James Buchanan to John A. Rockwell, *A Compilation of Spanish and Mexican Law in Relation to Mines, and Titles to Real Estate, in Force in California, Texas, and New Mexico*, 2 vols. (New York: 1851), I, p. 421.

24 Los Angeles *Ayuntamiento* session of July 18, 1849, in William Wilcox Robinson, ed., "The Story of Ord's Survey as Disclosed by the Los Angeles Archives," *Historical Society of Southern California Quarterly*, Vol. 19 (September, December 1937), p. 123.

25 Guinn, I, p. 266.

26 Ord's contract with the Los Angeles *Ayuntamiento*, July 22, 1849, pp. 124–125.

27 Los Angeles *Ayuntamiento* sessions of November 6 and December 24, 1849, Robinson, pp. 124–125.

28 See notes 24 and 27.

29 Guinn, I, pp. 266–269.

30 Ord to General Bennet Riley, Monterey, December 30, 1849, quoted in Philip T. Tyson, *Geology and Industrial Resources of California* (Baltimore: 1851), p. 126.

31 Guinn, I, pp. 266–269.

32 Ord, "Diary, 1850–1856," p. 39.

33 Guinn, II, p. 251.

34 *Ibid.*, pp. 289–290.

35 *Ibid.*, p. 272.

36 *Ibid.*, p. 273.

37 *Idem.*

38 *Ibid.*, p. 274.

39 *Ibid.*, p. 273.

40 *Ibid.*, pp. 273–274, 353–358.

41 *Ibid.*, p. 361.

42 *Ibid.*, p. 159.

43 Guinn, I, p. 273.

44 Bancroft, *California*, I, p. 661, n. 35.

45 Sir George Simpson, *Narrative of a Journey Round the World During the Years 1841 and 1842*, 2 vols. (London: 1847), I, p. 420.

46 See Santa Fe section, note 115.

47 Lansford W. Hastings, *The Emigrant's Guide to Oregon and California* (Cincinnati: 1845), p. 108.

48 Duran to Governor José Figueroa, San Diego, July 3, 1833, quoted in Zephyrin Engelhardt,

O.F.M., *The Missions and Missionaries of California*, 4 vols. (San Francisco: 1908–1915), III, pp. 477–478.

49 Eugene Duflot de Mofras, *Exploration du Territoire de l'Oregon, des Californies, et de la Mer Vermeille*, 2 vols. (Paris: 1844), I, p. 356.

50 Los Angeles *Ayuntamiento* session of March 13, 1847, CA, *Los Angeles Archives, Ayuntamiento Records*, II, pp. 430–431.

51 Bancroft, *California*, I, p. 659; on p. 666 he says population of the area was 675 whites and 4,000 converts.

52 Guinn gives the lower figure; Hastings the higher.

53 The first, third, lower figures for 1830–1840, and last four figures are from Guinn, p. 365.

54 Bancroft, *California*, IV, p. 633.

55 Richman, p. 126.

56 *Ibid.* Richman claims the first church was on the east side of the plaza, among the government buildings.

57 Guinn, I, p. 348.

58 *Ibid.*, p. 353.

59 *Ibid.*, pp. 264, 266.

60 *Ibid.*, p. 266.

61 Quoted in J. M. Guinn, "From Pueblo to Ciudad, the Municipal and Territorial Expansion of Los Angeles," *Publications of the Historical Society of Southern California* (1908), p. 218.

62 *Ibid.*, pp. 218–219; Los Angeles *Ayuntamiento* session of January 28, 1837, CA, *Los Angeles Archives, Ayuntamiento Records*, I, p. 395.

63 Guinn, p. 218.

64 Arguello to Alvitre, Los Angeles, October 3, 1840, CA, *Los Angeles Archives, Ayuntamiento Records*, II, p. 477.

65 Los Angeles *Ayuntamiento* session of July 22, 1847, CA, *Los Angeles Archives, Ayuntamiento Records*, II, pp. 437–438.

66 Guinn, p. 218.

67 Los Angeles *Ayuntamiento* session July 22, 1847, *op. cit.*

68 Hastings, p. 108.

69 Los Angeles *Ayuntamiento* session of July 26, 1845, *op. cit.*, p. 281; *ibid.*, pp. 367–385.

70 Pico and Bandini, Los Angeles, April 23, 1845, CA, *Departmental State Papers*, Los Angeles, III, pp. 111–112.

71 Los Angeles *Ayuntamiento* session of July 3, 1847, CA, *Los Angeles Archives, Ayuntamiento Records*, II, pp. 435–436.

72 William R. Emory, *Notes of a Military Reconnaissance from Fort Leavenworth in Missouri to San Diego in California* (New York: 1848), p. 161.

73 Edwin Bryant, "What I Saw in California in the Years 1846–1847," Manuscript, Bancroft Library, University of California, Berkeley.

74 Guinn, I, p. 274.

75 *Ibid.*, pp. 351–352.

76 *Ibid.*, p. 279.

77 Reps, 1965, p. 51.

78 Unless otherwise noted, water data is from Guinn, I, pp. 390–397.

79 Reyner Banham, *Los Angeles: The Architecture of Four Ecologies* (New York: Harper and Row, 1971), p. 415.

We have examined in this part three cities of the continental United States that shared an early impetus from the Spanish concepts, laws, and physical manifestation of Renaissance urbanism. Santa Fe was founded very early in the seventeenth century, during the drive to complete the dominance of tribes to the north of Mexico City; it had all the advantages of a vigorous city-founding tradition and of relatively ample budgets for defense and supplies. Both Los Angeles and St. Louis were founded at the end of the eighteenth century, nearly 200 years later, when the urban tradition of the Spanish Renaissance was exhausted. Yet in these two very different geographical and climatic and demographic situations, the Spanish managed to set up viable urban centers. Even more impressively, they managed to leave in each place the image of what a city should be, so that each city has in our own time rediscovered certain aspects of that image and worked to realize them. Especially in the concepts of the plaza and communality, traces of the Spanish city persist to this day.

Like other 19th century cities, St. Louis and Los Angeles exhibit rapid exploitation of their central business district as "real estate," rather than its preservation as urban nucleus. In size and in importance, St. Louis far outgrew the simple, early arrangements by and for a group of "neighbors." Loss of the Place Publique may symbolize the commercialism and loss of innocence of the first half or two-thirds of the 19th century. The Beaux Arts courthouse and its square, to the north of the old one, began to repair the crudeness. But only in the period since 1950 has the city begun to question that urgent 19th century culture, and seek to recapture some of the urban virtues of the Spanish days.

The fact that all three of these cities were peripheral to the Spanish (later Mexican) territory allowed them even in their beginnings more freedom than other more centrally located sites. Further, when the Anglo culture overran them, only St. Louis was integral to this new culture, and it has preserved the least trace of Spanish impact of the three; Los Angeles and Santa Fe again were peripheral and so developed their own unique blends of the old and new cultures.

To examine the early plan and history of Los Angeles is to catch the echo of Renaissance planning and the even

4
CONCLUSION

fainter echo of distant Roman or more distant Greek ideas of urban form. The spaces and buildings of the city in their haphazard preservation and in their persistant arrangements, speak to us of the long experience of civilization and of the continuity of cultural patterns of civic life.

The fact that Los Angeles was peripheral to Spanish territory allowed it more freedom than other more centrally located areas. Further, when the Anglo culture overran it, Los Angeles was once again peripheral and so developed its own unique blend of old and new cultures. Bit by bit, the amenities envisioned by the Laws of the Indies have crept back into Southern California life so that the influence of Felipe de Neve and Junípero Serra is felt almost two hundred years later.

Study of the experience of Spanish colonization in California shows us what happened to this tradition in the nineteenth century. By then, the political and economic revolutions shaking Western society had their impact even on this distant outpost. This process of disintegration is the subject of part III.

Few of the Spaniards who participated in the overland explorations to California during the early years of the colonization would have been surprised to find bustling cities and thriving agricultural towns within a span of less than a century. The land's natural amenities had long been recognized, but only in the twilight of Spain's decline as an imperial power did she undertake the final northward expansion of the vice-royalty of New Spain; it marked her last colonization effort in the Americas after nearly three centuries of hegemony.

The geographical and chronological limits of this material warrant explanation. The area of the colonization, known as Alta California, was confined to only a small portion of today's Golden State. Settlement occurred within a swath of land that was generally within thirty miles of the coast, although much of the interior was explored by the Spanish. Their territory did not extend more than a few miles north of San Francisco Bay, and San Diego marked its southernmost establishment. Baja California had been first occupied in 1697 by the Jesuits, though with no intention to colonize Alta California. The year 1769 clearly marks the beginning of Spanish control of Alta California, but it is more difficult to delimit an appropriate closing date. The treaty of Guadalupe Hidalgo in 1848 ended the Mexican War and, as such, defines the official termination of the Hispanic era. Yet events of importance, such as surveys, ordinances, and plans occurred after that date. As a result, 1850, the year that California attained statehood, will serve as an unofficial chronological boundary.

Alta California was occupied during the reign of Charles III (1759–1788), a period characterized by a perpetual state of war that effectively offset the concurrent economic recovery wrought by his able ministers. Charles's ill-advised foreign policy in New Spain necessitated the formation of a permanent colonial army in 1765, which cost 600,000 pesos and prompted one faction at the royal court to argue that the American possessions had become an insupportable burden. Thus, the Conde de Aranda recommended that all the American colonies be granted their independence with the exception of Cuba, Puerto Rico, and another unspecified possession in the Southern Hemisphere, which were to be retained as way stations for

III

DISINTEGRATION IN CALIFORNIA

commerce. By 1787 efforts to pacify the northern frontier of New Spain had become prohibitively expensive, and the treasury of the Viceroyalty showed a yearly deficit of 1 million pesos with debts of 20 million.[1]

The insolvency of the Spanish exchequer helps clarify some of the circumstances that characterized Spanish colonization in California. For one thing, it explains the emphasis placed upon missionary settlement; the cost of the Franciscan spiritual conquest was absorbed by the Pious Fund, a private endowment that had been administered by the Jesuits prior to their expulsion from the Spanish colonies in 1767. The expenses involved in maintaining the presidios, which was the responsibility of the government, was kept to a minimum by establishing civilian settlements. These pueblos were intended to provide agricultural products at nominal cost and thus eliminate the expensive and uncertain journey of the supply ships from Mexico. However, when this agricultural surplus failed to materialize and the expenses of maintaining the frontiers increased due to maladministration, Indian uprisings, and the threat of foreign military intervention, the Spanish could no longer effectively sustain a marginal undertaking such as the Californian colonization.

The Mexican government similarly was unable to support California or to invest capital in order to encourage its development. Additionally, Mexico could not populate her remote northern territory, which was coveted by the Americans, British, French, and Russians. The problems precipitated by independence left her preoccupied with internal dissention and the divisive legacy of three centuries of colonial rule. By the 1840s Mexico could not retain what had already been lost.

The northward advance of the Spanish from Mexico City was rapid in matters of discovery, arduous in the arena of conquest, and decentralized and entrepreneurial in terms of settlement. Chevalier has observed that the geography of Mexico "imposed . . . a haphazard pattern of development," conditioned by the availability of resources, primarily mineral, which resulted in "an uneconomical pattern of colonization thinly spread out over large areas."[2] The establishment and extension of the Spanish Empire in North America reflect the various ramifications brought to bear by the physical setting of the three processes of discovery, conquest and settlement.

The search for sudden and fabulous wealth was a primary force underlying early ventures into the vast and unknown hinterland. Both legend and the promise implied in the exaggerated reports of the early explorers commissioned by Hernan Cortés spurred Spaniards to feats requiring awesome endurance and "supreme indifference to difficulties."[3] Another key objective pursued by the Spanish was the discovery of the strait that was believed to connect the New World with the South Sea and the empires of the Orient. Although the Spice Islands were far distant, maritime efforts resulted in the discovery of the peninsula of Baja California in 1533 and the establishment of a brief and unsuccessful settlement at La Paz in 1535.

The Cortesian voyages of discovery were brought to an end by the assertion of royal authority in the person of Antonio de Mendoza, the first viceroy of New Spain. It would have been unthinkable to allow Cortés, the immensely powerful Marqués del Valle de Oaxaca, to establish another fiefdom on the frontier of the newly organized viceroyalty. A second factor which undermined the position of Cortés as a *descubridor* was Fr. Marcos de Niza's report of the seven cities of Cíbola, based on erroneous and wildly exaggerated information from Alvar Nuñez Cabeza de Vaca. The deranged Franciscan priest claimed to have seen one of the cities, that, according to his report, exceeded Mexico City in all respects; it was in reality a wretched Zuni village. By 1536 Cabeza de Vaca had explored much of the territory between Florida and Culiacán, in Sinaloa, nearly 1,000 miles from Mexico City. He had never seen the legendary cities, but had merely reported the myth of their existence.

Following the eclipse of Cortés, Francisco de Coronado became Viceroy Mendoza's candidate for the pursuit of glory in exploration and discovery. In 1540 he set out for the interior and points north with a party of 200 Spaniards and 1,000 Indians.[4] Smaller detachments were sent to Baja California and to the Colorado River while the main force established a base camp near the Río Grande Valley. Tales of Quivira, a kingdom of magnificent riches, brought Coronado as far as the dusty plains of eastern Kansas, where he found little more than a few tepees. Concurrently, there were supporting maritime efforts, and one of these voyages, under Hernando de Alarcon, sailed up the Gulf of California and navigated a portion of the Colorado River. However, the only tangible result of the expedition was an excellent chart of the Baja California coastline. Another laudable attempt was Hernando de Soto's search for an empire in the area north of the Gulf of Mexico. Although de Soto died in 1542, the remainder of the expedition trekked from the Mississippi River to Mexico City.

The Spanish had overextended themselves during their remarkable explorations. The widespread Indian uprising of 1540–1541, known as the Mixtón War, threatened to drive the Spanish back into the sea. This revolt was made possible in part by the vacuum left by the massive exodus of men on expeditions of discovery. The loss of population was most acutely felt in Nueva Galicia, the province from which Coronado had launched his enterprise. Subsequent efforts were chiefly directed at the extension of government control and at the development of sparsely settled areas.

After the 1540s the penetration of the north proceeded at a more deliberate pace, though with one notable exception. The discovery of silver at Zacatecas in 1546 precipitated a rush to the mines. The establishment of a town there heralded an era of urban settlement in areas of mineral wealth and from the secular point of view, made the mining towns the principal urban centers.[5] Subsequent discoveries of subterranean wealth provided the main impetus for the colonization of the north. Urban settlement was stimulated also by the need for defense; farms, convents, and agrarian towns were supplanted by presidios and missions in order to meet the challenges of a more truculent and less sedentary Indian population. Later, towns arose that served as markets and as administrative centers.

Colonization in the north flourished in the absence of the strong central government that had been established in southern and central Mexico. North of Zacatecas, the authority of the *Audiencia* of Guadalajara was rarely obeyed, a situation that the *Audiencia* itself readily acknowledged.[6] This area was ruled by individuals of wealth and power who had gained their fortunes from mines, land holdings, and commerce. The growth of this oligarchy coincided with the desire of a hard-pressed Spanish monarchy to allocate authority to wealthy private individuals.[7] As Chevalier has observed, the 1573 town planning and colonization ordinances reflect the necessity of entrusting expansion to men of experience and means.[8]

Mining was chiefly responsible for the northward expansion, and the dates of foundation of mining towns reflect the pace at which the penetration proceeded: Zacatecas (1546), Durango (1563), Parral (1631), and Chihuahua (1709). North of those areas there was little economic motivation to extend settlement, and what Gibson terms the "momentum of town foundation" slowed and ceased entirely.[9] As the result of an additional northward thrust, Santa Fe dates from about 1610 and the settlement of the Río Grande Valley began in 1598. It is remarkable that in less than a century, Spanish settlement had extended to an area more than 1,000 miles distant from the capital.

Baja California, discovered in the 1530s, remained uninhabited by Spaniards. From 1535 until 1683, the only attempt to establish settlement were sporadic and unsuccessful efforts to develop a pearl fishing industry. The most significant attempt to found a colony occurred in 1683, but it failed after two years.[10] The Jesuits entered Baja California in 1697 under Fr. Juan Maria Salvatierra. The order had secured for itself full control in spiritual, economic, civil, and military matters, but it was never able to make the peninsula flourish. The society's vigorous opposition excluded all Spanish settlers, a policy that probably made little difference owing to the sterility of the soil and the sparse rainfall. In addition, the difficult voyage across the Gulf of California made supply a major problem.[11]

Northward expansion from Mexico City took three principal directions: northwest to Sonora and the Californias; up the central plateau to Nueva Vizcaya and New Mexico; and northeasterly to Coahuila and Texas.[12] By the time Alta California was colonized, the northern frontier of Mexico was populated with about 150,000 individuals, consisting of Spaniards, *castas* (people of mixed race), and converted Indians.[13]

The discovery of San Diego Bay a mere fifty years after Columbus's first voyage belies Alta California's status as the last American frontier to be colonized by Spain. In

September 1542 Juan Cabrillo, a Portuguese sailing under the Spanish flag, reached what is today San Diego and took notice of its superb anchorage. However, no serious effort was made at that time to extend the Spanish domain northward. The midsixteenth century was characterized demographically by the initiation of westward Iberian emigration, and there was no need to dilute the limited resource of population for a dubious strategic consideration.

Additional knowledge of the California coast was drawn from the Manila-Acapulco route, which was inaugurated in 1565. In 1584 Acapulco-bound Francisco Gali sighted Cape Mendocino; eleven years later, the voyage of Sebastian Rodríguez Cermenho ended catastrophically in a shipwreck at Drake's Bay. The Spanish also had access to information of Sir Francis Drake's own voyage to the California coast. In 1602 Sebastian Vizcaino sailed northward from Acapulco on an expedition of discovery chronicled by Fr. Antonio de la Ascensión.[14] After a leisurely six months at sea, they reached San Diego, and Ascensión noted that it was a fine site for a settlement. He was impressed with the possibilities the location offered for a great seaport and hastened to include the further enticement of hidden mineral wealth.

Vizcaino, on the basis of experience, would have been a prime candidate to establish a settlement on the California coast, but the Spanish colonial bureaucracy had already determined otherwise. He was made *alcalde mayor* of Tehuantepec and his viceregal patron, the Conde de Monterey, was transferred to the southern viceroyalty at Lima in 1603. Unaware of this turn of events, the Council of the Indies recommended to Philip III in 1606 that a port be established on the California coast as a way station for the Manila galleon and that the responsibility for this be entrusted to Vizcaino. But a shipwreck intervened, and the order did not reach Mexico until April 1607; Vizcaino had already sailed from Veracruz in the previous fleet.

However, opinion was not unanimous concerning the desirability of a California port. The Marqués de Montesclaros, Monterey's successor as viceroy of New Spain, opposed the founding of a settlement in California, contending that practice had established that once an Acapulco-bound vessel sighted the coast of North America, the policy was to make directly to port; certainly, the long-

suffering crews would have endorsed such a sentiment. To
the contrary, Montesclaros argued, the real danger to the
galleons lay in the Orient as did two mythical treasure
isles, Rico de Oro and Rico de Plata. Thus, he diverted the
20,000 pesos that had been appropriated for California to
a search for the legendary islands. After being reluctantly
pressed into service to conduct those explorations, Vizcaino wrote in 1614 that such islands never existed. Thereafter, the matter of colonization lay dormant for more
than a century.[15]

California was once again brought to the attention of
the Spanish authorities in 1719. On the advice of Julio de
Oliban, a member of the Audiencia of Guadalajara, the
newly enthroned Philip V ordered that a settlement be
founded on San Diego Bay, describing the area as "capa-
cious, pleasant, and well-situated." He considered the project to be a matter of some importance as he felt that Spain
must take some action in California "before the enemies
of my crown occupy it."[16] But with the nation prostrated
following the War of the Spanish Succession, policies of
colonial expansion were not items of high priority, and
once again the question of settlement in California was
postponed.[17]

It was not until the reign of Charles III that serious
attention was devoted to the settlement of California. During this period, characterized by what has been termed his
"illustrious despotism," the king wrought an industrial
and commercial renaissance. Charles's abilities were well
suited to the centralization of power initiated in Spain as
a result of the Bourbon Family Pact and her ensuing close
relation to French absolutism in the years following Col-
bert and Louis XIV. The primary French objective in the
alliance was the strengthening of her Spanish ally in response to the growing power of England. In the 1760s this
consideration became especially acute as England emerged,
aggrandized at France's expense, from the Seven Years
War. In addition, Britain had succeeded in ousting the
Spanish temporarily from the Philippines, posing a threat
to the Pacific Coast. Furthermore, colonial ambitions were
read into English expeditions by Wallis-Carteret, Byron,
Bougainville, and Cook in the Pacific.[18] On another front,
there were reports of Russian incursions southward from
Alaska and Siberia; a rumor that 300 Russians were killed

in a battle with Amerinds lent some credence to Spanish suspicions. By 1768 there was considerable uneasiness "concerning repeated attempts which the Russians have made to open communication with North America."[19]

Considerations other than the threat of foreign intervention were also of importance in the decision to colonize California. The 1760s were a decade of major imperial and economic reforms in Spanish America. Foremost among these was the introduction of the French-inspired intendant system and the gradual freeing of commerce from its archaic bonds and restrictions.[20] The latter policy was designed to increase income and improve economic conditions both in Spain and in the colonies, and the appointment of a visitor-general was a step toward the implementation of these reforms.[21] José de Gálvez was chosen by Charles III to conduct the visitation and "to act as his personal representative in the inception of the new imperial rejuvenation."[22] The formal powers of the visitor-general eclipsed those of the viceroy in many areas of jurisdiction.[23] However, the *visitador*'s position could be made unassailable only by dint of his personal qualities, and Gálvez was imbued with such qualities.[24] Indeed, according to Bobb, "The aggressiveness this man displayed during his visitation is surprising, and there is no better example of his methods than the California occupation."[25]

It is probable that Gálvez intended to occupy California as early as 1767 as part of his broad conception of his responsibilities in New Spain, for "there was no phase of the frontier problem with which Gálvez . . . was not concerned or which he did not attempt to solve."[26] In January 1768 the Spanish minister of state, the Marqués de Grimaldi, ordered Viceroy de Croix to take measures to check Russian encroachments. Croix wrote of this to Gálvez on 30 April 1768, enclosing Grimaldi's order, and Gálvez replied on 20 May:

Recalling to mind the many conversations and reflections which we have previously had concerning the supreme importance and utility of taking possession of the port of Monterey and establishing there a presidio, I am obeying your order to take such measures as I deem fitting for reaching that place by land or sea. As you leave me discretion for the fulfillment of this order, it has seemed to me both fitting and necessary that I should inform you from here of the resolution which it was thought proper in this weighty matter.[27]

Thus, it appears that the Russian incident was only an excuse. Gálvez's task remained primarily one of reform and of increasing revenues. It was in that light that he saw California.

Although the legacy of the Franciscan missionaries is the most visible and romantic vestige of the Spanish period in California, it is ironic that at first the order maintained a fierce opposition to Gálvez's idea to establish several missions in the north. They believed that such a project was foolish, dangerous, and not feasible in light of the resources that Spain could make available.[28] The College of San Fernando, which had been authorized to fill the void in the Californias caused by the expulsion of the Jesuits in 1767, had intended to found five missions in Baja California between Velicata and San Diego and three missions in Alta California. Within a few years, however, the Fernandinos' ideas on the matter had undergone considerable revision. When the Dominicans relieved them of their obligations south of San Diego, the Franciscans warmed to their task in Alta California. By 1774 plans were articulated for a far more ambitious spiritual conquest than had been conceived at the outset. In that year, Junípero Serra posed his argument for a continuous chain of missions (figure 52). The missions, he theorized, if placed along the coast at regular intervals, would make travel more convenient, aid in communication, and foster the establishment of a more secure environment.[29]

It is to the credit of Gálvez that such a turnabout could be possible. In enlisting Serra's support, he forged an alliance between Church and State which, although short-lived and oftentimes precarious, furnished the necessary enthusiasm and momentum for this final northward thrust of the frontier of New Spain. "And yet," Priestley wrote, "with all the poverty, the hardship, and imminent failure of the expeditions [to California], the remarkable thing is that they were undertaken at all. Only an invincible will like that of Gálvez could have brought them about."[30]

Despite the vigorous momentum generated by Jose de Gálvez in the 1760s, by the beginning of the nineteenth century, progress in the economic sphere in California had

fallen far short of what the *visitador* had envisioned. It is
evident that Adam Smith's maxim, "What encourages the
progress of population and improvement, encourages that
of real wealth and greatness," was effectively ignored.[31]
There was certainly no lack of suggestions designed to
stimulate the colony's dormant economy. For example, in
1794 Miguel Costansó stressed, though to no avail, the
necessity for an outlet for the produce that the land yielded
and cited the promising future for salmon and tuna
fisheries.[32]

A detailed and comprehensive program for economic
development was proposed for California in 1805 by the
Conde del Valle de Orizaba. He suggested that mineral
wealth was present but that efforts to locate it would have
to be made. Sulfur was to be found near San José from
which alum and vitriol could be manufactured. The sea
and coastline constituted another lucrative source of
wealth if properly exploited. Salmon, tuna, cod, sardines,
perch, and the gray whale were all readily available if there
were seaworthy vessels at hand in which to pursue these
abundant resources. Similarly, turtles, seals, otters, and
pearls were present offshore, but the lack of boats of any
size left these prey mostly to foreign interlopers, chiefly
Russians.[33] The land, too, was capable of producing goods
that were in demand for export. Meat, oil, tallow, and
leather could be obtained from cattle; and from sheep,
bristles and wool. Bears and deer abounded in the mountains; the former's skins were in great demand, and the
latter were a source of chamois.[34] Only cattle were ever to
be exploited on a large scale by the Californians , but in
a manner more noteworthy for its waste and improvidence
than for its productivity.

Another arena in which the government was remiss was
in providing both a satisfactory market and outlet for the
exchange of the pueblos' agricultural produce. In 1797,
for example, San José and Los Angeles had a combined
excess of 2,000 *fanegas* (bushels) of wheat and corn.[35] But
even if a colonist received fair compensation for his crop,
he was still unable to obtain many of the goods that he
desired. One potential solution for this consumer vacuum
could have been the Manila Galleon, but it anchored at
Monterey only on rare occasions and all trade with it had
been prohibited in any event.[36]

This overall situation was called to the attention of Viceroy Branciforte in 1796 by Fr. José Señan:

It is my opinion that the formation of settlements and their prosperity would be greatly enhanced if the inhabitants were permitted, through certain advantages and privileges, to enjoy the fruits of their own labor and make some profit therefrom. Thus, the heavy tasks of agriculture would be made less burdensome and their application to other industries encouraged. . . . Their lack of enthusiasm for their work is not surprising, inasmuch as they regard most of it as fruitless. . . . Even if he were paid in cash for grain the colonist would still be unable to obtain the things he needs . . . and his very real unhappiness remains as keen as ever.[37]

It was this feeling of frustration and futility that conditioned the "indolence" so frequently remarked by foreign visitors. The settlers' only option was to wait for clandestine foreign traders, greedy for easy money, who supplied the goods-hungry Californians with useless and frivolous merchandise. As a result, Señan continued, "Vanity among our women and intemperance among our men are fostered."[38]

When colonists were able to sell their produce, it was at "absurdly low" prices fixed by the government. And since the government was the only legitimate source of import goods, it was able to charge more than 50 percent higher than their corresponding cost in Mexico.[39] Furthermore, as agriculture expanded, the increasing supply of produce resulted in still lower prices offered by the government.[40] The missions, too, were victims of this policy. Lasuén complained that

the missions not only sell their fruit and produce at the reduced price mentioned, and also the fact that the price is subject to regulation every year, and every season during the year. We tolerate the fact that for the most part it will be the price that best suits the purchaser rather than the missions.[41]

Legitimate trade was effectively inert outside the framework of the government monopoly. The *Recopilación*'s traditional strictures against commercial relations were applied to California with more vigor than was customary in Spanish America.[42] The colony's geographical isolation emphasized the effectiveness of this quarantine, which, in the years prior to Mexican independence, contributed much to the steady erosion of political and economic ties to the mother country. In 1816 Kotzebue remarked that the province "has remained neglected, without any importations from Mexico, during the six or seven years of the war between Spain and its colonies."[43] Yet, he observed, "A little liberty would make California the granary and market of the northern coasts of these seas, [for] industry and navigation, the offspring of liberty, would speedily transfer a profitable share of this trade to California."[44]

By 1820 the government in Monterey had recognized that it would have to take the initiative in order to promote commerce and thereby strengthen California's moribund economy. Governor Pablo Vicente de Sola lamented that "there is no communication with outsiders because of the absolute lack of ships."[45] In addition, José Bandini warned that "those foreigners who have been naturalized in this territory, recognizing that in the future they will be unable to find a means of support, will abandon a country that offers only misery."[46] Accordingly, the Mexican government declared Monterey and San Diego open to foreign trade in December 1821.[47] The conspicuous omission of San Francisco was perhaps not an insurmountable obstacle for commerce; other "unofficial" arrangements invariably were made. Wilkes observed that "great partiality is shown to those . . . who have a full understanding with his excellency the governor."[48]

The chief beneficiaries of this policy were the seaborne traders and those foreigners who were engaged in commerce on shore. Having been accustomed to more than half a century of peaceful, agrarian life, the Hispanic population continued in its pastoral and unhurried ways. In 1829 Governor José María de Echeandía reported that there was little hope of the settlers earning any more than a base subsistence living. A few years later Dana remarked that "the Californians are an idle, thriftless people, and can make nothing for themselves."[49] In January 1835 he could recall that there were only two ships operated by Californians.[50]

Even though California was eventually opened to trade, its prior development had been charcterized and retarded by the neglect of the colonial government in matters relevant to its prosperity. The colonizing population's oft remarked indolence and lack of vigor represented a pattern of life that was in harmony with the benign climate and fertile land. The settlers were not a strongly motivated group, and the Spanish government provided them with few economic incentives. The astounding failure of the Monterey government in 1835 to encourage appropriately the teachers and artisans of the dispersed Híjar colony is yet another instance of its inability to foster even a minimal program to further California's economic and demographic development.[51] That the Monterey authorities failed to capitalize on the colony's presence in California is indicative of the regime's blundering ineffectuality. Not only did the tradesmen and teachers represent a source of skilled labor and economic self-sufficiency, but, politically, they would have helped to offset the growing number of foreign settlers in California.

In comparing Spanish America to French Canada, Sir George Simpson of the Hudson's Bay Company wrote that both governments "regarded [their colonists] as soldiers than as settlers, rather as the instruments of political aggrandizement than as the germ of a kindred people."[52] While the French erred in pursing "the golden dreams of the fur trade . . . to overrun half of the breadth of the continent," Spanish America, "with its sierra of silver, became the asylum of idlers, holding out to every adventurer . . . the prospect of earning his bread without the sweat of his brow."[53] However, with the discovery of gold a few years later, similar delusions swept through the Anglo world as well. But by that time, Hispanic California had long been lost to more energetic and able forces than those that has spawned her.

NOTES

1 Justo Sierra, *The Political Evolution of the Mexican People*, trans. Charles Ramsdell (Austin & London, 1969), pp. 165–168.

2 François Chevalier, *Land and Society in Colonial Mexico*, trans. Alvin Eustis, ed. Lesley Byrd Simpson (Berkeley & Los Angeles, 1963), p. 12.

3 Charles Gibson, *Spain in America* (New York, 1967), p. 36.

4 Herbert I. Priestley, *The Mexican Nation, A History* (New York, 1924), p. 58.

5 Gibson, p. 191.

6 Chevalier, p. 149.

7 Ibid., p. 150.

8 For example, the agreement made with Juan de Oñate in 1596 for the colonization of New Mexico was modeled after the 1573 regulations (*ibid.*, p. 158). See "Ordenanzas sobre descubrimiento nuevo y Población", (Segovia, July 13, 1573), *Colección de Documentos Inéditos Relativos al Descubrimiento, Conquista y Organización de las Antiguas Posesiones Españolas de América y Oceanía sacados de los Archivos del Reino* (42 vols; Madrid, 1864–1884), VIII, pp. 484–537.

9 Gibson, p. 191.

10 Charles E. Chapman, *A History of California: The Spanish Period* (New York, 1939), p. 11.

11 *Ibid.*, p. 17.

12 *Ibid.*, pp. 2–3.

13 *Ibid.*, pp. 4–5.

14 Fr. Antonio de la Ascensión, "Descubrimiento y Demarcación de la California," (Mexico, October 12, 1620), *Colección de Documentos Inéditos . . .*, VIII, pp. 537–574.

15 Sebastian Vizcaino, "Relación del Viaje hecho para el Descubrimiento de las Islas llamadas 'Ricas de Oro y Plata,' situados en el Japon . . .," (n.pl., January 22, 1614), *Coleción de Documentos Inéditos . . .*, VIII, pp. 101–199.

16 Quoted in William Lytle Schurz, *The Manila Galleon* (New York, 1939), p. 243.

17 The war was precipitated by the death of the heirless Charles II, the most illustrious of the Hapsburg genetic disasters. The first of the Spanish Bourbons, Philip V, had been placed on the throne as part of the war's settlement; a grandson of Louis XIV, he proved to be an ineffectual ruler, but judicious ministerial appointments laid the groundwork for a resurgence from the decadence and stagnation into which Spain and her empire had fallen.

18 Schurz, p. 245.

19 José de Gálvez to Viceroy Charles Francois de Croix, San Blas, May 20, 1768, quoted in Herbert I. Priestley, *José de Gálvez, Visitor-General of New Spain, 1765–1771* (Berkeley, 1916), p. 246.

20 Priestley, *Galvez*, p. 25.

21 *Idem.* It is interesting that the need for sweeping changes had been recognized and that prophetic proposals were made well before 1760; their salient features were adopted and implemented in 1765. The need for a general visitation in the colonies was of primary importance in the eyes of earlier writers (*ibid.*, p. 37).

22 *Ibid.*, p. 45. Gálvez was, according to Priestley, "with the possible exception of the second Revillagigedo, the most able representative of the Spanish crown in New Spain during the eighteenth century" (*ibid.*, pp. vii–viii).

23 *Recopilación de Leyes de los Reynos de las Indias*, 4th ed. (3 vols; Madrid, 1791), Book II, Title 34, I, pp. 512–523. Thus, in. Charles's instructions to Gálvez, the king wrote, "I grant you . . . the powers and jurisdiction which you need to give your commission entire fulfillment. To this end I desire that my viceroy and captain-general of New Spain shall take all measures which you ask and give you the assistance you need" (Instrucción reservada al visitador general José de Gálvez," Madrid, March 14, 1765, quoted in Priestley, *Gálvez*, pp. 404–412).

24 *Ibid.*, p. 59.

25 Bernard E. Bobb, *The Viceregency of Antonio Maria Bucareli in New Spain, 1771–1779* (Austin, 1962), p. 158.

26 Charles E. Chapman, *The Founding of Spanish California* (New York, 1916), p. 80; Priestley, *Gálvez*, p. 268.

27 Gálvez to Croix, San Blas, May 20, 1768, quoted in Priestley, *Gálvez*, p. 246.

28 *Ibid.*, p. 254.

29 Serra to Viceroy Bucareli, Monterey, August 24, 1774, Serra, *Writings*, ed. Antonine Tibesar, O.F.M. (4 vols; Washington, D.C., 1955–1966), II, p. 143.

30 Priestley, *Gálvez*, p. 254. However zealously he supported Gálvez, Serra had nothing to do with the initial plan to occupy California. Priestley alleged that he was chosen to be president of the California Missions "without his own knowledge, and sent thither without the opportunity of refusal." However, no missionary could be sent into pagan regions without his explicit consent (*ibid*; Serra, I, p. xxxv).

31 Adam Smith, *An Inquiry into the Nature and Causes of the Wealth of Nations*, ed. James E. Thorold Rogers, 2nd ed. (2 vols; Oxford, 1880), II, p. 146.

32 Miguel Costansó, "Informe de Don Miguel Costansó al Virrey, Marqués de Branciforte, sobre el Proyecto de Fortificar los Presidios de la Nueva California," *Noticias y Documentos acerca de las Californias, 1764–1795* (Madrid, 1959), p. 237. (This document has been subsequently translated by Manuel P. Servin in the *California Historical Quarterly*, 49 (September 1970), 221–230.

33 Conde del Valle de Orizaba to Felipe de Goycoechea, Mexico, December 20, 1805, *Provincial State Papers*, XII, pp. 18–19. See also Adele Ogden, *The California Sea Otter Trade, 1784–1848* (Berkeley & Los Angeles, 1941).

34 Conde del Valle de Orizaba to Goycoechea, *op. cit.*

35 Governor Diego de Borica to Viceroy Branciforte, Monterey, November 16, 1797, *Provincial Records*, III, pp. 384–385.

36 Pedro Fages, Monterey, February 26, 1791, *Provincial State Papers*, VI, p. 160.

37 Señan to Branciforte, Mexico, May 14, 1796, José Señan, *Letters, 1796–1823*, trans. Paul D. Nathan, ed. Lesley Byrd Simpson (San Francisco, 1962), pp. 2–3.

38 *Ibid.*, p. 4.

39 *Ibid.*, p. 3. Borica to Viceroy Miquel José de Azanza, Monterey, October 25, 1798, *Provincial Records*, III, p. 428.

40 For example, a list of items whose abundance required reduced prices offered by the government, dated August 3, 1803, may be found in *Provincial State Papers*, XI, pp. 249–250.

41 Lasuén to Borica, Mission San
Carlos, August 16, 1795, Fermín
Francisco de Lasuén, *Writings*,
ed. & trans. Finbar Kenneally,
O.F.M. (2 vols; Washington,
D.C., 1965), I, p. 345.

42 See *Recopilación de Leyes de
los Reynos de las Indias*, 4th ed.
(3 vols; Madrid, 1791), IX:27:5–
7 for official thought on this matter (III, p. 327).

43 Otto von Kotzebue, *A Voyage
of Discovery, into the South Sea
and Beering's Straits* (3 vols; London, 1821), III, p. 42.

44 *Idem.*

45 Sola to José de la Guerra,
Monterey, March 25, 1820,
*Provincial State Papers. Benicia.
Military*, III, p. 242.

46 José Bandini, *Descrision de
l'Alta California en 1828*, trans.
Doris Marion Wright (Berkeley,
1951), p. 13.

47 Hubert Howe Bancroft, *History of California* (7 vols; San
Francisco, 1884–1890), II, p.
473.

48 Charles Wilkes, *Narrative of a
United States Exploring Expedition during the Years 1838, 1839,
1840, 1841, 1842* (5 vols; Philadelphia, 1845), V, p. 459.

49 Bancroft, II, p. 665. Dana, p.
77. But Dana also acknowledged,
"The Americans . . . and English-
men who are fast filling up the
principal towns, and getting the
trade into their hands, are indeed
more industrious and effective
than the Spaniards; yet their children are brought up Spaniards in
every respect, and if the 'California fever' (laziness) spares the first
generations, it always attacks the
second" (*Ibid.*, p. 170).

50 *Ibid.*, p. 83.

51 See C. Alan Hutchinson, *Frontier Settlement in Mexican California: The Híjar-Padrés Colony
and its Origins, 1769–1835* (New

Haven & London, 1969), pp.
181–351, for a definitive account
of the colony's formation and
dissolution.

52 Sir George Simpson, *Narrative
of a Journey Round the World
during the Years 1841 and 1842*
(2 vols; London, 1847), I, p. 296.

53 *Ibid.*, pp. 295–296.

The presidio, or fort, and the mission are the characteristic institutions of the Spanish-American frontier. (figure 63) The presidio's ancestor was used to great martial advantage over vast areas by the Romans, and the Spanish continued its use in the Americas as an effective instrument of pacification and defensive expansion. In the course of two centuries, the herculean task was accomplished of extending a line of these fortifications across the entire North American continent, from St. Augustine (1565) to San Diego (1769). The strategic role of these agents is illustrated in a 1758 report by a Spanish treasury official:

1

THE PRESIDIO AND THE SPANISH BORDERLANDS FRONTIER

Presidios are erected and missions founded in *tierra firme* whenever it is necessary to defend conquered districts from the hostilities and invasions of warlike, barbarian tribes, and to plant and extend our Holy Faith, for which purposes *juntas de guerra y hacienda* are held.[1]

Reflected in this statement is the cumulative wisdom of nearly three centuries of bridging new and unknown frontier environments. The appearance of the 1573 *ordenanzas* was a response to the numerous and complex problems posed by Spanish colonization toward the end of its first century in the New World. Just prior to that time, the great theologians and jurists of the era had locked horns in a debate of profound significance. The issue in question was the manner in which Spaniards were to establish themselves in the Americas.

Counterposed in philosophical deadlock were the views of armchair jurists, most notably Palacios Rubios, and jungle-seasoned churchmen, principally the Dominican missionaries Las Casas and Vitoria. The compromise reached involved neither domination by force of arms nor exclusive evangelical action, but the carefully considered policy of *pacificación*. If peaceful behavior on the part of the Indians permitted, colonization would be the domain of religious authorities. However, if resistance were to be encountered, then the military would assume control. At all times, though, and circumstances permitting, the most mild and Christian means should be substituted for those that were violent and irreparable. Thus, the Spanish presence was to be circumscribed by considerations respecting the integrity of Indian dominion within the region. As we shall see, this most humane and well intentioned of all colonial legislation was either frequently ignored or deemed impractical.

Whatever the outcome, the tandem of military and religious personnel formed the spearhead of colonization. Toward the end of the colonial era, most expansions of Spanish jurisdiction occurred in sparsely populated areas characterized by hostile populations and difficult terrain. Thus, for example, in order to blunt the effects of Apache raids, a line of six presidios was established in Chihuahua before 1720 extending as far north as El Paso; these posts, "some of them moved from time to time according to need, kept the province from utter ruin though there was hardly a mission, hacienda or *real de minas* (mining settlement) that was not at one time abandoned."[2] Later, in 1771, we find a notation from Viceroy Charles Françoix de Croix concerning the establishment of "una linea ó cordon" of fifteen presidios in a troubled frontier area, although there is no indication of their location.[3]

The *Recopilación* is curiously reticent in its treatment of presidios.[4] The detailed instructions addressed to so wide a variety of problems associated with site selection, town planning procedures, and the physical layout of civil settlements are stark in their absence in the section devoted to presidial matters. Most of the legislation relates rather to specific instructions at locations of great logistical concern long before the problems of the northern frontier attained any importance. These were seaports of the legendary Spanish Main (such as Havana, Cartagena, Santo Domingo, and so forth) and were prominent in plans designed to ensure the safe passage of the treasure fleets.[5] It is puzzling that in light of the "great importance to our Royal Service, defense of said Provinces, and punishment of enemies and Pirates," that presidial site selection and operational instructions do not appear in the *Recopilación*, even in an edition as late as 1791, when the full scope of both maritime and frontier problems was well understood.[6] Presidial legislation, then, was apparently the responsibility of a decentralized authority, which was best able to diagnose and prescribe the appropriate measures suited to the particular challenges posed by the borderlands environment. Charles III expressed confidence in this approach to presidial affairs in his California-oriented *reglamento* of 1772. He wrote in its concluding section,

I declare that the presidios of California are to continue for the present on their actual footing according to the provisions made by my viceroy after the conquest and reduction had been extended to the port of Monterey. . . . I order . . . that my viceroy sustain and aid by all possible means the old and new establishments of said province, and inform me of all that he may deem conducive and useful to their progress.[7]

The absence of a coherent body of legislation for presidios is perhaps responsible for some of the difficulties encountered in distant frontier regions. Problems of supply and sustenance were among the foremost obstacles to survival that could have been mitigated by legislative guidance, if not common sense. In 1781 Geronimo de la Rocha, an engineer, reported that "unless presidios are located in terrains capable of producing crops for their provision and consumption, at the same time that there is being encouraged, in them and in their shelter, agriculture and the raising of herds," they will not be able to perform their garrison function adequately.[8] This was a correct assessment and indicated that the maintenance of presidios was a major problem for even eighteenth-century colonial administration.

The specific role of the presidio is illustrated by the founding of the first Spanish outposts at San Diego in 1769. The objectives of the effort were stated by Visitor-General José de Gálvez:

It is of primary consideration that this expedition establish the Catholic Religion, extend the domain of the King, and protect this peninsula from the ambitious schemes of a foreign nation; the honor of Spain rests upon the successful undertaking of a plan ordered by Philip III as early as 1606. Therefore, no effort can be spared without offense to God, King, or Country.[9]

Upon arrival at San Diego, the Indians were to be pacified (recalling the circumstances of the 1573 ordenanzas), and a site was to be chosen for the presidio and mission. The need for amity with the Indians was stressed, and advice was offered should resistance be encountered. If necessary, force could be used to overcome belligerence, and constant precautions would have to be exercised to avoid surprise attacks, peaceful appearance notwithstanding.[10] Such advice was both sound and prophetic. The San Diego mission was burned and several Spaniards slaughtered during an uprising in 1775. Earlier, Fr. Juan Crespi had observed that local Indians there were "too clever, wide-awake, and businesslike for any Spaniards to get ahead of them."[11]

Survival was the most pressing problem faced by the presidios in their first years. Everything necessary had to come from Mexico via the long and treacherous sea route from San Blas; for many years the supply ships were the sole source of this sustenance. In 1770, 1772, and 1774 the province faced extinction, only to be saved by the arrival of the ships at the eleventh hour.[12] This problem was brought to the attention of Viceroy Antonio María de Bucareli by Miguel Constansó in 1772:

I cannot disguise the utility of this discovery from the keen insights of Your Excellency; however, the lands in the north of the Californias are poor and barren of fruit, and consequently, they cannot furnish even the least assistance to the new establishment of San Diego and Monterey; if some assistance has been received by land, it was from the Presidio of Loreto and was sent by the governor of said peninsula [Baja California] instead of the grain and other effects sent from San Blas.[13]

Two years later Felipe de Neve was appointed governor and upon his arrival in Alta California in the winter of 1776 he conducted a tour of inspection. He reported his findings to Teodoro de Croix, commandant-general of the newly-created *Provincias Internas*:[14]

When I came to these new establishments in February last, I found the three presidios [San Diego, Monterey, and San Francisco] open, without any defense other than their garrisons. . . . Considering the importance of these presidios and that they are exposed to sudden attacks of the numerous Gentiles . . . . I have ordered in accordance with the Royal Regulations . . . that they are to be formed . . . by building three walls of the square whose circumference is to be 480 *varas* outside of the foundations . . . and the four bulwarks at the corners at a height of three *varas*.[15]

Events on the frontier moved slowly, and progress during these early years was measured in terms of crises survived. The decade prior to 1780 "formed a period rather of preparation than of accomplishing, of theories rather than practice in matters affecting the general interests of the country."[16] In 1784 a royal order directed that in peacetime, lookout points (*puestos*) should be fortified so that in case of sudden or unexpected attack the installation in question would be prepared.

The first specific legislation that provided the basis for the urban development of presidial towns was issued on 22 October 1791, though not approved by the viceroy until January 1793. It first reached California in June 1792; at that time Governor José de Arrillaga authorized presidial commandants to distribute land to soldiers and colonists who petitioned for it and wished to settle in the vicinity of the presidios.[17] The text of the order reads,

In conformance with the opinion of the assessor of the *commandancia general*, I have determined . . . that . . . presidial captains may grant and distribute houselots and land to soldiers and settlers who solicit them in order to establish their residences. And considering the area of four common leagues, measured from the center of the presidio plaza . . . two leagues for each wind . . . I have determined, so as to avoid doubts and disputes in the future, that presidial captains restrict their grants to within the four leagues already mentioned, without exceeding in any way those boundaries.[18]

Prior to this instruction, Arrillaga had made several provisional grants near Monterey on the Salinas River to *inválidos* in order to encourage argriculture; he indicated that such a practice was desirable and that his predecessors had not made any similar grants. Ironically, there is no clear evidence that any grants were issued under the provisions of the 1791 regulations.[19] Nevertheless, settlements at the presidios were developing. In 1790 Monterey had a non-Indian population of 216, of whom less than a third were women; San Francisco had 124 residents, of whom almost two fifths were women; and San Diego and Santa Barbara had better balanced totals of 222 and 157, respectively.[20] In light of these statistics, it is difficult to understand the misinformation about California compiled by Alexander von Humboldt during his travels in the Americas from 1799 to 1804. He wrote,

The population of New California would have augmented still more rapidly if the laws by which the Spanish *presidios* have been governed for ages were not directly opposite to the true interests of both mother-country and colonies. By these laws the soldiers . . . are not permitted to live out of their barracks and to settle as colonists.[21]

It is doubtful that these findings were the result of personal observations; there is no official record from California concerning his presence in the territory. His information is probably the result of hearsay and superficial knowledge of old legislation.

Fear of foreign invasion was the primary consideration underlying events in California in the 1790s. British incursions in the Pacific were long a matter of record, and Spain could ill afford a military confrontation with England. Her range of alternatives was limited further by the unilateral termination of the Bourbon Family Pact by the French Revolution. Lacking a powerful ally, Spain could do little more than brace herself and fortify her meager Pacific Coast defenses. The most significant feature of Spain's defensive program was the founding of the Villa de Branciforte, a military and civil settlement. Defensive entrenchment was the only realistic policy the Spanish could sustain, and this realization is reflected in Viceroy Revilla Gigedo's instructions to his successor, the Marqués de Branciforte: "It is in the ports of Monterey, San Diego, [and] San Francisco . . . where it is necessary to establish a regular defense by constructing sufficient batteries if we are to be able to put an end to the intentions of those nations who might wish to establish themselves there." [22] Branciforte then commissioned Miguel Costansó to report on California's defenses, and he advised that additional fortifications at the presidios be constructed:

What is most important to us now is to avoid spending large sums of money while also avoiding the damage that threatens us and that we must justly fear from foreigners already established on the coasts of California. We recognize to great effect the activity of the British nation, its skill, courage, and audacity in the direction and execution of all its undertakings. [23]

Indeed, the outlook was bleak, as the Spanish expected war. Constansó lamented, "All concurs to favor the designs of England, who surely will know how to profit from such propitious circumstances." [24] Spain was weak, bankrupt, and incapable of effectively defending her far-flung possessions. Constansó feared the "sorry consequences that will necessarily result from our neglect or indifference in a matter of such importance." [25] It is surprising that the British did not see fit to strike at California. Vancouver's reports gathered during 1792 and 1793 provided unequivocal evidence of California's vulnerability:

If these establishments are intended as a barrier against foreign intruders, the object in view has been greatly mistaken, and the most ready means have been adopted to allure other powers, by the defenseless state of what the Spaniards consider as their fortresses and strongholds. Should the ambition of any civilized nation tempt it to seize on these unsupported posts, they could not make the least resistance, and must inevitably fall to a force barely sufficient for garrisoning and securing the country.[26]

Yet by 1796 nothing substantial had been done to strengthen Spanish defenses. In that year, Engineer Extraordinary Alberto de Córdoba inspected the presidios and found them virtually useless. He believed that the cost of constructing enough effective defenses would be prohibitive and urged that the number of troops assigned to California be increased and that one or more warships be used to patrol the coast.[27] Córdoba's suggestion to send more troops to California was realized in the establishment of the new town of Branciforte.

The futility of military solutions to California's defensive problems is illustrated by the fact that the significance of the presidios gradually diminished after 1800, and the emphasis became one of solely civil settlement. José Bandini, a prominent Californian, wrote in 1828,

The presidio buildings were probably suited to their original purpose, since the object was to afford protection against the surprise attacks of the nearby gentiles; but as this need no longer exists I believe they should be demolished, for the buildings are threatening to fall into complete ruin, and the cramped living quarters can only discommode those who live in them. Outside the presidios, private individuals have constructed adequate houses, and as more building of this kind may be seen every day it is certain that substantial towns will soon appear in California.[28]

Certainly, if the buildings had not been demolished, time would have taken its toll. Alexander Forbes described what remained of them in the early 1830s:

Those fortifications resemble the innumerable others which the Spaniards thought necessary to erect in all their colonies. A fort was always thought absolutely necessary at every supposed vulnerable point. . . . With a few guns of heavy metal . . . the duty of the government and commandant for the time being was considered as fulfilled; and the rot and the rust were forever after left to their natural province of destruction.[29]

By that date the presidios were in ruins, but the towns that had slowly grown about them were ongoing entities. The coming of the Yankees had a profound impact on life in the presidial towns that was noticeable well before the frenzied hysteria of the gold rush. Americans were specifically attracted to these coastal towns and their trade and commerce. Monterey, the provincial capital and site of the customs house, was the focal point of mercantile activity. Its growth under three flags—those of Spain, Mexico, and then the United States—provides a case study of improvisation within the rhetoric of a venerable tradition of urban settlement.

1 Quoted in Herbert E. Bolton, *The Mission as a Frontier Institution in the Spanish-American Colonies*. Reprinted from the *American Historical Review*, XXIII (October, 1917), pp. 42–61 (El Paso, 1962), p. 11.

2 Hubert Howe Bancroft, *History of California* (7 vols; San Francisco, 1884–1890), I, p. 28.

3 Croix, Mexico, July 18, 1771, *Provincial State Papers*, I, p. 75.

4 *Recopilación de leyes de los Reynos de las Indias*, 4th ed. (3 vols; Madrid, 1791), Book III, Title 9, I, pp. 592–597.

5 *Idem*. The other fortifications in question are St. Augustine, Puerto Rico and Guayra (Venezuela).

6 *Ibid.*, III:9:1, I, p. 592.

7 Charles, III, Madrid, September 10, 1772, "Reglamento é Instrucción para los Presidios que se han de formar en la linea de frontera de la Nueva España," quoted in Bancroft, I, pp. 206–207.

8 Quoted in Alfred Barnaby Thomas, *Teodoro de Croix and the Northern Frontier of New Spain, 1776–1783* (Norman, Okla., 1941), p. 188.

9 José de Gálvez to Vicente Vila, La Paz, January 5, 1769, *Provincial State Papers*, I, pp. 23–32.

10 Gálvez to Pedro Fages, same place and date, *ibid.*, pp. 32–44.

11 Crespi to Francisco Palou, San Diego, June 9, 1769. Palou, *Noticias de la Nueva California*, ed. & trans. Herbert E. Bolton (4 vols; New York, 1966), IV, p. 257. The requirement of vigilance, ever present in borderlands colonization, knows no compromise.

12 Charles E. Chapman, "The Alta California Supply Ships, 1773–1776," *Southwestern Historical Quarterly*, XIX (October, 1915), p. 184.

13 Miguel Costansó to Bucareli, Mexico, September 5, 1772, Romulo Velasco Ceballos, ed. *La Administración de D. Frey Antonio María de Bucareli y Ursua* (2 vols; Mexico, 1936), II, p. 205.

14 On August 22, 1776, California and six other territories on the northern frontier of New Spain, collectively called the *Provincias Internas,* were formed into a *comandancia general,* which was separately administered from the viceroyalty. Teodoro de Croix, nephew of Charles François de Croix, who had preceded Bucareli as viceroy, was named commandant general; his headquarters were at Arispe, Sonora. California was returned to viceregal jurisdiction in 1793.

15 Felipe de Neve to Teodoro de Croix, Monterey, September 19, 1777, *Provincial records*, I, pp. 18019.

16 Bancroft, I, p. 317.

17 José de Arrillaga to Monterey commandant, Loreto, June 3, 1792, *Provincial State Papers*, VI, pp. 211–212.

18 Pedro de Nava, Commandant General of the Internal Provinces to Arrillaga, Chihuahua, January 19, 1793, *State Papers. Missions and Colonization,* I, pp. 317–319. However, two leagues for each wind would have resulted in an area of sixteen square leagues! This is a very common error.

19 Bancroft, I, p. 503, p. 611.

20 *State Papers. Missions*, I, pp. 73–75.

21 Humboldt, *Political Essay on the Kingdom of New Spain*, trans. John Black (4 vols; London, 1811), II, p. 347.

22 Juan Vicente Guemes y Pacheco de Padilla, Segundo Conde de Revilla Gigedo, *Instrucción Reservada al Marqués de Branciforte* (Mexico, 1966), p. 249.

23 Miguel Costansó, "Informe de
Don Miguel Costansó al Virrey,
Marqués de Branciforte, sobre el
Proyecto de Fortificar los Presi-
dios de la Nueva California,"
*Noticias y Documentos acerca de
las Californias, 1764–1795*
(Madrid, 1959), pp. 225–226.

24 *Ibid.*, p. 227.

25 *Ibid.*, p. 229.

26 George Vancouver, *Voyage of
Discovery to the North Pacific
Ocean and Round the World* (3
vols; London, 1798), II, p. 501.

27 Alberto de Córdoba, "Informe
al Virrey sobre defensas de California," December 27, 1796,
cited in Bancroft, I, p. 541.

28 José Bandini, *Descrision de
l'Alta California en 1828*, trans.
Doris Marion Wright (Berkeley,
1951), p. 4.

29 Alexander Forbes, *A History
of Upper and Lower California*
(San Francisco, 1937), p. 127.

The port of Monterey was among those landmarks discerned by Sebastian Vizcaino during his voyage along the coast of California in 1602. It was the subject of much discussion in the following century and a half by virtue of its assumed connection with the elusive Northwest Passage. Hence, Monterey's importance to the Spanish was a matter of long standing, and its settlement was the first objective they pursued after the founding of San Diego.

A land expedition under Gaspar de Portolá left San Diego in July 1769 with the intention of reaching Monterey and establishing a presidio there. They arrived at the shores of Monterey Bay on 1 October, but the port they expected was not recognized even though it lay at their feet. Portolá was convinced they had failed to find Monterey: "What should be the Río Carmelo is only an *arroyo*; what should be a port is only a little *ensenada*; what were great lakes are lagunitas."[1] His doubts were supported by the fact that Vizcaino, and later, Cabrera Bueno, had both recorded the incorrect latitude for the port. Another explanation offered was that over the years the port had gradually been filled with sand.[2] However, the most likely reason for Portolá's befuddlement was that the harbor and anchorage at Monterey fell far short of the popular ideal that had conditioned his expectations.[3]

The search for Monterey was renewed in April 1770, and the destination was reached on May 24. This time there was no mistake; the leaders of the expedition, Portolá, Fr. Juan Crespi, and Lieutenant Pedro Fages, unanimously agreed: "This is the port of Monterey which we seek, just as Vizcaino and Cabrera Bueno describe it."[4] The presidio was established on 3 June 1770, and its beginnings were described by Palou:

Hand was put to building a stockade and inside of it some humble habitations for the royal presidio. . . . For a site a level place was chosen on the shore of an estuary. . . . Engineer Don Miguel Costansó made his measurements . . . and drew the plan of the presidio . . . all the people moving to it.[5]

The plan of the presidio called for a square of about 200 feet by 200 feet with an interior plaza of 160 feet. By November the stockade enclosure was completed and a plan of the layout was sent to the viceroy (figure 63c). A powder magazine was constructed, and the buildings were whitewashed inside and out.[6] The presidio was completed by December 1773, as is indicated by Palou's description:

> It has a stockade of wood with four ravelins, and on each of them a bronze cannon. Inside the stockade there is a church of adobe with its flat roof of plaster, and near it a room of the same materials for a dwelling unit for the fathers . . . On the front face there is a dwelling for the captain, also of adobe, with two small rooms . . . There is another room built of adobe which serves as a jail, a granary, quarters for the volunteer soldiers and the leather jackets, and other rooms for the muleteers and servants. All of the latter are made of logs with a flat roof of earth.[7]

At this point in its history, there was little to differentiate Monterey from San Diego, already constructed. However, on 1 January 1774 it was made the seat of the political and military governments of Alta California, and a little more than three years later, the capital of the entire California peninsula was transferred from Loreto, in Baja California, to Monterey.

One of the initial problems encountered at Monterey was that of its site, which, apparently, lacked some key amenities. Richard Morse has written that abandonment or transfer is a characteristic of Spanish colonial settlements. Such drastic acton would sometimes become necessary due to poor site selection, Indian raids, or changes in the patterns of trade.[8] However, considerations of strategy were the criteria for selection of presidial sites rather than the usual standards of water, arable land, and sufficient building materials. Monterey, like San Diego, was to be the victim of an inflexible decision concerning its location. Fernando de Rivera y Moncada, its commandant in 1774, stated that he did not consider the presidio's site to be a convenient one and urged that it be moved to a spot near the Salinas River, four or five leagues distant. Viceroy Bucareli tentatively approved the move, but a royal order from Spain commanded that under no circumstances should the presidio be moved because the port of Monterey must be protected at all costs.[9] However, Geiger has claimed that the plan was not taken seriously and that Bucareli's underlings never saw fit to even mention the matter to him.[10] This claim arises from Serra's remark, "I was told that he [Rivera] was not allowed to leave the port, nor to transfer the presidio elsewhere," although

Serra continues that "it was general gossip that the new Captain was going to move the presidio, as if that had been the main object of his appointment." [11]

But the presidio was to remain, and by March 1776 Monterey was growing at a rate that the garrison's walls could not contain for long. The establishment of the town itself was imminent and would have occurred earlier if the inhabitants had been sufficiently industrious. This is indicated by Fr. Pedro Font's account:

Its buildings form a square, on one side of which is the house of the commander. . . . On the other two sides there are some huts of small houses of the families and people who live there. All are built of logs and mud, with some adobe; and the square or plaza of the presidio, which is not large, is enclosed by a stockade. . . . It is all a very small affair, and for lack of houses the people live in great discomfort. Nor is this for want of materials, for there is lime and timber to spare, but for lack of effort directed to the purpose. [12]

However, Governor Felipe de Neve's arrival in 1777 was responsible for a flurry of activity, and by July 1778 a stone wall 537 yards in circumference, twelve feet high, and four feet thick had been completed.

California's physical and economic isolation was a hindrance to the colony's development, though the material and psychological effects of this situation evidently caused little governmental concern. The Manila Galleon was required to call at Monterey, but the commanders preferred, with rare exceptions, to absorb the financial penalty and make directly for Acapulco. However, the order served little purpose even if obeyed since all trade with the Philippines ship was prohibited. In 1791 Governor Pedro Fages reiterated the earlier directive that forbade commerce with the galleon on the few occasions it anchored at Monterey. He insisted that the colonists were provided with all that was necessary, and he believed that if business was allowed to be transacted with the Manila ship, the soldiers and settlers would barter their clothing and other needed effects for "immoderate luxuries which cannot be sustained." [13] Seven years later, Governor Diego de Borica took exception to this statement, citing the desirability of supplying California with "effects for daily use," [14] but it would be a matter of decades before this situation was remedied.

Knowledge of Monterey, as of the other California settlements, is augmented substantially by the accounts of foreign travellers. Lapérouse, in 1786, was the first to visit Monterey, but his observations were chiefly of a scientific nature. The first visitor of note in California was George Vancouver, who was in Monterey for much of December 1792. His description of the presidio is not especially revealing, and he was not impressed by its "lonely uninteresting appearance"; nor was he much taken with its worth as a fortification. But his comments on its situation vindicate, to a degree, Rivera y Moncada's desire to relocate the presidio:

The presidio . . . does not appear to be much benefitted by its vicinity to fresh water since in the dry season it must be brought from a considerable distance, as the Spaniards had not been at the pains of sinking wells to insure a permanent supply. There were many delightful situations in the immediate neighborhood of the presidio, with great diversity in the ground . . . and a soil that would amply reward the labour of the industrious, which our Spanish friends might with equal ease have sat themselves down; more comfortable, more convenient, and I should conceive more salutary than their present residence appeared to be.[15]

The appearance of the settlement was documented by a French captain, M. Péron, who attributed the slow progress being made in California to lack of motivation:

The aspect of the town shows ignorance in the arts and a stationery state of the country. The houses and cabins are constructed without taste, the furniture coarse, the utensils imperfect—an absolute lack of the conveniences of life. . . . Industry is in general the feeble side of Spanish establishments and it is for this that they cost so dear to their government. The governer . . . avowed only that he had to regret that he had proposed different methods of amelioration without avail.[16]

The population of Monterey at this time was close to 400;[17] the size of the garrison during the decade never fell below 50 and was as high as 62.[18] A document of December 1797 indicates that 30 individuals paid tithes, but that is not necessarily an accurate indication of the number of households.[19]

The first years of the nineteenth century found the presidio in a deteriorating condition, for it had never been of sound construction. In March 1801 the main gate was demolished by a storm and the rest of the establishment was tottering on the insufficient foundation built after a fire in 1789.[20] In 1801, 298 pesos, 7 reales, were spent in efforts to repair the chronic damage.[21] It appears that there was pressure at this time applied in Mexico to rebuild the entire presidio; however, no action was taken on this item of pork-barrel appropriation.[22]

From the period of revolutionary turbulence in Mexico, about 1811 to 1820, virtually no information about California remains. There were no official communications, nor did the soldiers receive their pay. The missions produced their usual surplus and disposed of it according to the ethics and acumen of the padre in charge, for the missionaries realized it was the lesser of two evils to support the military force. The soldiers suffered the most as they had nothing to sell; everyone else fared as best they could.[23]

Monterey appears to have been the first presidio in Alta California to have produced urban settlement outside the walls of the fortification. Peter Corney's description in the summer of 1815 indicates that by that time it was becoming a substantial town; it had about fifty houses and the surrounding plain provided a lush carpet for the new dwellings.[24] Under the circumstances, the presidio continued to exist in fair condition. In April 1818 Governor Pablo Vicente de Sola noted that the north and east walls had been rebuilt but that the south side still wanted improvement. Plans were also articulated to bring water to the presidio via an aqueduct from the Carmel River, but there were no resources available for such a project.[25] In November 1818 Monterey was attacked by Hippolyte Bouchard, a pirate bearing letters of marque issued by José de San Martín. He demanded that California surrender and launched his assault upon receipt of a negative answer. Isolated from the mainstream of events in Latin America, the Californians were neither impressed by the tenets of revolution nor by credentials issued by a great revolutionary, and they refused to respond. However, no significant damage occurred, and the situation was back to normal within five months.[26] At the time of Duhaut-Cilly's visit in March, 1827, Monterey had grown to somewhat less than 500 in population; Robinson's estimate of about 1,000 two years later appears to be an exaggeration.[27] The Frenchman's account of Monterey indicates that growth around the presidio was continuing and that its position as capital of California, despite a brief San Diego interregnum in the 1820s, had become further enhanced by attracting foreign, chiefly Anglo, commercial activity:

To the right of the Presidio, on a small verdant plain, one sees, scattered here and there, about forty houses of quite an attractive appearance, uniformly roofed with tile and with whitewashed exteriors. There, with about as many cabins with thatched roofs, is all which consists of the capital of Upper California.[28]

He was misinformed, however, in his assumption that all the houses dated from a period after 1821, the era of Mexican independence.[29] But he did notice that many of the houses belonged to foreigners; a census taken in 1829 indicated that there were forty-four *estranjeros* in the Monterey area.[30]

The transition from military to civil government at Monterey was accomplished quietly and with little fanfare; there was none of the acrimony that was to accompany the *coup* at San Diego. There the establishment of a purely civilian form of government was precipitated in 1833 by a near-rebellion against the regime of Santiago Arguello, commandant of the presidial company. Arguello was frequently at odds with the townspeople, whose final recourse was a petition to Governor José Figueroa on 22 February 1833. It addressed itself to the termination of military control and the formation of an *ayuntamiento*:

It is sad to know that in all the pueblos of the Republic the Citizens are judged by those whom they themselves elect for this purpose, and that in this port alone one has to submit himself, his fate, fortune and perhaps existence, to the caprice of a military judge, who being able to misuse his power, it is always easy for him to evade any complaint which they might want to make of his conduct . . . and there is no other formula than the imperious words of I command it.[31]

Figueroa upheld the petition and ruled that under Mexican law, San Diego was entitled to an *ayuntamiento*; on 4 May 1834 he recommended that the town be designated a pueblo. Three months later he authorized the election of one *alcalde*, two *regidores* (four were requested in the petition), and one *síndico procurador*.[32] The organization of the pueblo was formally begun on 21 December 1834, and the *ayuntamiento* assumed its powers on New Year's Day 1835.[33]

The institutional cause for this inevitable civil versus military friction lies in the fact that the Spaniards considered a presidio a permanent installation. Its strategic importance was a constant factor, although, in the case of San Diego, this was not necessarily so. Davis wrote, "The location of the presidio was chosen from a military point of view, to protect the citizens of this miniature city from the ferocious and savage Indians of those days."[34] The *Recopilación* made no provision for the transition to a civil form of government at the presidios, nor did Spanish legislation of the eighteenth century provide relevant statutes in that direction.

At Monterey in 1820 an order was issued to form an *ayuntamiento*, but the circumstances surrounding it are not clear; Bancroft suggested that the action was "for purposes largely experimental."[35] *Alcaldes* were in office in 1823 and 1826, but there is no further information concerning the functioning of the government. The *ayuntamiento* appears to have assumed its full responsibilities following an election in December 1826.[36] The first of its documented acts was a series of municipal ordinances promulgated in December 1828.[37] Public morality seems to have been its chief concern. Three of the legislation's fifteen articles were devoted to matters of temperance and two were concerned with the use of firearms; also noted were the problems of excessive card playing, theft of horses, panhandling, idleness, and vagabondage. Curfews and business hours were specified, and pawnshops were condemned as usurious. Monterey's population of 502 in 1830 represented a slow but steady growth; more than 100 of that number was assigned to the presidio.[38]

A second series of ordinances was promulgated in 1833 by Marcelino Escobar, constitutional *alcalde*. However, these were directed at environmental considerations. The owner of hogs that were caught running in the streets would be fined twelve reales for a first offense. Settlers would have to clean in front of their houses at least twice weekly, and the garbage was to be used as landfill for holes caused by erosion and the manufacturing of adobes;

further, bricks were to be made in restricted areas or on one's own property. Another article warned against cutting trees on public land for personal gain.[39]

A steady stream of foreign visitors passed through Monterey after the mid-1830s. Their descriptions reflect their varying degrees of empathy or, more usually, antipathy for Spanish California. But despite their prejudices, a picture of Monterey emerges from which conclusions can be drawn. Richard Henry Dana's account of his travels along the California coast is the best-known description of Hispanic California available to the general public. He visited only the four presidial towns and was led to believe erroneously that "every town has a presidio in its centre; or rather, every presidio has a town built around it.[40] His description of the Monterey presidio in January 1835 indicated that it was "entirely open and unfortified. There were several officers with long titles, and about eighty soldiers, but they were poorly paid, fed, clothed, and disciplined."[41] As for the town itself, Dana was perhaps the only writer to prefer it to Santa Barbara, its younger and more elegant sister:

The town lay directly before us, making a very pretty appearance; its houses being plastered, which gives a much better effect than those of Santa Barbara, which are of a mud-color. The red tiles, too, on the roofs, contrasted well with the white plastered sides and with the extreme greenness of the lawn upon which the houses—about an hundred in number—were dotted about here and there, irregularly. There are in this place, and in every other town I saw in California, no streets, or fences . . . so that the houses are placed at random upon the green, which, as they are of one story and of the cottage form, gives them a pretty effect.[42]

A year later, Faxon Atherton counted but twenty or thirty houses. He observed that Monterey, once again capital of California after a year's hiatus, had "no streets, no hotels . . . and the ground [was] covered with the bones of cattle and the air almost filled with carrion crows and vultures."[43] Ruschenberger's population estimate of about 500 in 1836 is more in line with Dana's observations and presents a more accurate description of the size of the town than Atherton's.[44] Petit-Thouars also noticed that the houses "were scattered here and there, without order," and did not perceive "the slightest trace of culture." He

estimated its population to be no more than 200.[45] Francis
Simpkinson, a seaman of H.M.S. *Sulphur,* commented,

The town, though it looks rather neat and comfortable
from the anchorage, is a miserable spot when one enters
it. The few houses there are scattered over the plain without the least order or regularity, and carcasses of bullocks
and horses give the same character of indolence to the
place as San Francisco.[46]

With the exception of Dana, these sophisticated and
well-traveled men expressed prejudices that reflected their
intolerance and lack of understanding of a latino culture.
Atherton was particularly eager in all his descriptions of
California to vent his contempt on what he saw. Of Monterey he wrote, "We . . . took a stroll about the town if
twenty or thirty houses can be called such."[47] That Monterey was a territorial capital seemed ludicrous to Petit-
Thouars and Simpkinson. The latter wrote, "On the whole
the place did not impress a very grand idea of the capital
of a beautiful country like California."[48] The Frenchman's
idea of a center of polity could not be reconciled with
what he found at Monterey. The houses composed "by
virtue of their agglomeration . . . that which is called the
city of Monterey, doubtless in deference to its seat of
government." He continued, "It serves no purpose to add
that there is no other monument than the church of the
Presidio."[49]

By 1840 Monterey's population had risen to about 700,
and it is possible that a certain amount of attention had
been paid to the city's physical plan.[50] This is indicated by
Duflot de Mofras's description of the town in 1841:[51]

The city is composed today on two parallel streets and of
several groups of houses dispersed on the plain. Almost all
the houses are built with bricks dried in the sun . . . with
roofing, floors and balconies of wood; some are quite nice.
Since they all have a garden and a large yard, the town
occupies a vast area, and from a distance one is deceived
by its importance; but the population is only six hundred,
mostly foreigners. All the houses have their main facade
turned towards the southeast in order to avoid the dam-
ages of the north-west wind which blows for half the year.
Seen from the sea, the situation of Monterey is truly ad-
mirable; there is no position more picturesque and more
favorable for the establishment of a great city.[52]

However, he remarked that "there is at Monterey no build-ing worthy of attention." The presidio had been demol-ished, but the *castillo* had three serviceable cannons, "which had been cast in Manila or Lima in the seventeenth century"; the presidial force numbered about sixty.[53] Sir George Simpson of the Hudson's Bay Company dispelled all illusions about planning and street arrangement that Duflot had suggested:

The town . . . is a mere collection of buildings, scattered as loosely on the surface as if they were so many bullocks at pasture; so that the most expert surveyor could not possibly classify them into crooked streets. What a curious dictionary of circumlocutions a Monterey Directory would be.[54]

He also observed that

the habitations have a cheerless aspect, in consequence of the paucity of windows, which are almost unattainable luxuries. Glass is rendered ruinously dear by the exhorbi-tant duties . . . After all, perhaps the Californians do not feel the privation of light to be an evil. . . . It cannot, by any possibility interfere with the occupations of those who do nothing.[55]

The activities of US Consul Thomas O. Larkin were in large part responsible for a mild business boom in Mon-terey. In 1841 he successfully agitated for the construction of a wharf, and although he contributed much of his own funds to the project, he was never reimbursed. Larkin was also the prime mover behind the reconstruction of the customs house, "which promises to be a small range of decent offices; for though it has been building for five years, is not yet finished," as Simpson had observed.[56] The wharf and customs house provided the necessary atmos-phere to foster a modicum of commerce. We are certain that Larkin did not neglect his own interests. After the wharf was completed, he acquired a number of nearby lots, on which he built stores that were offered for rent.[57] After the arrival of the US fleet in 1846, Larkin invested in a parcel opposite the customs house, which later became one of Monterey's most important business blocks.[58] La-place's estimate of the population in 1842 was 1,500, a rather exaggerated figure, but he observed that many of the town's leading citizens were American and British merchants, an occupation that Monterey residents had theretofore monopolized. The town boasted two newspapers, one in English and one in Spanish, which underscored the binational character of the California capital. Lafond was impressed by "the newly-constructed buildings which give this town an air of youth and freshness, which charms and seduces as much as the amiable hospitality of its inhabitants.[59] Even Hastings was struck by the size and vigor of Monterey (figure 62):

Including those within its suburbs, it contains about one hundred buildings. . . . There are many more foreigners at this place, than at any other town in the country. They . . . are chiefly Americans. This town is situated upon one of the most beautiful sites for a town, or even for a city, that I have ever beheld . . . This is, in all respects, a most delightful and favorable site, for a great commercial emporium, as which it is undoubtedly destined ultimately to be occupied.[60]

The original presidio had almost entirely disappeared by 1844; a dozen artillerymen and three or four guns in working order were all that remained of the fortification and its garrison.[61] By 1845 Mexico was bracing for war with the United States, leaving the California government weaker and more chaotic than usual. In July 1845 Juan Alvarado issued a proclamation declaring that Monterey had been lacking in civilian authority for a substantial period of time.[62] One *alcalde* owed the municipal treasury thirteen dollars, while another had left town when his resignation was refused. A Captain Torre was appointed to act temporarily, but many would not recognize his authority.[63]

The character of Monterey appeared to have undergone a change by mid-1846 when the Americans seized California. Walpole wrote, "Many of the more respectable inhabitants had left on its occupation by its new masters; but others, and they not a few, were very glad of it, for the Mexican rule had become intolerable."[64] In addition, the commercial axis of California had shifted to Yerba Buena, the rapidly growing settlement on the eastern shore of the San Francisco peninsula. Outwardly, at least, Monterey remained as it had been. Larkin reflected, "Monterey is about the same. It will not increase fast. It will, I think, be a good, moral, gentle town for California. . . . Yerba Buena and other places in and about San Francisco will be the busy, bustling, uproar of places."[65] In January 1847 General William T. Sherman wrote, "Everything on shore looked right and beautiful . . .; the few adobe houses, with red-tiled roofs and whitened walls, contrasted well with the dark pine trees behind. . . . Nothing could be more peaceful in its looks than Monterey."[66] Furthermore, he continued, "not a single modern wagon or cart was to be had in Monterey, nothing but the old Mexican cart with wooden wheels, drawn by two or three pairs of oxen, yoked by the horns."[67]

As for Monterey's town plan, Duflot's observation of two parallel streets was not substantiated by any other account. Juan Bandini wrote that "there is a small promenade near the dock," but that is hardly the *plaza mayor* specified by the *Recopilación*.[68] With reference to the chaotic physical development of the town, he noted that "although quite a few large houses have been constructed, these buildings have all been situated without hope of forming a street, since there has been no method for the builder other than whim."[69] A somewhat more understated comment was forwarded by Larkin, who reported in 1843, "The streets are not very straight and about twenty-one yards wide."[70]

The first effort to impose an uncluttered pattern on the Monterey street system was made on 1 March 1847, by William Robert Garner, an Englishman, and Walter Colton, who in 1846 had become the town's first American *alcalde*. Garner wrote,

Some attempts were made to-day to regulate the streets in the town of Monterey. This is a difficult matter, as each person has built his house on the spot and in the form he thought proper, without any attention to regularity. . . . however, after some considerable difficulty, we succeeded in laying off two handsome streets, both of which will form a front line extending in a North and South direction. One of these streets is nine hundred yards long, and the other eleven hundred yards from one extremity to the other.[71]

The area between the two streets was divided into building lots, and their spirited sale furnished "sufficient proof that Monterey is destined to increase rapidly in population, and consequently in improvement and wealth."[72] Accordingly, the demand for land "had increased beyond credulity." He observed in a letter dated 5 March 1847 that in Monterey "so great had been the demand of late, that it was found necessary to set aside sufficient land for a jail, a market place, a burial place, and a public square."[73] This could be read as a sweeping indictment of, and explanation for, the chaotic physical development present in California's towns. It is, no doubt, an accurate report since Craig asserts that Garner's letters "are the most authoritative and complete description of the customs and life of the Californians . . . . to reach the general American public before the Gold Rush."[74] On the other hand, it is reasonable to suggest that the requisite land for these uses may have been so designated long before, however informally. But only at that particular time did it become necessary to identify those sites clearly in response to pressures exerted by private individuals. Visual evidence supports this interpretation, for the required open space is readily apparent in contemporary views of the town. However, Garner's comments emphasize the fragile basis of the Hispanic urban pattern in all the California settlements.

It was finally decided that a comprehensive and orderly blueprint for growth and the alignment of existing structures had to be put into operation. On 27 August 1849 the *ayuntamiento* enacted the following regulations: First, a plan of the town was to be drawn with the boundaries of existing houses and walls in one color; house lots that had been granted but not developed, in a second color; and streets, alleys and plazas, in a third color. Second, the person commissioned to draw the plan would be compensated with grants of house lots if there were, as was likely, insufficient funds in the municipal treasury. Third, if there were lands that had been granted where streets, alleys, or plazas were designated, and if there were no foundations or houses on them, the *ayuntamiento* would name three individuals to determine fair compensation for the obstructing territory. Fourth, if developed lands were in conflict with the arrangement of public walkways, the owners of those properties would be compensated according to the same procedure. And last, no one would be permitted to build foundations or erect fences on land without the council's permission.[75]

This was the first indication of any plan since the presidio was constructed in 1770. Although the town of Monterey began after effective Spanish rule in Mexico had terminated, it is curious that no plan for its development was formulated by the Mexican authorities. Were any plans for new towns drawn up in Mexico during the post colonial era? In California, such actions did occur with reference to activities associated with the founding and growth of Sonoma. Perhaps planning is a function of a government with sufficient scope, resources, and authority, which was not the case in California until the American conquest.[76] Monterey was perhaps the only colonial Hispanic capital without a plan.

If urban chaos was to govern Monterey's physical development, then much the same would be said for Santa Barbara, its sister presidio 200 miles to the south. An early historian of Santa Barbara County has told us that

as the settlement grew stronger, houses were built outside of the inclosure, and the walls were suffered to go down, and in places were removed to make room for buildings. The courts of the Noriega and Carillo houses were laid out partly outside and partly within the presidio walls.[77]

The lack of a plan in those days was noticeable to all. Juan Bandini wrote that in 1847 "in town were lately built houses of some taste, all scattered about without order and according to the caprice of the owner."[78] Another writer was of the opinion that "the town was laid out by means of a huge blunderbuss loaded with adobe houses." And a third thought Santa Barbara "resembled a family of pigs of all ages around the maternal swine"[79] (figure 64).

The first remedy for this chaotic situation was proposed in 1851 when Salisbury Haley was commissioned to conduct a survey; the town was to be arranged in the familiar grid pattern with blocks 150 yards square.[80] Each street was to be sixty feet wide, and the two major thoroughfares, eighty feet wide; however, the blocks that emerged had unequal dimensions. Haley's surveying chain contained rawhide thongs that stretched in damp weather and contracted in the sun so that when the blocks were subdivided, property owners found that their land extended well into the street or into adjoining lots.[81] The survey, however, maintained the implicit pattern stamped on the town by the old presidio. The streets were slanted at an angle of 48°30' west, which was in close conformance to the *Recopilación*, which specified that the corners of the

plaza should be oriented toward the four points of the
compass so that the streets would not be exposed to the
inconvenience of the four winds, a scheme already followed at Monterey. That is, the streets were to bisect the
four quadrants of the compass.[82] In order to avoid further
urban chaos, the town council passed an ordinance in July
1852 requiring that

each person who has the intention of building a house on
unoccupied land must obtain from the *Comisionado* a
certificate which indicates that the house will not obstruct
the lands and thoroughfares of the city. . . . Whether the
owner of land wishes to construct a house or houses . . .
[he] must first advise the *Comisionado* who will inform
the Municipal Council.[83]

Another ordinance of similar vintage provided that those
who held land "during a period of twenty years without
receiving a title for same may do so without any additional
costs other than the gratuities of executing such a
document."[84]

Fortunately, such procedures were not made any more
urgent by the crush of events. The pressures of population
and the demand for land remained external to Santa Barbara. Rather, it was Los Angeles that had to grapple with
these problems as the state's southern locus of urbanization. Instead, Santa Barbara remained one of the final
outposts of California's pastoral era, when a steamship
would call twice a month with a surf-soaked sack of mail.

Monterey, too, quietly found itself removed from the
mainstream of events. During the Gold Rush, it was virtually abandoned. Even though there was a state constitutional convention in session in Monterey in October
1849, Bayard Taylor found it deserted: "Few people were
stirring in the streets, business seemed dull and stagnant;
and after hunting half an hour for a hotel, I learned there
was none."[85] In April 1852 Bartlett reported, "Many of
its houses are now deserted, or in a dilapidated state, and
the grass may be seen growing in the streets."[86] What was
to be Monterey's fate? San Diego, mired in arid isolation,
helplessly waited for the railroad to bridge the continent.
Taylor reflected that the growth of San Francisco and the
depopulation following the gold hysteria were not to be
cause for uneasiness. Monterey may have been dull, but
"it [was] . . . in the sense that Nice and Pisa are dull

cities."[87] Bartlett predicted that "Monterey will become the residence of gentlemen of fortune on account of its more genial climate and its distance from the noise and bustle of a great city. It will be to San Francisco what Newport is now to New York."[88]

What can be concluded about Monterey and its modest niche within the Hispanic urban tradition? First, as observers have noted from the days of Bartlett to the present era when the whole of Monterey's environs are an affluent riviera, the Spanish were expert judges of terrain. They knew where to begin their settlements. If these were not nurtured, it was for reasons of resources and the constraints of an unwieldy, vast, and declining empire. These factors were particularly relevant in California, 1,500 miles distant from Mexico City. Spain's colonial possessions were a vast incubator of colonizers who, though not always steeped in the juridicial tradition of codified legislation, were imbued with the ability to recognize terrain with urban pretensions. If they could not provide site selection criteria per the *Recopilación's libro, título,* and *ley,* they could at least recognize where possibilities were most promising.

Second, while abandonment and transfer of a settlement is a traditional adjustment within Spanish settlement practices, the presidio, in its strategic role, was not afforded the flexibility of other urban institutions. The mission could be moved if its terrain or surrounding population proved too hostile. The pueblo was frequently subject to recalibration; flooding, attacks, or natural disasters were an expected component of its pedigree. But the presidio, in its noncompromising physical location, had to endure. If a location is of great strategic value, then it is a military problem and there is no need to consider issues such as changes in urban form or political authority due to civilian succession. Such issues are built into the situation.

For example, urban settlements, the *Recopilación* cautions, should not be situated in maritime locations where the tumult and temptation of the port of call runs contrary to the presumed industriousness of urban life. But in California inland waterways are not a characteristic of the landscape, especially on the central and southern coasts, where most colonization took place. The *Recopilación* strongly recommends river locations for urban settlements

since they favor transportation, lack the diversions of seaports, and often have access to a fertile hinterland. With
this major option lacking, population centers in California
would have to be located in a maritime situation. As a
result, many travelers never ventured inland. The two
pueblos, San José and Los Angeles, languished in the bountiful amenities of their isolation, forgotten and removed
outposts of California Pastorale.

If the *Recopilación* did not create civilian settlements
from military forts, provincial governors could. And once
this occurred, the presidios were quick to assert their control over the problems of municipal management; Monterey, for example, gave prompt attention to morality and
environmental considerations. Although this intensity was
not sustained, by 1847 planning and land titles were foremost in the town's attention. This was necessary because,
as Juan Bandini recalled for San Diego,

as it was not customary at that time for [Governor] José
María Echeandía to give [written] titles,[89] nor until now
was the plan of the town determined (today it has been
made and the town has taken its proper form), it was
necessary for me to obtain the documents which authorized the legitimacy of my possessions[90] to the effect that
a square of one hundred *varas* on each side was conceded
to José Antonio Estudillo and myself divided between both
of us.[91]

Two conclusions may be arrived at based upon the information in Bandini's account. First, the presidio and then
pueblo of San Diego grew up quite haphazardly. There
was no plan or systematic procedure for development until
after the American conquest. The *Recopilación* was, if you
will, *hors de combat* in this instance. Yet there was at least
one copy of it in California during the Spanish period, as
a letter of Junípero Serra indicates, and a minimal degree
of familiarity with it on the part of lower-echelon officials
is not an unreasonable assumption.[92] On the other hand,
it did not contain legislation pertinent to the development
of presidial towns. The most plausible and simple explanation that can be offered is that there was no competent
authority present to exercise control over all but the most
rudimentary matters on a day-to-day basis. Uniform and
consistently applied principles of town planning were at
best a remote possibility on a frontier such as California.

As an American observer wrote in 1841, "Although I was prepared for anarchy and confusion, I was surprised when I found a total absence of all government in California, and even its forms and ceremonies thrown aside."[93] Accordingly, the absence of a plan for San Deigo was noted by its many foreign visitors. Second, the lack of authority did not preclude the existence of individual written titles; it was not merely the custom of convenience that dictated that "grants of that class were made verbally."[94] The *Recopilación* specifies that grants of house lots and other lands be entered in the "libro de Cabildo," sometimes referred to as the "libro de Población," and that it was to serve as the permanent record of title.[95] If such a record was not maintained, then it could be said that an anarchic situation prevailed in California. However, a verbal title does not exlude the existence of a written entry, however insufficient it may have been in the eyes of some Anglo lawyers. It is doubtful that any of these *libros* still survive.

Though lacking the orthodox accoutrements of strong central control and a standardized adherence to the model colonial plan, Monterey demonstrates that it is within the tradition of Spanish colonization. Indeed, three and a half centuries after its colonization, this remote outpost has maintained a semblance of its heritage, albeit one rooted in ephemeral custom rather than rigorous adherence to laws long submerged by revolution, miscegenation, and immeasurable distance.

1 Gaspar de Portolá, "Diario del Viaje á la California," quoted in Hubert Howe Bancroft, *History of California* (7 vols; San Francisco, 1884–1890), I, p. 151.

2 Junípero Serra to Francisco Palou, San Diego, February 10, 1770, Serra, *Writings*, ed. Antonine Tibesar, O.F.M. (4 vols; Washington, D.C., 1955–1966), I, p. 159.

3 Bancroft, I, pp. 153–155.

4 *Ibid.*, p. 169.

5 Francisco Palou, *Noticias de la Nueva California*, ed. & trans. Herbert E. Bolton (4 vols; New York, 1966), II, pp. 292–293.

6 James Culleton, *Indians and Pioneers of Old Monterey* (Fresno, 1950), pp. 44–45.

7 Palou to Viceroy Antonio María de Bucareli, Monterey, December 10, 1773, Palou, III, p. 229.

8 Richard Morse, "Latin American cities: Aspects of Function and Structure," *Comparative Studies in Society and History*, IV (July, 1962), pp. 473–493.

9 Bancroft, I, p. 309.

10 Maynard J. Geiger, O.F.M., *The Life and Times of Fray Junípero Serra* (2 vols; Washington, D.C., 1959), I, p. 443.

11 Serra to Bucareli, Monterey, September 9, 1774, Serra, II, p. 175.

12 Pedro Font, *Diary of an Expedition to Monterey by Way of the Colorado River, 1775–1776*, ed. & trans. Herbert E. Bolton (Berkeley, 1933), pp. 289–290.

13 Fages, Monterey, February 26, 1791, CA, *Provincial State Papers*, VI, pp. 159–160. Henceforth, *Provincial State Papers, Provincial Records, Departmental State Papers,* and *State Papers* refer to California (CA).

14 Borica to Viceroy Miguel de Azanza, Monterey, October 25, 1798, *Provincial Records*, III, p. 428.

15 George Vancouver, *Voyage of Discovery to the North Pacific Ocean and Round the World* (3 vols; London, 1798), II, p. 43.

16 M. Péron, "Monterey in 1796," trans. Henry R. Wagner, *California Historical Society Quarterly*, I (October, 1922), p. 176. The authenticity of the account as a first-hand narrative has been questioned, but it is nonetheless sufficiently accurate in its content to warrant inclusion here.

17 Bancroft, I, p. 677.

18 *Ibid.*, p. 467.

19 *Provincial State Papers*. Presidios, pp. 174–175.

20 Raymundo Carrillo, "Los Edificios de Monterey," Monterey, December 31, 1800, *Provincial State Papers. Benicia. Military*, II, pp. 126–127.

21 *Provincial State Papers*, XI, pp. 194, 172.

22 Bancroft, II, p. 143.

23 *Ibid.*, p. 196.

24 Peter Corney, *Early Voyages in the North Pacific, 1813–1818* (Fairfield, Wash., 1965), pp. 129-130.

25 *Provincial Records*, IV, p. 429. José de Jesus Vallejo, *Reminiscencias Historicas de California* (Bancroft Library MS, 1874), p. 77.

26 Bancroft, II, p. 234.

27 Alfred Robinson, *Life in California* (Oakland, 1947), p. 9.

28 Auguste Duhaut-Cilly, *Voyage Autour du Monde* (2 vols; Paris, 1834–1835), I, pp. 362–363.

29 The account of Duflot de
Mofras, published about a decade
later, appears to have drawn
upon Duhaut-Cilly's dating of the
emergence of the town of Monterey: "It was only in 1821 that the
town which has been given the
pompous title of capital city
began to form. The first house
was built by an English merchant
named [William] Hartnell"
(Eugene Duflot de Mofras, *Exploration du Territoire de l'Orégon,
des Californies, et de la Mer Vermeille* [2 vols; Paris, 1844], I, p.
403).

30 *Departmental State Papers*, I,
p. 292.

31 Quoted in Richard F. Pourade,
The History of San Diego (5 vols;
San Diego: 1960–1965, III, p. 14.

32 William Heath Davis, *Seventy-
five Years in California*, (San
Francisco, 1929), p. 258.

33 *Departmental State Papers.
Los Angeles*, IV, p. 620. The
Recopilación provides for a maximum of 12 *regidores* in principal
cities and 6 in the others
(IV:10:2, II, p. 33). No more
than 2 *alcaldes* are permitted
(IV:10:1, *ibid*). The *sindico procurador* is specified in IV:11:1 (II,
p. 37).

34 Pourade, III, pp. 14–15.

35 Bancroft, II, p. 611.

36 *Idem*.

37 Monterey *Ayuntamiento*,
Monterey, December 6, 1828,
Departmental State Papers, I, pp.
239–242.

38 Mariano Soberanes, Monterey,
July 12, 1830, *State Papers. Missions*, II, p. 7. Bancroft, II, p.
609.

39 Marcelino Escobar, Monterey,
January 6, 1833, *Departmental
State Papers. Monterey*, pp. 61–
65; *Departmental State Papers*, II.
pp. 159–161.

41 *Idem*.

42 *Ibid.*, p. 72.

43 Faxon Dean Atherton, *California Diary*, ed. Doyce B. Nunis,
Jr. (San Francisco & Los Angeles,
1964), pp. 3–4.

44 Ruschenberger was a surgeon
assigned to the United States war-
ship, "Peacock." William S. W.
Ruschenberger, *A Narrative of a
Voyage round the World during
the Years 1835, 36 and 37* (2
vols; London, 1838), II, pp. 400–
404.

45 Abel du Petit-Thouars, *Voyage
autour du Monde* (10 vols; Paris,
1840–1844), II, pp. 84, 110.

46 Richard A. Pierce and John H.
Winslow, eds., *H.M.S. Sulphur at
California, 1837 and 1839* (San
Francisco, 1969), p. 28.

47 Atherton, p. 3.

48 Pierce, p. 28.

49 Petit-Thouars, II, p. 64.

50 Bancroft, III, p. 667.

51 Californian opinions of M.
Duflot were of great variance.
Alvarado found him to be "a
young man of great literary repu-
tation, of spirited character, and
of generous inclinations," while
at the same time having "very
false ideas about our character"
(Juan B. Alvarado, *Historia de
California* [5 vols; Bancroft
Library MS, 876], IV, p. 175).
On the other hand, Dona Teresa
(de la Guerra) Hartnell, wife of
the English merchant to whom
Duflot had referred, had more
strenuous objections to the
Frenchman:

While at my table he found fault
with every one of our dishes,
however, he did full justice to the
wine. . . . Unfortunately in his
sleeping room I had deposited a
barrel of the choicest wine which
my father had sent me from Santa
Barbara to be given to the priests.
. . . Next morning at breakfast

my guest, not making an appearance, I detailed a servant to call him; but Mr. Mofras not giving any answer to call him; I ordered the door to be broken; and there stretched upon the floor my Frenchman lay dead drunk, bedding in a filthy state and many gallons of wine missing from the barrel.
(Quoted in Susanna Bryant Dakin, *The Lives of William Hartnell* [Stanford, 1949], p. 257.)

52 Duflot de Mofras, I, pp. 403–404. The large yards, or corrals, were a custom derived from the *Recopilación*; similarly, the orientation of the houses are a logical component of legislation dictating the corners of a town plaza face the cardinal points of the compass (*Recopilación de leyes de los Reynos de las Indias*, 4th ed. [3 vols; Madrid, 1791], IV:7:17, II, p. 23; IV:7:9, II, p. 21).

53 Duflot de Mofras, I, pp. 405, 325.

54 Sir George Simpson, *Narrative of a Journey Round the World During the Years 1841 and 1842* (2 vols; London, 1847), I, p. 344.

55 *Ibid.*, p. 345.

56 *Ibid.*, p. 346.

57 Reuben L. Underhill, *From Cowhides to Golden Fleece: A Narrative of California, 1832–1858* (Stanford, 1939), pp. 56–57.

58 *Ibid.*, p. 126.

59 Victor Laplace, *Campagne de Circumnavigation de la Fregate L'Artémise pendant les Années 1837, 1838, 1839 et 1840* (6 vols; Paris, 1841–1854); Gabriel Lafond, *Voyages autour du Monde* (2 vols; Paris, 1843), I, p. 208.

60 Lansford W. Hastings, *The Emigrants' Guide to Oregon and California* (Cincinnati, 1845), p. 108.

61 Bancroft, IV, p. 656.

62 *Ibid.*, p. 654.

63 *Idem.*

64 Frederick Walpole, *Four Years in the Pacific . . . from 1844 to 1848* (2 vols; London, 1849), II, p. 205.

65 Thomas O. Larkin to Samuel J. Hastings, Monterey, November 16(?), 1846, Thomas O. Larkin, *The Larkin Papers*, ed. George P. Hammond (10 vols; Berkeley & Los Angeles, 1951–1964), V, p. 279.

66 William Tecumseh Sherman, *Recollections of California, 1846–1861* (Oakland, 1945), pp. 9–10.

67 *Ibid.*

68 Juan Bandini, *Historia de la Alta California, 1769–1845* (Bancroft Library MS, 1874), p. 64. *Recopilacion*, IV:7:9, II, p. 21.

69 *Ibid.*, pp. 64–65.

70 Larkin to Andrew Johnstone, Monterey, June 3, 1843, Larkin, II, p. 19.

71 William Robert Garner, *Letters from California, 1846–1847*, ed. Donald Munro Craig (Berkeley, Los Angeles & London, 1970), pp. 193–194. The streets in question are Alvarado and Castro (later Tyler). The visual effect recalls Duflot de Mofras' apparently incorrect description of 1841.

72 *Ibid.*, p. 194.

73 *Ibid.*, pp. 198–199.

74 *Ibid.*, pp. 1–2.

75 Ignacio Esquer and Ambrosio Gomez, Monterey, August 27, 1849, *Unbound Documents*, pp. 181-182.

76 See Woodrow J. Hansen, *The Search for Authority in California* (Oakland, 1960).

77 Quoted in Jesse D. Mason, *History of Santa Barbara and Ventura Counties, California* (Oakland, 1883), p. 53.

78 Juan Bandini, *Historia de la Alta California, 1769–1845* (Bancroft Library MS, 1874), p. 46.

79 Both quoted in Mason, p. 53.

80 The order reads: "It is authorized that the land surveyor of the city require all owners of house-lots situated within the limits of the survey of the City; and that Salisbury Haley mark off the boundary lines of each houselot in order to facilitate the conclusion of the Map of the City" (*Santa Barbara Archivo*, p. 103).

81 Yda A. Storke, *A Memorial and Biographical History of the Counties of Santa Barbara, San Luis Obispo and Ventura, California* (Chicago, 1891), p. 63.

82 *Recopilación de leyes de los Reynos de las Indias*, 4th ed. (3 vols; Madrid, 1791), IV:7:9, II, p. 21.

83 *Santa Barbara Archivo*, pp. 87–88.

84 *Ibid.*, pp. 99–100.

85 Bayard Taylor, *Eldorado, or Adventures in the Path of Empire* (2 vols; New York, 1850), I, p. 133.

86 John Russell Bartlett, *Personal Narrative of Explorations and Incidents in Texas, New Mexico, California, Sonora, and Chihuahua* (2 vols; New York, 1854), II, p. 72.

87 Taylor, I, p. 137.

88 Bartlett, II, pp. 74–75.

89 The first actual written title granted by an *alcalde* was said to have been issued to Tomasa Alvarado in 1838. (Bancroft, III, p. 612).

90 From 1850 to 1854 the United States Land Commission challenged both individual claims of land as well as the town's claim to its area of four square leagues. In December of 1849 the San Diego *ayuntamiento* resolved that "all titles of house lots which are now in the archives of this court of those which may hereafter be presented with *good evidence of their legality* are and shall be admitted by the council as proof of good faith and right of property" (*Documentos para la Historia de California, 1826–1850: Originales y copiados de los Archivos del Condado de San Diego*, pp. 465–466). An act in 1851 provided that the existence of a town on July 7, 1846, should be regarded as *prima facie* evidence of a land grant. San Diego obtained confirmation for its pueblo lands as a result of an official survey by Capt. Henry Delano Fitch in 1845. Santiago Argüello testified that the boundaries of the survey "were designated by myself previous to the survey. I have known them since the year 1818" (quoted in Pourade, III, p. 15). The survey was approved in substance in 1870 and a patent was issued in 1874 (Bancroft, IV, p. 567).

91 Juan Bandini, San Diego, January 30, 1850, *Documentos para la Historia de California, 1826–1850: Originales y copiados de los Archivos del Condado de San Diego*, p. 52.

92 Serra to Rafael Verger, Monterey, August 15, 1774, Serra, *Writings*, ed. Antonine Tibesar, O.F.M. (4 vols; Washington, D.C., 1955–1966), III, p. 353.

93 Charles Wilkes, *Narrative of the United States Exploring Expedition during the Years 1838, 1839, 1840, 1841, 1842* (5 vols; Philadelphia, 1845), V, p. 152.

94 *Documentos para la Historia de California . . .*, p. 8.

95 *Recopilación*, IV:12:8, II, p. 41.

Few will dispute historian Lewis Hanke's observation that "no European nation . . . took her Christian duty toward native peoples so seriously as did Spain." [1] Despite this national commitment, however, Spanish colonial officials of Church and State found it difficult to agree as to how this broad consensus would be translated into policy on the local level. This was especially apparent in Spain's frontier territories where the guiding beacon of statutory orthodoxy was eclipsed by distance and compromised by the pragmatic considerations of the business of empire. Thus arose the classic blanket rejoinder of the theoretically culpable but nevertheless autonomous secular official, "Obedezco pero no cumplo" ("I obey but I do not comply"). The immunity effectively built into these local decisions frequently came at the expense of the missionary orders, particularly in the more remote areas of the sprawling American empire. Despite the central role played by the aspiring missionary church in the course of empire in the sixteenth century, the institution increasingly became a perennial thorn in the side of a resource- and revenue-hungry colonial government.

By the waning years of the colonial era, the vulnerable and impoverished Spanish empire could no longer afford the luxury of an ecclesiastical establishment which clung to the anachronistic mandate of paternalistic stewardship that it had secured nearly three centuries earlier. Monumental in their achievements under conditions which stretched the limits of human endurance, the missionary orders proved equally tenacious in their resistance to any perceived incursion into their hegemony. Although the nature of colonial society had undergone massive change by the eighteenth century, the missionaries remained intransigent in their determination to thwart adjustments in their equilibrium with the secular world. The formal expulsion of the Jesuits from the colonies in 1767 was only the most dramatic blow which the State finally leveled at the missionary orders; it reflected a situation of much greater cumulative enmity.

3
CHURCH-STATE BOUNDARY DISPUTES

This chapter originally appeared as "Power and Priorities: Church-State Boundary Disputes in Spanish California," *California History* (formerly *California Historical Quarterly*) 57:4 (Winter 1978/79), 364–375.

The eighteenth-century colonization of California provides a case in point in Spain's Church-State conflict. The specific issue around which larger antagonisms surfaced was the objection by missionaries to the choice of locations for the pueblo of San José de Guadalupe in 1777 and the Villa de Branciforte two decades later. This happened, in part, because the three forms of urban settlement in California—the mission, presidio, and pueblo— were distinct yet symbiotic entities. Missions were reconstituted Indian villages centered around a church and a strictly-supervised regimen of agriculture and crafts.[2] Their purpose was the introduction of Spanish civilization and the proselytization of the Catholic faith to Native Americans. Presidios, or forts, were to provide protection for mission communities as well as serve as coastal sentries and ports of entry; they were dependent on the missions for their sustenance. Pueblos or the more exalted villas (at least in title) were civilian agrarian settlements; their presence in California reflected the need to establish agricultural self-sufficiency in the province and to eliminate their dependence on the missions, as well as to increase the province's sparse Spanish population. From the beginning of the colonization effort, carefully drawn regulations prescribed where pueblos could be located with respect to Indian mission communities. In theory, this policy of separation of the mission from the secular world was to be vigorously enforced until such time as the mission completed its educational and evangelical tasks among the natives.

The mission-pueblo boundary disputes in later-eighteenth century Spanish California illustrate three dimensions of the Church-State problem. First, it becomes apparent that the acrimony of successive generations of conflict had made impossible harmonious dialogue between the clergy and secular interests, not only in matters of major impact (such as the timing of mission secularization), but also in rather minor if not wholly avoidable issues (such as boundary disputes). Second, it is revealed that secular interests chose to proceed with town foundings in a manner not only patently illegal, but also designed to tread heavily upon, if not humiliate, the Franciscan missionaries. Thirdly, it is evident that the California friars actively kindled the flames which were eventually to consume them by strenuously opposing the establishment of such secular communities from the very beginning. By turning a deaf ear on the needs of the State, the missionaries sowed the fateful seeds of exasperation and vindictiveness among their military and agrarian brethren.

It is therefore not surprising that tensions often ran high in the early years of the settlement of California. For example, following the midnight Indian uprising at the San Diego mission in November, 1775, Junipero Serra, father president of the missions, quarreled with Captain Fernando de Rivera y Moncada concerning measures to deal with rebellious and hostile Indians. Both parties had cause for anger because deteriorating relations between Rivera's soldiers and the mission community had led the missionaries to insist that the troops withdraw from the immediate area. This left the mission virtually defenseless against the surprise attack. Concurrently, the padres constantly bridled at the government-imposed prices at which their grain was to be sold to the military, and they retaliated by withholding spiritual services from the troops; these services they regarded as voluntary charity, not a prescribed duty. The military, in turn, could counter by providing decreased protection to the missions, thus inviting the possibility of another tragedy like that at San Diego. Behind these squabbles was the difficulty of separating policies from the individuals empowered to carry them out. In these years personalities in conflict produced frequent disagreements which, according to historian Hubert Howe Bancroft, were "often petty in all their phases, and such as might easily have been avoided by slight mutual concessions and efforts to promote harmony."[3] For example, it required two years to resolve the seemingly trivial issue of State-sanctioning of the missionaries' power to administer the sacrament of confirmation. Father Serra and Governor Felipe de Neve battled from 1779 to 1781 on this issue alone.[4]

Although the role of individual personalities should not be minimized, the sources of the boundary conflict in California were as cumulative as they were circumstantial. In the sixteenth century, the Spanish monarchy realized that the secular clergy were more malleable than the religious orders whose primary ties were to Rome rather than to the Crown. Philip II thus sought to minimize the role of the regular clergy in the colonies, but he was never able to achieve this end due to the scarcity of secular priests. This perpetual condition insured the continued sway overseas of the regular clergy, a fact which sorely vexed successive sovereigns, particularly the eighteenth-century Bourbon monarchs.[5]

The overriding factor in Church-State discord was not abstract conflicts of authority and allegiance, but rather the control of territory and population. As early as 1530, royal governors were instructed to respect the integrity of Indian communities, their organization, and their customs, excepting what was deemed justifiable intervention in matters involving pagan customs or barbarous practices.[6] The implications of territorial integrity extended to other fronts as well. It was very early viewed as a necessity, writes historian J. Preston Moore, "to protect the Indians against legal injustices at the hands of the *encomenderos*, caciques, and pettifogging attorneys."[7] Through the centuries, the rationale for this almost too fiercely protective attitude remained remarkably consistent. An early spokesman, the Franciscan mystic Géronimo de Mendieta (1525–1604), similarly wrote:

The Indian with respect to the Spaniards is like a small dog in front of a mighty lion. The Spaniards have both the evil desire and the strength to destroy all the Indians in New Spain, if they were ever given the chance. The Indian is so phlegmatic and meek, that he would not harm a fly. Consequently, one must always assume in case of doubt that the Spaniard is the offender and the Indian is the victim.[8]

Considerably later, at the virtual end of the colonial era, Father President Fermín Francisco de Lasuén reiterated the separatist attitude long fostered by missionary rule. Articulating much the same fears as did Mendieta, Lasuén brought the matter still closer to the outright proprietary paternalism to which the friars had so accustomed themselves. "If in some mission, or in all of them," he wrote,

certain Indian men and women are sometimes denied permission to associate with certain individual people *de razón*, it is for precisely the same reasons as those for which every good father of a family in every civilized nation should forbid his children to go with bad companions.[9]

The specifics which may be read into this attitude extended to include actions of vigorous resistance to any and all perceived incursions of the secular society into the broadly-defined sphere of interest which the missionaries took as their mandate. These included opposition to institutional changes relevant to internal mission organization such as governance and land uses. Although attempts to manipulate mission internal affairs were loudly contested by the friars, it was a relatively simple matter for them first to resist and then to put on a show of compliance, while absorbing only a minimum of change. Thus, in 1778 when Governor Felipe de Neve ordered that mission Indians commence electing their own *alcaldes*, or mayors, and *regidores*, or councilmen, Lasuén countered with narrow objections based on technicalities, then quietly yielded. However, in the end, he cleverly dodged de Neve's directive by lengthening the interval between elections and then by eliminating them entirely, substituting municipal officers appointed by missionaries.[10]

But not all threats to the missionary realm could be quite so easily parried. Supreme in a land where they dominated both resources and population, the friars were content to maintain the *status quo*. But the larger objectives of empire, specifically the populating of the province and the encouragement of agrarian endeavor, dictated a change in this hegemony. Felipe de Neve realized that the introduction of civil agricultural settlements was essential to California's security, if not survival, and his term as governor was to witness the founding of two pueblos, San José de Gaudalupe in 1777 and Nuestra Señora de Los Angeles de Porciúncula in 1781. It was with the establishment of San José that a new tale of acrimony began.

Father Junípero Serra was outspoken in his opposition to the introduction of secular establishment in California. The presidios he acknowledged as a necessary evil; but as for "pueblos composed of Spaniards, or of people of mixed blood," he had "never been able to see or recognize any advantage in it whatever, either on the temporal or spiritual side."[11] Serra believed that establishing more missions offered a better means of attaining agricultural self-sufficiency, for not only would they "be the means of supplying foodstuffs for themselves and for the Royal Presidios," but they would "accomplish this far more efficiently than these pueblos without priests."[12] However, the problem of populating the country remained, and Serra's ideas drew de

Neve's sarcasm: "He forgets," wrote the governor, "that this would not people the land with Spanish subjects."[13] Pragmatically, therefore, Serra could not easily dismiss the idea of civil towns in California. Not surprisingly, however, he relegated their advent to a date far in the future when "the gentiles that are spread throughout these lands have become Christian, and when they are settled in their various reservations or missions, . . . then will be the proper time for introducing towns of Spaniards." He warned, too, that the people must "be of good conduct and blameless life."[14]

If San José's colonists did not meet Serra's rigorous standards, then far less could be said for the site selected for California's first civilian settlement. In both 1778 and 1779 unseasonable flooding had inundated the pueblo, and in the latter year it languished under three feet of water. In his efforts to correct the situation, de Neve relocated the town's agricultural lands, relating that he had found a site "more suitable and closer to the population, changing the distribution which I have made."[15] However, this action failed to remedy the immediate circumstances and instead initiated a prolonged round of acerbic sparring with the clerics which was to endure for twenty years.

The bitter controversy with the nearby mission at Santa Clara began to flare in earnest by the early summer of 1778. De Neve observed, "Said pueblo has not only encountered difficulties with the sowings, but also with the bad arrangement in which its lands were distributed, all in the direction in which the Mission of Santa Clara is situated."[16] In June, 1778, Father Serra reiterated his vehement opposition to civil settlement to Viceroy Antonio María de Bucareli. Serra once again asserted that increasing the number of missions would provide a satisfactory solution to the problem of agricultural supply and suggested, "The settlers who can suitably fit into such a scheme—and at present their numbers are few—should be distributed until more promising times among the missions."[17] Serra took a necessary precaution in preparing the missionaries for the anticipated struggle with the secular authorities. In August, 1779, he wrote to his superior, the Guardian of the College of San Fernando, requesting that

. . . the *Recopilación de Leyes de Indias* (Code of Laws) [be] brought at the expense of all the missions and placed at this mission, where the President has his residence. The gentleman [Governor de Neve] has a copy, and he is out-matching us with his quotations. Although I remember quite an amount from the time I read these laws, I have also forgotten a great deal—especially the quotations. And so I would appreciate it if they came, and we can let him know he is not dealing with ignorant men.

The truth is that he will always get the better of us because of the knack he seems to have of getting around any law.[18]

Serra's fears not withstanding, however, the body of laws enabled the missionaries to argue their case from an unassailable position, and their enventual defeat stemmed not from the intrinsic merits of the issue, but from the uncompromising and stubborn determination of the secular authorities to win their case.

The missionaries' "brief" may be divided into two distinct sections. One pertained to the rights of Indians and the prerogatives of Indian settlements, and the other consisted of statutes which limited the location of Spanish towns. In summary, the case presented by the religious observed that all royal officials were charged with the duty to protect and defend the rights of Indians and to punish transgressors vigorously, while the ecclesiastics' function was to insure their jurisdictions were not jeopardized in any way.[19] Consequently, Indian settlements were to have sufficient lands and water, as well as a commons of one league in length where cattle could be pastured without interference from herds belonging to Spaniards.[20] Once Indians were reduced to a settlement, they were to remain on that land for at least five years in order to learn to cultivate it and profit thereby, and so they would learn the proper mode of government.[21]

With respect to limiting the settlement activities of Spaniards, the missionaries probably inadvertently omitted from their case key statutes which prohibited the founding of towns on sites that were not vacant or that were prejudicial to the interests of Indians.[22] But equally appropriate was their citation of a prohibition against distributing land in newly-founded towns which adversely affected Indian holdings.[23] Infractions involving livestock were items of particular rancor with the missionaries, who invoked legislation which stipulated that ranches and other lands granted to Spaniards must not be in opposition to the interests of Indians, and if granted, such lands must be returned to their rightful owners.[24] More specific, however, was the stipulation that cattle ranches must not be situated within one and one-half leagues of older Indian settlements or within three leagues of new ones; otherwise, severe penalties for violations were to be exacted.[25] The presence of a pueblo adjacent to an Indian settlement constituted a far greater threat, or at least annoyance, than an *estancia*, or ranch, they continued. The missionaries' contentions, as it turned out, were all valid, and none were offered in rebuttal by the secular authorities.

Despite Father Serra's undisputable position, however, nothing was done to remedy what he considered to be an unjust state of affairs. Of Governor de Neve, Serra wrote, "Common sense, laws, and precedents mean nothing to him."[26] Further, although de Neve surely realized the sound basis on which the religious grievances rested, he

went ahead with his project, even though he often changed the plans and details of its development, and even the people who lived there, But it remained on the same site. . . . On one occasion the gentleman in question [de Neve] went so far as to admit that everything had been . . . carried out contrary to the laws. But he excused himself by saying that his instructions had not been obeyed, that his wishes were that it should be in a different town. He even went so far as to hint that it would be changed.[27]

Serra continued that neither de Neve nor any other official had ever made the effort to set a boundary between the mission and pueblo because "justifiable complaints would be made and lawsuits started."[28] Such complaints were lodged by the missionaries at Santa Clara in 1782. They wrote to Pedro Fages, de Neve's recent successor as governor:

When we recall how short a distance there is between the two, we can see how much annoyance and damage will be caused to our poor convert Christians, and what a source of constant friction it will be to them. . . . It is contrary to His Majesty's laws that any land should be owned by citizens of the said pueblo. . . . This is clear from the measures Your Lordship might order to be made and also when you compare your findings with the laws contained in *La Nueva Recopilación de Indias*.[29]

Serra, however, realized that righteous anger in an isolated province such as California would not convince the secular authorities in Spain to change the location of the town. Accordingly, he wrote to his superiors in frankness, "If the laws dealing with such matters, and they are very specific, are of no account, then everything else is to no avail."[30]

Unhappily, the civilian authorities were equally frustrated in their intents. Flooding continued to plague San José despite the considerable efforts and tribulations which earlier difficulties had exacted from the settlers. In early 1785 it was first suggested that it would again be necessary to move the town to a higher elevation, but *Comisionado* José Moraga hesitated to initiate such drastic action. However, the sentiment of the settlers was in favor of relocation, and in August, Governor Fages wrote to Jacobo Ugarte y Loyola, commandant general of the *Provincias Internas*, requesting permission to move the town to a small nearby hill. The change of site would not have represented a major dislocation for the settlers, because at the time their houses were only palisade structures with earthen roofs.[31] Ugarte approved the idea "as it would be more useful and advantageous," but warned that it must be done "without altering or varying . . . the limits and boundaries of the lands or districts assigned to said Town or to the contiguous Mission of Santa Clara since there is no just reason for it to claim said site."[32] In other words, Ugarte stressed that the transfer of land uses must not jeopardize in any way the uneasy *modus vivendi* with the mission. Furthermore, while he intended to give the missionaries no satisfaction in their dispute of past years, he believed it was important for the location of San José to stay within the area, presumably four square leagues, which it had been assigned (figure 65).

Despite the decade or so of contemplation, the move was not undertaken until 1797. In January of that year, *Alcalde* Marcos Chavoya officially requested that the town be transferred, "recognizing the deplorable situation in which the Pueblo has found itself owing to the flooding of the arroyos which surround it."[33] Governor Diego de Borica assented, but he wrote in the margin of the document, "Determination of the matter reserved until the engineer Alberto de Córdoba returns from San Diego to examine the terrain and informs me of what he has seen."[34] However, even before Córdoba's arrival, the Santa Clara missionaries were protesting that the change would adversely affect their interests and prerogatives.[35]

When Córdoba arrived he was ordered to "reconnoiter carefully the environs of San José and indicate within its boundaries the site which is most proper for its transfer which is close to its tillage lands, and require the settlers to mark it off with stakes."[36] After Córdoba's work had been completed, Governor Borica attempted to mollify the missionaries by explaining to them how the determination had been made. Córdoba, after taking testimony from both sides "on their reciprocal claims," then proceeded to set the official boundary "not far from the land which it today occupies, because these have been determined by the higher authorities." It was within these limits that "the settlers of said pueblo must immediately locate themselves."[37] The *pobladores*, or settlers, were then instructed to "go to construct their houses on the other side of the river in case of flooding."[38]

Despite their earlier defeat, the missionaries seized the opportunity to press their case once again. They wrote to Governor Borica, citing Libro VI, Título 3, Ley 9 of the *Recopilación*, "which prevents and prohibits Indians from leaving the lands which they had previously possessed."[39] At that time the friars claimed that the mission had 1,434 Indian neophytes, with 4,000 more living in surrounding *rancherías*, and thus, much more land would be required by the mission. They also argued that livestock from San José would stray from the pueblo's commons and destroy the mission's pastures.[40] Additionally, the validity of Córdoba's boundary determination was questioned.[41] Complaints concerning trespassing by San José livestock had only recently been registered, which the missionaries believed to be in violation of "various royal *cédulas* (statutes) and the law," and they threatened to take their case to a superior court of appeal.[42] But despite their apparent legal justification, even the viceroy did not see fit to take action and the matter was not broached again.[43]

The two decades of sustained acrimony experienced in the Santa Clara Valley provided a hard-earned lesson in tactics to the secular authorities. Accordingly, in their plans of 1796–97 to found the Villa de Branciforte on the northern rim of Monterey Bay, the subterfuge of a *fait accompli* was embraced. Although there is no indication of any overt effort to conceal the plans to establish Branciforte, it must nevertheless have been a well-kept secret. The missionaries, in fact, learned of the proposed founding only two weeks before the first colonists were scheduled to arrive. Accordingly, Lasuén wrote to the president of his missionary college that the villa was "the greatest misfortune that has ever befallen mission lands. . . . This is a flagrant violation of all law. If any remedy can be found, it would be wrong not to apply it."[44] A few days later Lasuén wrote Governor Diego de Borica, politely suggesting his disapproval of the matter. Lasuén argued:

The King knew the situation quite well, and so did his Excellency the Viceroy, and Mission Santa Cruz had already been founded with royal approval. Hence it appears to me impossible that his Majesty should wish, ordain, or approve of a villa or pueblo in the immediate neighborhood, or that his Excellency should attempt it.[45]

The College of San Fernando lodged its formal protest with the office of the viceroy in August, 1797.[46] As with the case of San José, the missionaries substantiated their case with appropriate citations from the *Recopilación*, and in light of the similar circumstances underlying the two conflicts, it is perhaps worthwhile to make some comparisons. Again the friars' argument may be divided in two parts, one relevant to the protection of the rights of Indians, the other limiting the sites where towns of Spaniards might be established. In this instance the latter approach was not stressed to the viceroy, possibly because "the explanation given suffices to convince us that Your Excellency was not informed with the sincerity and truth, which the matter required, as to the site or location on which the new pueblo is projected against the express intent of such grand and equitable laws."[47] More conciliatory than before, the missionaries emphasized:

The College regards the project itself with favor as something useful. Nor does it venture to make representation in order to hamper or embarrass your Excellence. It merely desires to see the plan executed in accordance with the laws. Otherwise there will arise disputes, disorders and delays.[48]

Three statutes from the *Recopilación* were cited in the Villa de Branciforte dispute which were not cited previously by the missionaries in the course of the San José–Santa Clara boundary squabble. (A second treatment of those statutes mentioned in both is unnecessary, as they are discussed above.) The first of these—Libro IV, Título 21, Ley 8—was obviously an error;[49] the law which precedes it, No. 7, appropriately forbade the founding of new towns in areas which were already populated or which were in situations contrary to the interests of existing inhabitants.[50] Ley 12 safeguarded territory assigned to Indians from cattle pastures used by Spaniards.[51] It should be emphasized that the villa and the Santa Cruz Mission were separated by the narrow San Lorenzo River and were "scarcely a stone's throw away" from each other.[52] Libro VI, Título 3, Ley 6 was another error, and probably the missionaries meant to refer to Ley 8, which provided for each mission "a location which has the convenience of water, arable lands . . . and a commons of one league in every direction."[53]

The missionaries' protest, however, was unfortunately timed, and in light of international tensions and the viceroy's resolution to found a town bearing his name, it is unlikely that there was any possibility of a significant change in the situation. But the protest did cause a delay and compel Borica to defend his actions. He argued in rebuttal that the mission had sufficient land for its declining Indian population and further suggested that the villa would be able to purchase whatever surplus the mission produced.[54] However, it was not until December, 1800, a hiatus of nearly three years, that the objections were laid to rest; finally, in March of 1801 the cost of the project was given final approval by the *Junta Superior de Real Hacienda* (Royal Treasury).[55]

What is the explanation for the circumstances which precipitated these conflicts? In 1778 Viceroy Bucareli had reported the founding of San José to Charles III. One of the items in the report which both men must have noticed was the specific indication that the new town was but three-quarters of a league from a mission, a rather suspicious proximity.[56] Nevertheless, the purposes for which the town had been established received unquestioned precedence, and it is doubtful that the king would have seen fit to intervene in a dispute over a minor provincial settlement. Governor de Neve was the real culprit, because his unilateral decision to locate San José near the mission was ill-advised and contrary to law. Indeed, he had the entire Santa Clara Valley at his disposal for a site. Nevertheless, the decision was subject to higher approval, and if it had been reversed, San José would not have been the first Spanish colonial town to have been relocated during its early years. It was upon Viceroy Bucareli that the responsibility ultimately devolved, and although in him "Serra did not have a better friend," Bucareli did not see fit to take action with respect to San José.[57] Teodoro de Croix, commandant general of the *Provincias Internas*, was directly responsible for affairs in California. Though a religious man, Croix was not an ally of the missionaries. For these reasons the decision stood to maintain San José near its original site, and there existed no further avenue for appeal for the clergy.

Similarly, a feared confrontation with England, which led to the founding of the Villa de Branciforte,[58] dictated a course of action oblivious to the niceties of statutory orthodoxy as well as to the costs of internecine squabbling. Indeed, the California boundary disputes demonstrated that missionary (and presumably Indian) interests were of such low priority that even modest accommodations were spurned in favor of wholly uncompromised attainment of secular goals. This in turn reflects the continuing intransigence of the missionaries' attitudes concerning Indian stewardship and their chronic inability to define the well-being of the mission Indian in a context any broader than the societal isolation of the mission community. It was the increase of the Spanish population and the founding of Spanish towns, regardless of prior intents, that had become the only real goals of the California colonization. The missionaries and Indians may have been quite indispensable to the maintenance of California in the latter three decades of the eigheenth century, but their voices were rarely heard or heeded beyond the pale. For all their illusory power based on the domination of population and agricultural resources, the missionaries could never, or more correctly, would never establish their credibility as interpreters of the general welfare.

The CITY of MONTEREY, California 1842.

62 View of Monterey, 1842. From a painting by Gildmeister, drawn, according to the legend under the view, for Señor Larkin, the American counsel whose house stands at right front. The sketch suggests its pastoral setting and haphazard arrangement, "on a green lawn." Many of the adobe houses shown here are preserved and can be visited at Monterey. What is probably the presidio is the large two-storey complex to the left of center with a flagpole on the roof; only the presidio chapel and some wall survives of this complex. The present-day presidio was built later in the nineteenth century, on the wooded hill at right, or even farther to the right where the house stands on a rather steep hill. (Courtesy of the Huntington Library, San Marino, Cal. Originally used as frontispiece in vol. 3 of the Larkin papers)

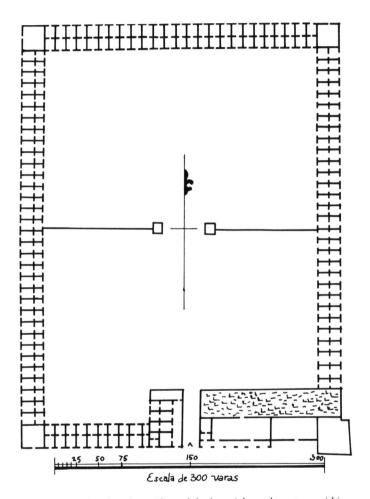

63 Four Spanish colonial presidios of the late eighteenth century within the United States. All of these plans date from the end of the eighteenth century. The similarity between Santa Fe and the California group indicates that this form was the standard answer to problems of defense all along the frontier.

(A) Santa Fe, 1791. The Governor's Palace is at lower right. This plan is redrawn from one done by Jack Mills of the Museum of New Mexico; it was compiled from a 1791 map by Juan de Pagasaurtundua and other sources found in the Archives in Mexico City.

Plan del Real Presidio del Canal de Santa Barbara, y actual estado de sus obras que el Teniente Comandᵗᵉ de el S.ᵒ M.ᵉˡ Goycoechea a cuyo cargo han corrido, manifiesta al Sᵒʳ Gʳˡ de esta Peninsula y Comandᵗᵉ Inᵗ S.ᵒʳ Pedro Fages, en expresion individual de su construccion, y por nota lo qᵉ falta a su complimento

(B) Even earlier is the plan of the presidio of Santa Barbara, from 1788. The entrance was at the top of the plan and a military chapel stood opposite the doorway. At Santa Fe the protruding bastion at lower right was used as the chapel. (Courtesy of Bancroft Library at the University of California at Berkeley)

(C) Earlier still is the plan of the Royal Presidio of Monterey, dating from about 1771. The original and the new churches are at A and B, respectively; neither of these is located axially opposite the doorway. As usual, the rooms around the edge of the central court were assigned to both domestic and official use. All four corners, rather than two as at Santa Barbara or one as at Santa Fe, are in the form of bastions. This presidio is much smaller than Santa Fe, measuring only 100 *varas* on the entry side. (Courtesy of the San Diego Historical Society/Title Insurance & Trust Collection)

(D) Presidio of San Francisco, dated by Bancroft to 1792. The same distribution of rooms within an encircling wall is followed. The large room at 3 may be the church, which stands next to a minor entrance and opposite the major one between 4 and 5. Some buildings, such as 4, have interconnecting rooms. One set, at 1, has its own enclosed outdoor space and may then be construed as the governor's house. Apparently the fourth side was not completed. (Courtesy of the Bancroft Library at the University of California at Berkeley)

Plano del Real Presidio de
S.ⁿ Carlos de Monterey.
Explicacion.

A Yglesia actual
B Yglesia nueva
C Sacristia
D Quartel de la Tropa de Cuera
E Quartel de la Partida de Voluntarios
F Cuerpo de Guardia
G Almazen del Presidio
H Almazen del Rey
Y Almazen de la Mision
J Vivienda del Oficial
K Vivienda de los RR.ᵒˢ Misioneros
L Herreria, y Fragua
M Carpinteria
N Casa del Horno de Regua

O Casa del Tisanero
P Enfermeria
Q Casa p.ª las Gentiles de Cuera
R Hospicio p.ª los nuebos Christianos
S Casa p.ª las Mugeres Gentiles
T Corral para las Gallinas
V Chiquero de Cerdos
X Cosinas en General
I Casa de la Division del Castillo de Tierra
Z Lugares Comunes
& Troneras

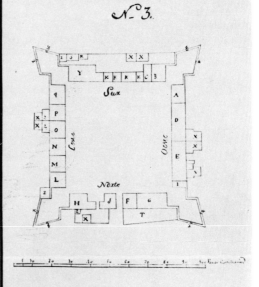

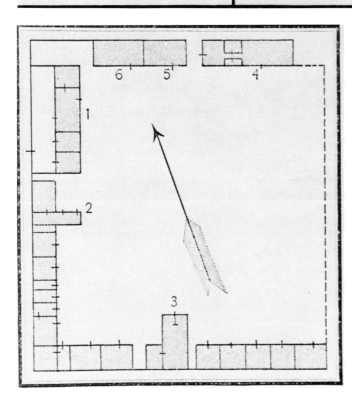

64 View of Santa Barbara in 1839 (from Alfred Robinson, *Life in California*). The mission church sits on the hill, dominating the town. Unity of architecture is evident even in the schematic treatment of the houses of various sizes. Ocean-going vessels like the one in the foreground were the most important means of communication with the wider world. (Courtesy of the California Historical Society, Los Angeles/Title Insurance & Trust Co. Collection of Historical Photographs)

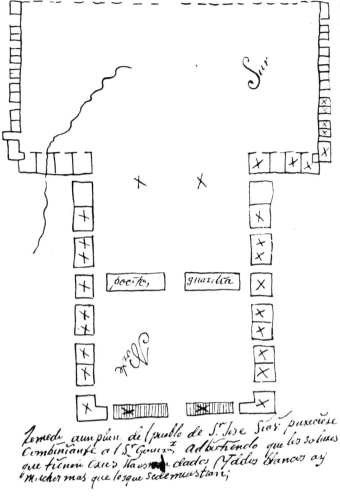

65 Earliest plan of San Jose, probably before 1780 [for the first *commissionado* (military supervisor) of the pueblo]. The plaza lies at the bottom of the plan, surrounding the word *Norte. Norte* and *Sur* show that the plaza is properly oriented with its angles at the points of the compass. Streets apparently enter the plaza near the angles, except that the major openings bisect the space on an NW-SE axis, separating *pocito* from *guardiá*. X may indicate occupied houses, except that two X marks float out in space toward the south, and three sets of marks are paired within the rectangles of the houses, without separation lines to denote attached houses. A stream extends across the eastern part of the site.

Very eighteenth century is the open, axial arrangement, allowing for easy expansion, and giving a dynamic quality to the settlement. Many eighteenth-century sites in colonial Brazil are similar. This plan may have been made by Jose Moraga, who tells us in the caption that "there is much more there than can be shown". (Courtesy of Western Title Insurance Co., San Jose, California)

NOTES

1 Lewis Hanke, *The Spanish Struggle for Justice in the Conquest of America* (Boston, 1965), p. 175.

2 See Herbert E. Bolton, "The Mission as a Frontier Institution in the Spanish-American Colonies," *American Historical Review*, 23 (October, 1917): 42–61.

3 Hubert Howe Bancroft, *History of California* (7 vols.: San Francisco, 1884–1890), I: 407. Occasionally, however, aberrant behavior transcended personal disharmony. The contentious existence of Fernando de Rivera y Moncada in California was apparently due to pathological causes. Fr. Pedro Font observed "he does not like to take suggestions from anybody about anything" (Pedro Font, *Diary of an Expedition to Monterey by Way of the Colorado River, 1775–1776*, ed. & trans. Herbert E. Bolton [Berkeley, 1933], p. 226). While attending to the distress of the San Diego Mission following the Indian uprising of 1775, Rivera's extreme course of action in dealing with one of the culprits caused Frs. Fuster, Lasuén, and Amurrio to excommunicate him (Bancroft, I: 266–267). Even Moncada's relations with his military colleagues were tempestuous. An observer of his interaction with the highly respected Juan Bautista de Anza believed that Rivera was mad; José Moraga shared this opinion (Bancroft, I: 270–271). Bancroft's assessment was perhaps more charitable: "Rivera was evidently a weak man. Whether insane, or influenced solely by a spirit of childish jealousy . . . is a question." (Bancroft I: 272).

4 Edwin A. Beilharz, *Felipe de Neve: First Governor of California*. (San Francisco, 1971), pp. 55–61.

5 Frederick B. Pike. *The Conflict Between Church and State in Latin America* (New York, 1964), p. 6.

6 J. H. Parry, *The Audiencia in Nueva Galicia in the Sixteenth Century: A Study in Spanish Colonial Government* (Cambridge, England, 1948), pp. 59–60.

7 J. Preston Moore, *The Cabildo in Peru Under the Hapsburgs, 1530–1700* (Durham N.C., 1954), p. 234.

8 Quoted in John Leddy Phelan, *The Millennial Kingdom of the Franciscans in the New World* (Berkeley, 1956), p. 61.

9 Lasuén, Mission San Carlos, June 19, 1801, Fermín Francisco de Lasuén, *Writings*, ed. & trans. Finbar Kenneally, O.F.M. (2 vols.; Washington D.C., 1965), II: 212.

10 For a discussion of this point, see Daniel J. Garr, "Planning, Politics and Plunder: The Missions and Indian Pueblos of Hispanic California," *Southern California Quarterly*, 54 (Winter, 1972): p. 296.

11 Serra to Teodoro de Croix, Monterey, August 22, 1778, Junípero Serra, *Writings*, ed. Antonine Tibesar, O.F.M. (4 vols.: Washington, D.C., 1955–1966), III: 263.

12 *Ibid.*, 255.

13 Quoted in Bancroft, I: 314. See also Daniel J. Garr, "A Rare and Desolate Land: Population and Race in Hispanic California," *Western Historical Quarterly*, 6 (April, 1975): 133–148, and the next chapter.

14 Serra, III: 255.

15 Felipe de Neve to Teodoro de Croix, Monterey, August 11, 1778, California Archives, Bancroft Library (CA), Provincial Records (5 vols.), I: 92.

16 *Ibid.*, 9. The mission had been founded the months earlier in January, 1777.

17 Serra to Bucareli, Monterey, June 30, 1778, *Serra Writings III:* 199.

18 Serra to Fr. Rafael Verger, Monterey, August 15, 1779, *Serra Writings* III: 133.

19 *Recopilación de leyes de los Reynos de las Indias*, 4th ed. (3 vols.: Madrid, 1791), II: Libro IV, Título 4, Ley 5, 13; II: Libro VI, Título I, Ley 189–190.

20 *Ibid.*, II: Libro VI, Título 3, Ley 8, 209. An ordinance promulgated by Philip V in 1713 was also listed. It differed from the preceding in that the commons had to consist of one league in every direction; this regulation is not listed in the annotations in the *Recopilación* to the ley cited above (ordinance cited in Maynard J. Geiger, O.F.M., *The Life and Times of Fray Junípero Serra* (2 vols.; Washington, D.C., 1959), II: 196.

21 *Ibid.*, II: Libro VI, Título I, Ley 20, 194; II: Libro VI, Título 3, Ley 8, 209.

22 *Ibid.*, II: Libro IV, Título 5, Ley 6, 16; II: Libro IV, Título 7, Ley 1, 19.

23 *Ibid.*, II: Libro IV, Título 12, Ley 7, 41.

24 *Ibid.*, II: Libro IV, Título 12, Ley 9, 41.

25 *Ibid.*, II: Libro IV, Título 3, Ley 20, 211–212.

26 Serra to Fr. Francisco Pangua and the Discretorium, Monterey, December 8, 1782, *Serra Writings*, IV: 169.

27 *Ibid.*

28 *Ibid.*, 169–171.

29 Frs. José Antonio Marquia and Tomás de la Peña to Governor Pedro Fages, Santa Clara, November 2, 1782, *Serra Writings,* IV: 397.

30 Serra to Pangua, *et al., Serra Writings*, IV: 169.

31 Bancroft, I: 479.

32 Ugare y Loyola to Fages, Arispe, June 21, 1787, CA, State Papers, Missions and Colonization (2 vols.), I: 271.

33 Chavoya to Governor Diego de Borica, San José, January 10, 1797, CA, Provincial State Papers (13 vols.), IX: 25–26.

34 *Ibid.*

35 Fr. Francisco Sánchez to Borica, Mission Santa Clara, April 30, 1797. CA, State Papers, Missions and Colonization, I: 269. There is a document from about 1790 which indicates that the land to the south of what is presumably Coyote Creek belongs to the pueblo and that on the north side to the mission. (Anonymous, n. pl., n.d. (c. 1790), CA, Departmental State Papers. San José (2 vols.) I: 45.

36 Borica to Córdoba, Monterey, May 11, 1797, CA, Provincial State Papers, Indices, 257.

37 Borica to Sánchez, Monterey, May 11, 1797, CA, State Papers. Missions and Colonization, I: 92–93.

38 Ignacio Vallejo to Borica, San José, September 26, 1797, CA, Provincial State Papers, VIII: 344. The move was to the east side of the Guadalupe River.

39 *Recopilación*, II: Libro VI, Título 3, Ley 9, 208.

40 The first of these documented incidents appears to have occurred in 1794 (José Pérez Fernandez to Borica, San Francisco, December 1, 1794, CA, Provincial State Papers, VII: 34).

41 Frs. Magín Catala and José Viader to Borica, Mission Santa Clara, August 6, 1797, CA, State Papers. Missions and Colonization, I: 276–280.

42 Frs. Isidoro Barcenilla to Ignacio Vallejo, San José, October 9, 1797, CA, Provincial State Papers, VIII: 351–352.

43 De la Peña to Viceroy Miguel José de Azanza, Mexico, Colegio de San Fernando, July 27, 1798, CA, State Papers. Missions and Colonization, I: 46–51.

44 Lasuén to Fr. Pedro Callejas, Mission San Carlos, May 1, 1797, Lasuén, II: 26.

45 Lasuén to Borica, Mission San Carlos, May 5, 1797, ibid., 27.

46 College of San Fernando to Viceroy Branciforte, Mexico, August 30, 1797, cited in Zephyrin Engelhardt, O.F.M., The Missions and Missionaries of California (4 vols.: San Francisco, 1908–1915), II: 517–519.

47 College to Viceroy, ibid.

48 College to Viceroy, ibid.

49 Recopilación, II: Libro IV, Titulo 12, Ley 8, 41.

50 Ibid., II: Libro IV, Titulo 12, Ley 7, 41.

51 Ibid., II: Libro IV, Titulo 12, Ley 12, 42.

52 College to Viceroy, Engelhardt, Missions and Missionaries, II: 517–519.

53 Recopilación, II: Libro VI, Titulo 3, Ley 8, 209.

54 Borica to Branciforte, Monterey, February 6, 1798, cited in Bancroft, I: 572.

55 Fiscal to Viceroy Felix Berenguer de Marquina, Mexico, December 11, 1800, cited in Florian F. Guest, O.F.M. "The Establishment of the Villa de Branciforte," California Historical Society Quarterly, 41 (March, 1962): p. 43.

56 Bucareli to Charles III, Mexico, July 27, 1778, La Administración de D. Frey Antonio Maria de Bucareli y Urusa, ed. Romulo Velasco Ceballos (2 vols.; Mexico, 1936), I: 436–437.

57 Quoted in Serra Writings, I: xvi.

58 For more information on the international pressures on Spain, see Guest, "Villa de Branciforte"; Daniel J. Garr, "Villa de Branciforte: Innovation and Adaptation on the Frontier," The Americas, Summer, 1978; and William Ray Manning, The Nootka Sound Controversy (1905).

The settlement of California was an effort crippled by the logistic difficulties inherent in a remote frontier and by the steadily declining resources and determination of the Spanish and Mexican colonizers. They were unable to populate a land which in many cases offered the colonist little incentive. Hispanic settlement efforts contrast with the covetous and timely enterprise of the Anglo-American frontiersmen drawn across the Great Divide by mineral riches, fertile and sparsely populated territories, and the magnet of the Pacific. In practice, Hispanic population policy in California was primarily one of channeling a reluctant and frequently unstable population to secure the distant hinterland while simultaneously purging the Mexican heartland of those whose presence was deemed undesirable. In sharp contrast, we find the Spanish juristic mandate that respectable and industrious soldiers and settlers, accompanied by their families, should populate the frontier provinces. The fact that the program of expedience embodied the extraofficial goals of both viceregal and, later, national governments was ignored, though hardly overlooked. As so often occurred in the annals of Spain overseas, the best designs of those who formulated policy were thwarted and compromised by circumstances beyond their ken and control. Also woven into this coarse fabric was the characteristic Latin American preoccupation with matters pertaining to socioracial stratification. This is a key variable in frontier population policy as well as in official attitudes concerning unstable social conditions.

The earliest California settlers were soldiers, followed by civilians recruited from northern Mexico after the decision had been made to establish the pueblos of San José and Los Angeles. The presence of a military contingent posed two related problems: first, the social composition of the frontier population; second, and more crucial, the characteristic absence of women in a military environment. The latter was indeed a factor remiss in the desired augmentation of the non-Indian population, especially since the missionaries were faced with the unenviable task of segregating indigenous women from theoretically celibate

4

POPULATION AND RACE IN HISPANIC CALIFORNIA

This chapter originally appeared as "A Rare and Desolate Land: Population and Race in Hispanic California," *Western Historical Quarterly* 6:2 (April 1975), 133–148.

soldiers. These unyielding circumstances affecting the coexistence of missionaries and military were further exac-
erbated by the nature of the frontier army's troops. Ideally,
enlistment was voluntary and limited to men of sturdy
character and physique. It was not, however, unusual for
authorities to resort to the conscription of "recycled" deserters, vagabonds, drunkards, and assorted criminals, all
of whom were invariably drawn from the scorned lower
strata of a racially mixed society.[1] Thus, the men of the
Army of New Spain were frequently other than what Teodoro de Croix specified in his instructions for the recruit-
ment of soldiers for the California presidios. Like the settlers, each was to be "healthy, robust, and without known
vice or defect that would make him prejudicial," in addition to possessing "greater strength and endurance for the
hardships of frontier service."[2]

The inherent difficulty with the frontier army was that
it provided a convenient outlet for the expulsion of un-
dersirables from Mexico. As early as 1773, Padre Junípero
Serra entreated the government "not to look upon Monterey and its missions as the *China* or *Ceuta* of exile for
the soldier. . . . Being sent to our missions should not be
a form of banishment, nor should our missions be filled
with worthless people who serve no purpose but to commit
evil deeds."[3] Although Viceroy Antonio María de Bucareli
saw to it that Serra's wishes were accommodated, subsequent administrations were not inclined to give high priority to missionary preferences. By the mid-1820s, the estate
of California had fallen so low in Mexico that in 1826 it
was proposed without further pretense that the army be
purged of its dead wood by recruiting virtuous citizens for
its ranks and exiling all the jetsam and flotsam to the
distant dependency. This policy was described by Alexander Forbes, British vice-consul at the port of Tepic:

Whatever soldiers are sent to California are the refuse of
the Mexican army, and most frequently are deserters, mu-
tineers, or men guilty of military crimes. Those presidios
are also appropriated as receptacles for transported felons;
so that California is the Botany Bay of Mexico.[4]

The situation apparently continued to deteriorate until the
era of American rule. For example, in 1845, Belden observed that the soldiers "committed all sorts of outrages
and were very apt to commit violence with their knives,

... and were a bad lot generally, ... very disagreeable with the native population, overbearing, and insolent."[5]

The implications for frontier settlement are both obvious and ominous. Since each mission required a protective military escort, the friars were presented with a trying problem—the security implicit in the soldiers' presence was often outweighed by their importunity. The first decade of California colonization saw the formation of military and missionary settlements exclusively; the acrid basis for subsequent discord was quickly established between hapless secular and embattled religious authorities. Neither side would reap much consolation from the fact that it was always difficult to attract a stable and balanced population to a frontier environment, but particularly for the defensive settlement of a remote colony.

The troublesome qualities of the initial contingent of soldier/colonists were immediately apparent during California's early years, especially between 1769 and 1779. One of the reasons for the relocation of the San Diego Mission was the missionaries' desire to avoid proximity to the soldiers at the presidio.[6] The military was well aware that California posed a difficult situation for the friars since, as even the anticlerical Teodoro de Croix acknowledged, not only did the priests require protection but they also had to shield their charges, "who are docile and without malice, like all Indians, to the first impressions of good or bad example set by the Spanish who settle among them."[7] Missionary accounts of insubordination and immorality were numerous, with emphasis on the latter. In 1773, for example, Serra confided to Bucareli:

Then, too, the presence of so many women . . . it would be a great miracle, yes a whole series of miracles, if it did not provoke so many men of such low character to disorders which we have to lament in all our missions; they occur every day; it is as though a plague of immorality had broken out.[8]

Although the missionary viewpoint may seem to belabor the obvious, it nevertheless delimits the full extent of the problem, and with it the shortsightedness of the secular authorities. Shortly after, dismayed but undaunted, Serra again informed the viceroy that "the soldiers, clever as they are at lassoing cows and mules, would catch an Indian woman with their lassos to become prey for their unbridled

lust."[9] However easily diagnosed were the symptoms of
the problem, the cure required measures as arduous as
they were evident. It was no mean task to lure single
women to a distant environment barren of cultural and
other societal amenities. Yet, a year later, as much without
warning as without permanence, the long awaited remedy
materialized. Serra's witty acknowledgment hardly concealed his relief:

> Don Rafael, the warehouse keeper at San Diego, brought
> his wife with him. So now the number of families is in-
> creasing. And the people here will now be rid of their
> belief that the Spaniards are the offspring of mules, a
> notion they previously had, seeing that mules were the
> only members of the female gender they saw among us.[10]

Not until 1795 was active government concern with
women manifested as both a factor in population growth
and as an agent of societal stability. At that late date,
Governor Diego de Borica noted the small number of
settlers in California and the enusing, if not dire, necessity
of encouraging population growth for reasons of both
security and sociability; unmarried soldiers were singled
out as the chief, however unwilling, culprits remiss in this
situation. He called upon the four presidio commandants
to promote marriage by all honorable means, and offered
a bonus of forty *pesos* to any soldier who took upon
himself the bonds of matrimony.[11] When the viceregal
government concurrently adopted the policy of sending
convicts to California, Borica requested equal numbers of
mujeres blancas. He also cited the need to supplement the
small number of "women of quality . . . since many would
forcefully resist emigration rather than consent to these
unions; their guardians can procure suitors of correct habits, and as there are few here, it appears to me that few
marriages of this kind will take place."[12] Therefore, he
continued, if women of social pretensions were unavailable, it would be advantageous to furnish ones of lesser
status with the trappings of respectability, such as a serge
petticoat, a serviceable shawl, and a linen jacket.[13] Although the viceroy, the Marqués de Branciforte, concurred
and indicated that he would send women to California at
government expense, it appears that his efforts were not
productive.[14] A similar project, which was never followed
through, brought nineteen female orphans to California in

1800. They were distributed among presidial families, and two girls had found husbands by the year's end.[15]

The only specific and sustained government program for populating California consisted of periodic shipments of vagabonds and convicts from the streets and jails of New Spain. The practice had a venerable past. In response to the startling growth of mestizo and mulatto vagrancy in the sixteenth century, Philip II advised his viceroys that "some men are incorrigible, inobedient, or harmful and are to be expelled from the land and sent to Chile, the Philippines, or other parts."[16] The populating of frontier areas certainly provided a convenient solution to the problem of idle urban masses. In eighteenth-century Mexico, trouble with the lower classes was chronic, particularly in the economically unstable mining regions. Visitor-General José de Gálvez was instructed that he and the viceroy, the Marqués de Cruillas, were to "confer on the matter of forming settlements in the provinces in suitable places with the idle, undesirable people who are in Mexico and other large towns."[17] However, Gálvez ordered that no vagabonds were to be sent to California. He sought to insulate the new colony against the time-tested methods of social purgation which were soon to prevail.[18] Later, in 1787, Governor Pedro Fages, yielding to the urgent need for more people, proposed that those imprisoned in Mexico, particularly craftsmen, be exiled to California in lieu of completing their sentences if they agreed to remain there as settlers.[19] In 1791, three *presidarios* arrived, and in the same year there is a report of a convict blacksmith instructing the Indians of the San Francisco Mission in his trade.[20]

The impact of the policy of populating California with convicts was felt within a short time. San José appears to have been the primary victim of the emigration. By the fall of 1800, several complaints of robberies, disputes, and other disorders had been recorded. An official report states that there were many vagabonds without useful employment "who have caused the *regidores* and *alcaldes* to patrol at night from eleven to one and from one to three."[21] Apparently, many of these were squatters who had named their own interim *Alcalde de Campo!*[22]

The initial attempt to deal with the problem resulted in a proposal to distribute the *presidarios* among "honest

vecinos." But Governor José de Arrillaga subsequently argued that such a plan was not feasible because "the settlers
are committing frequent scandals and are insolent, vicious,
buffoons, and immoral; it is asked that the transportation
of other new ones be suspended." [23] Fray Fermín de Lasuén, in rare but predictable unison, echoed the governor's
sentiments:

I have never known of anyone whatever of the convicts in
question who has the character, ability, skill, or trade
which is needed here. I do hear of crimes and scandals in
connection with them; and I see them in the presidios,
ranches and pueblos almost like tramps. . . . It seems to
me that sending convicts to these parts to serve as colonists
holds out no prospect of good, and has many disadvan-
tages for the service of God, the King, and of the common
good. [24]

It had been hoped initially that errant artisans in particular
would be rehabilitated in California if given the opportunity to practice their trade and to impart their skills to
mission Indians. However, the result of the policy, as noted
above, made a mockery of whatever aspirations the government had entertained.

The viceregal administration in Mexico City was made
well aware of the difficulties caused by its exported felons,
and it appears that no more were sent during the remaining
two decades of Spanish rule. In 1805, the policy of convict
immigration was roundly criticized by the Conde del Valle
de Orizaba. He reiterated that "the first need of this colony
is the increase of its population. The precedent of minor
criminals destined for this objective should not be construed as a solution." [25] He recommended instead that
families with children be sent to the frontiers and that, in
contrast to the previous settlers, legitimate tradesmen be
included among them. [26]

When, in 1825, republican Mexico reinstituted the policy of utilizing California as a penal colony, local opposition flared once again and the issue became a persistent
source of rancor between the central government and its
distant dependency. [27] Governor José María de Echeandía
accused the Mexico City authorities of "ignoring that in
the peninsula there exist decent families of education,"
and asserted that this program of exile constituted a grave
danger to California's prosperity and stability. [28] But by

1829, the force of this opposition dwindled to a mere request that only "useful" convicts be sent since California had no jails and the government could not be held responsible for the exiles.[29] However, Echeandía's protest was ignored; shipments continued, and one even deposited its reluctant emigrés on Santa Cruz Island where they were left to fend for themselves with only a supply of cattle and fishhooks.[30]

The Californians believed, Vallejo recalled, "that Mexico had no right to infest its growing towns with subjects who had a hatred for morality, who preferred lies to the truth, idleness to industry, murder to a peaceful life, and whose presence was a constant menace, terrible for the peace and tranquillity of honorable families."[31] Juan Alvarado opposed "this absurd project," and vowed that he would take "all necessary means to abort this plan of thieves."[32] However, this did not dissuade the central government. By 1835, Governor José Figueroa had authorized *alcaldes* to establish special tribunals for vagabonds so that speedy and efficient justice might be dispensed.[33]

However, it should be pointed out that not all the exiles were of the same parcel of rogues, nor did they all live up to the notoriety which had preceded their arrival in California. Many were banished to California for so-called political crimes. For example, an 1828 statute forbade secret meetings, and made the third offense punishable by four years' exile in California.[34] A native Californian and diarist, Mrs. Angustias de la Guerra Ord, recounted that in 1829 a shipload of about eighty convicts arrived at Santa Barbara. The men, "most of them naked," were exiled for "very grave offenses." She continued, "I am compelled to relate this episode by the desire to record that these unfortunate Mexicans never afterwards gave cause for complaint, but always conducted themselves well."[35] Vallejo, despite his opposition to the government's use of California as a penal colony, nevertheless claimed success in his efforts to assimilate convicts into his Sonoma community. "From 1834 until the arrival of Commodore Stockton [in 1846]," he recalled, ". . . the Sonoma frontier was the Ceuta of Alta California; it was customary to send all unruly and rebellious spirits here and with pleasure I can assure that without the use of severe measures I succeeded in converting all my involuntary guests!"[36]

Perhaps at times the plague of convicts was more imagined than real. Alvarado conceded that, since the perpetrator was "the government of a Republic of new creation, it was not easy to regulate all manner of those who were discontented in the territory."[37] Although there were more than a few incorrigibles included among all the convicts, many went on to live productive lives in California. Nevertheless, the situation does not speak well of the Mexican program to secure and develop the province.

The state of affairs in California brought forth additional proposals designed not only to increase its population, but also to improve its quality. As early as 1775, Serra advocated sending "soldiers from respectable stock, taking care that in their number would be some . . . families . . ., that two such families be placed in each mission, so that the wives of these soldiers should devote themselves to instructing the women of the missions."[38] This idea was echoed by Viceroy Revillagigedo in 1793, although circumstances compelled him to admit that finding families—and especially stable and industrious families—would be difficult.[39] The intent of this scheme was to relieve the presidios of the burden of supplying escorts for the missions while simultaneously promoting population growth and industry. It was also again suggested that artisans be sent to California in order to "instruct the Indians in the arts necessary to society . . . for there is no better way then to introduce families among them who are industrious and useful."[40] Although twenty artisans were sent to California, chiefly in 1792 and 1795, most returned to Mexico before 1800 upon the expiration of their contracts.[41]

Collaterally, a rather crude effort was made to upgrade the quality of the indigenous population. Viceroy Revillagigedo lamented in 1794 that there were no European immigrants "who might have improved the Indian race in many ways."[42] In that same year Miguel Costansó recommended that families of Spaniards, or of *individuos de casta mixtas,* be settled in the California missions, believing that intermarriage would benefit the Indians, who

when reduced to a civil life, procreate much less, and the mixture with the Spaniards or as we say with white people in general produces by the second or third generation individuals who scarcely retain the least defect of Indians inasmuch as having bred among Spaniards, their language, habits and customs hardly differ from ours.[43]

But the desired level of integration was not achieved since it was thought more important to bolster the population of the pueblos. As for eugenic modifications of the Indian population, Lasuén reported in 1801 that only twenty-four colonists had married California Indian women during the preceding three decades.[44]

Costansó's statement is particularly interesting since it shows that, even in an isolated frontier colony such as California, the characteristic Latin American preoccupation with matters of "purity of blood," or the lack thereof, was an essential feature of a stratified society. This standard enjoyed legal sanction until the end of the colonial period, but the aversion to miscegenation persisted beyond that time as a cultural practice.[45]

The state of racial affairs in California is best reflected in the socioracial census enumerations.[46] Mörner has observed that "the disdain of both Spaniards and criollos for mestizos and other 'castas' was as good as boundless," and this was reflected in the highly evolved socioracial terminology of the eighteenth century.[47] Such nomenclature, derived from New Spain, was used in several censuses of the 1780s and 1790s in California, and indicates the widespread importance attached to precision in racial distinction. The complexity of the various systems of ethnic classification indicates that they were "completely absurd, especially in dealing with people who more often than not were illegitimate."[48] Admittedly, few of the terms used in California went beyond the basic classifications and their derivatives which were drawn chiefly from physical appearance. But it is interesting that they were used and that some were even drawn from Peruvian nomenclature.[49]

Spanish colonization efforts—whether viewed in terms of quantity or quality of settlers, or by whatever standard population policy may be measured—failed to make a significant impact in California. In December 1793, Vancouver observed that "the mode originally adopted and since constantly pursued, in settling this country is by no means calculated to produce any great increase of white inhabitants."[50] Such a consideration had attained primary importance by 1795 as a result of the Nootka Sound controversy. Costansó stressed the importance of populating California if only for strategic reasons, since without additional colonists the province would not only be a liability but also an easy prey for an ambitious foreign power.[51]

It had always been recognized in California that military personnel represented the most economical source of manpower for colonization. The utilization of sailors who wished to settle on shore was especially advantageous since no transportation expenses were involved in their immigration. In 1785, Felipe de Goycoechea recommended that mariners be permitted to settle permanently—although twelve years earlier Serra had argued successfully, but without tangible results, a similar position before Viceroy Bucareli.[52] Later, in 1790, Viceroy Revillagigedo wrote that "it is a good, useful, and industrious custom for sailors to remain in the labor and founding of new missions."[53] Governor Pedro Fages recommended to José Antonio Romeu, his successor, that presidial and other soldiers be settled in pueblos.[54] And, in 1794, Costansó urged Viceroy Branciforte to permit sailors of the Manila Galleon to settle in Monterey if they so desired. This suggestion was thwarted by the crew's insistence that the ship make directly for Acapulco without further delay.[55]

Yet, despite the futility of government programs, the colonial era's sole private proposal to colonize California was not well received. An apparently advantageous proposition was made in 1802 by Lieutenant Luis Pérez de Tagle of Manila. He requested permission to bring a colony from the Philippines to California. In his petition to the king, Tagle stated that he had spent time in California and was familiar with the country's condition. The program which he proposed centered on the development of trade to counteract the English commercial influence in the Pacific. But the plan vanished in the maze of viceregal bureaucracy, and Bancroft speculated that it died a premature death because of Tagle's "modest demand" that he be placed in command of Monterey and the coast.[56] Not surprising, recommendations continued that the population be augmented by industrious persons who could flourish in the benign climate of California.[57] The failure to obtain even a modest number of desirable immigrants led not only to internal problems, but also to the eventual inundation of the country by ambitious foreign elements, particularly American.

The supreme irony of the population debacle was the rejection of precisely those measures so ardently awaited in earlier years. The persistent requests for skilled artisans and their families found belated fruition in the Hijar-Padrés Colony of 1834–35. Planned and organized by Mexican vice-president Valentín Gómez Farías, the colony was dispersed after it arrived in California. Predictably, this occurred because the colony threatened the dominion of decayed local interests which no longer were able to discern the difference between the welfare of their country and their own shortsighted objectives. Although traditionally viewed within the context of Mexican efforts to take advantage of the Californians, the dissolution of the colony by Governor José Figueroa only paved the way for the Yankee usurpation of California within the decade. Given the pervasive atmosphere of distrust sown by the policies set in Mexico City, the endemic political instability and intrigue afoot in California, and the basic fear that the colony would preempt secularized mission lands long coveted by the Californians, contemporary public opinion favored Figueroa's measures, although hindsight would lead us to question their sagacity.

The alternative of last resort, the promotion of settlement by non-Spanish colonists, quite naturally had long been discouraged by Spanish law and colonial policy.[58] Yet, as early as 1793, Vancouver recognized that Spain's own resources and those of her empire would not be sufficient to populate California. "Progress towards civilization seems to have been remarkably slow; and it is not likely to become more rapid, until the impolicy of excluding foreign visitors shall be laid aside," he commented.[59] On this issue, Mexican ideas differed sharply from those of Spain. Just prior to independence, Mexico City's first impulse was to work within the framework of Spanish law. Viceroy del Venadito wrote that the *Recopilación* allowed settlement by foreigners who "profess useful arts and trades," but no program to attract settlers was formulated.[60] In 1824 the Mexican Congress passed the first of a handful of colonization laws which gave liberal, albeit only rhetorical, encouragement to foreign settlement.[61] A similar enactment dating from 1830 provided not only transportation costs for both Mexican and foreign families, but also authorized that up to one hundred thousand *pesos* be allocated to sponsor foreign immigrants. However, this bill never got beyond the Senate.[62]

Nevertheless, a great many foreigners settled in California on their own initiative and soon managed to dominate the hitherto straitened commercial affairs of the province. Fernandez dates the beginning of this period from the year 1822.[63] By 1841, the Anglo-American commercial conquest was complete, and in trade-oriented northern California the foreigners had also gained political ascendancy. "By their monopoly of trade and their command of resources, to say nothing of their superior energy and intelligence," Simpson wrote of the mercantile community, "they already possess vastly more than their numerical proportion of political influence."[64]

It is therefore not surprising that xenophobic forces emerged in California by the late 1830s. In Los Angeles foreigners were forbidden to acquire land even if they chose to follow the secular and sacred legal dictates by becoming naturalized citizens.[65] Duflot de Mofras related two incidents in which foreigners were murdered—one of them a fellow Frenchman—without any attempt by the authorities to bring the culprits to justice.[66] But the days of Hispanic preponderance were numbered. Hastings heralded "a new era in the affairs of California, . . . about to rise . . . bursting forth in a day, as it were, into brilliant intelligence, commendable activity, and unbounded enterprise."[67] Two months later the imminent arrival of two thousand American families was announced by Vallejo, and like Texas twelve years earlier, California was virtually annexed to the United States by the abdication of an underpopulated and underfinanced Mexican nation.[68] Governor Pio Pico's reaction to the news was typical of many Californians. In a speech before the Departmental Assembly, he warned:

We find ourselves threatened by hordes of Yankee immigrants who have already begun to flock into our country, and whose progress we cannot arrest. Already have the wagons of that perfidious people scaled the almost inaccessible summits of the Sierra Nevada, . . . and penetrated the fruitful valley of the Sacramento. What that astonishing people will next undertake, I cannot say; but in whatever enterprise they embark they will sure to be successful.

Already these adventurous voyagers . . . are cultivating farms, establishing vineyards, erecting mills, sawing up lumber, and doing a thousand other things which seem natural to them.[69]

Pico's apprehensions were more than justified. The coming of the Yankees created a new social order. Despite the Americans' narrow values and denigration of Latin culture, they merely replaced, in a qualitative sense, Mexican California's well delineated hierarchical social structure. Writing of Monterey society in 1840, Arnaz found that it was "organized on the basis of separate classes, with gaiety and perfect order prevailing in its diversions."[70] Dana was struck by the efforts of the Californians to maintain their hierarchical society which was dominated by those families claiming "pure" Spanish blood. There were only a few of these families, he observed, and they vigorously defended their status

. . . intermarrying, and keeping up an exclusive system in every respect. They can also be told by their complexions, dress, manner, and also by their speech; for, calling themselves Castilians, they are very ambitious of speaking the pure Castilian language which is spoken in a somewhat corrupted dialect, by the lower classes. From this upper class, they go down by regular shades, growing more and more dark and muddy, until you come to the pure Indian, who runs about with nothing upon him but a small piece of cloth.[71]

But this societal configuration was to be short-lived as California was settled by overwhelming numbers of Yankee emigrants, persons who were to hold the caste-conscious Californians in contempt, much as they had despised the Indians and *castas*. Hastings deprecated his hosts' "dorment [sic] intelligence, inert energy, and dead and buried enterprise."[72] Indeed, the clash of basic values, antagonisms of religion and race, and the Anglos' catalog "of the venial and cardinal sins practiced in the province" underscored the divisions between the two groups.[73] Pitt has written that "judgmental is the word for Anglo-Saxon spirit in California in this period."[74] Perhaps this heavy-handed search for justification could not be avoided. The spoilation wrought by the gold hysteria rendered the bucolic past even more valuable than the ephemeral glitter of precious metal, for no amount of panning would produce even the smallest nugget of an irretrievable and fragile era.

One of Mexican California's shrewdest Yankee traders, Thomas O. Larkin, wrote in 1856, "I began to yearn after the times prior to July, 1846 and all their beautiful pleasures, flesh-pots of those days—halcyon days they were. We shall not enjoy the same again." [75]

The abrupt transition from pastoral Mexican backwater to booming American commercial emporium and mining frontier produced a social transformation in northern California as dramatic as it was transfiguring. Elsewhere, particularly in the south, the gold rush did not mark sudden death for the Hispanic culture. Los Angeles, Santa Barbara, and even Monterey maintained their cultural links with the past well into the final quarter of the nineteenth century. The shattered Hispanic heritage of California was at first the object of scorn and derision, and then of nostalgic, if overblown romanticism. Still visible in mission ruins, ersatz architecture, and place names enveloped by suburban sprawl, it is today less real than imagined. The gold seekers, the railroad builders, and the land speculators, ruthlessly pursuing their notions of progress, failed to cast even a hasty backward glance.

1 Lyle N. McAlister, "The Army of New Spain, 1760–1800" (Ph.D. dissertation, University of California, Berkeley, 1950), 194–95.

2 Teodoro de Croix, "Instrucción que debe observar el Capitán D. Fernando Rivera y Moncada para la recluta y habilitación de familias, pobladores y tropa . . . para el resguardo, beneficio y conservación de los nuevos y antiguos establecimientos de aquella Peninsula," Arispe, December 27, 1779, quoted in Historical Society of Southern California, *Annual Publication Commemorating the One Hundred and Fiftieth Anniversary of the Founding of Los Angeles, September 4, 1781* (Los Angeles, 1931), 192.

3 Padre Junípero Serra to Viceroy Antonio María de Bucareli, Mexico, June 11, 1773, Junípero Serra, *Writings,* ed. Antonine Tibesar, O.F.M., 4 vols. (Washington, D.C., 1955–1966), I, 383.

4 Alexander Forbes, *A History of Upper and Lower California* (San Francisco, 1937), 128.

5 Josiah Belden, *Memoirs and Early Letters,* ed. Doyce B. Nunis, Jr. (Georgetown, California, 1962), 66–67.

6 Richard F. Pourade, *The History of San Diego,* 5 vols. (San Diego, 1960–1965), II, 19–20.

7 Teodoro de Croix, "Instrucción," 192.

8 Serra to Bucareli, Mexico, April 22, 1773, Serra, *Writings,* I, 341.

9 Serra to Bucareli, Mexico, May 21, 1773, Serra, *Writings,* I, 363.

10 Serra to Melchor de Peramas, Monterey, June 14, 1774, Serra, *Writings,* II, 67.

11 Borica to presidio commandants, Monterey, April 13, 1795, California Archives (CA), Bancroft Library, Provincial Records, 5 vols., II, 405–6.

12 Borica to Viceroy Miguel de la Grúa Talamanca y Branciforte, Monterey, September 17, 1797, CA, Provincial Records, III, 379–80.

13 Borica to Branciforte, Monterey, September 17, 1797, CA, Provincial Records, III, 379–80.

14 Branciforte to Borica, Orizaba, January 25, 1798, CA, Provincial Records, VI, 55–56. Hubert Howe Bancroft, *History of California,* 7 vols. (San Francisco, 1884–1890), I, 605.

15 Bancroft, *History of California,* I, 606.

16 *Recopilación,* II, Libro VII Título 4 Ley 2, 359.

17 Julián de Arriaga to José de Gálvez, Madrid, March 26, 1765, quoted in Herbert I. Priestley, *José de Gálvez: Visitor-General of New Spain, 1765–1771* (Berkeley, 1916), 413.

18 Priestley, *José de Gálvez,* 259.

19 Bancroft, *History of California,* I, 605.

20 Bancroft, *History of California,* I, 605.

21 Macario de Castro to Hermenegildo Sal, San José, September 30, 1800, CA, Provincial State Papers, XI, 6–7. Sal to Governor José de Arrillaga, Monterey, October 2, 1800, CA, Provincial State Papers, XI, 5–6.

22 Sal to Arrillaga, CA, Provincial State Papers, XI, 6.

23 Arrillaga to Viceroy Félix Berenguer de Marquina, Loreto, April 29, 1801, CA, Provincial State Papers, Indices, 67–68.

24 Fermín Francisco de Lasuén to Arrillaga, Mission San Francisco, December 27, 1801, Lasuén, *Writings,* ed. and trans. Finbar Kenneally, O.F.M. 2 vols. (Washington, D.C., 1965), II, 285–86.

25 Conde del Valle de Orizaba to Felipe de Goycoechea, Mexico, December 20, 1805, CA, Provincial State Papers, XII, 17–18.

26 Del Valle de Orizaba to de Goycoechea, Provincial State Papers XII, 17–18.

27 A decree issued by President Anastasio Bustamente in 1830 provided that the government would pay for the transportation of convicts and their families. Said convicts would be employed in public works projects and would be eligible for grants of land and subsistence of one year upon the expiration of their terms. Anastasio Bustamente, Mexico, April 16, 1830, cited in John A. Rockwell, *A Compilation of Spanish and Mexican Law in relation in Mines, and Titles to Real Estate, in force in California, Texas and New Mexico*, 2 vols. (New York, 1851), I, 621.

28 Mariano G. Vallejo, Recuerdos Históricos y Personales tocante á la Alta California, 5 vols. (Bancroft Library MS, 1875), II, 70.

29 Bancroft, *History of California*, III, 48.

30 Bancroft, *History of California*, III, 48.

31 Vallejo, Recuerdos, II, 71–72.

32 Juan B. Alvarado, Historia de California, 5 vols. (Bancroft Library MS, 1876), IV, 9–10.

33 Figueroa, Monterey, May 18, 1835, CA, Santa Cruz Archives, 1 vol., 80.

34 Theodore H. Hittell, *History of California*, 4 vols. (San Francisco, 1897), II, 89.

35 Angustias de la Guerra Ord, *Occurrences in Hispanic California*, trans, and ed. Francis Price and William H. Ellison (Washington, D.C., 1956), 15.

36 Vallejo, Recuerdos, III, 293.

37 Alvarado, Historia, II, 120.

38 Serra to Bucareli, Monterey, January 8, 1775, Serra, *Writings*, II, 203.

39 Revillagigedo, "Carta de 1793," cited in Bancroft, *History of California*, I, 602.

40 Miguel Costansó, "Informe de Don Miguel Costansó al Virrey, Marqués de Branciforte, sobre el Proyecto de Fortificar los Presidios de la Nueva California," *Noticias y Documentos acerca de las Californias, 1764–1795* (Madrid, 1959), 231. Alvarado, Historia, I, 81.

41 Bancroft, *History of California*, I, 615.

42 Quoted in Bancroft, *History of California*,, I, 57.

45 Costansó, "Informe," 233.

44 Lasuén, Mission San Carlos, June 19, 1801, Lasuén, *Writings*, II, 212.

45 As late as 1806, the Council of the Indies endorsed the idea of a hierarchical, multiracial colonial society. See Magnus Mörner, *Race Mixture in the History of Latin America* (Boston, 1967), 75.

46 See, for example, CA, Provincial State Papers, VIII, 90 (San José, December 31, 1794); CA, State Papers: Missions, I, 5–10 (Santa Barbara, December 31, 1785), 61–64 (San José, October 5, 1790), 85–91 (San Francisco, October 2, 1790), 103–4 (Los Angeles, December 31, 1792); CA, State Papers: Missions and Colonization, II, 98–99 (Los Angeles, November 19, 1781).

47 Mörner, *Race Mixture*, 57.

48 Mörner, *Race Mixture*, 59.

49 See Mörner, *Race Mixture*, 58–59, for a listing of terms from both Mexico and Peru. In addition to the standard classification of Spaniard, Indian, mextizo, and

mulatto, the terms lobo, coyote, pardo, negro, and chino appear in California, as does the designation "de color quebrado," the latter in the San José census of December 1794.

50 George Vancouver, *Voyage of Discovery to the North Pacific Ocean and Round the World*, 3 vols. (London, 1798), II, 496.

51 Costansó, "Informe," 230.

52 Goycoechea to Governor Don Pedro Fages, Santa Barbara, August 9, 1785, CA, Provincial State Papers, III, 165. Serra to Bucareli, Monterey, August 24, 1774, Serra, *Writings*, II, 151.

53 Revillagigedo to Fages, Monterey, December 14, 1790, CA, Provincial State Papers, V, 243.

54 Fages, "Papel de varios puntos concernientes al Gobierno de la Peninsula de California é Inspección de Tropas . . . ," Monterey, February 26, 1791, Provincial State Papers, VI, 152–53.

55 Costansó, "Informe," 234–35.

56 Bancroft, *History of California*, II, 4.

57 Conde del Valle de Orizaba to Goycoechea, Mexico, December 20, 1805, CA, Provincial State Papers, XII, 20.

58 For a detailed statement of official thought on the problem, see Libro IX Titulo 27 of the *Recopilación* (III, 326–35). Only one statute is even mildly favorable with respect to foreign settlement (III, Libro IX Titulo 27 Ley 13, 329).

59 Vancouver, *Voyage of Discovery*, II, 498.

60 Viceroy del Venadito to Gov. Pablo Vicente de Solá, Mexico, October 20, 1819, CA, Departmental State Papers: Juzgados; Naturalization, 174. He probably was referring to Libro IX Titulo 27 Ley 13 of the *Recopilación*.

61 "Decreto del Congreso Mejieano sobre Colonización," Mexico, August 18, 1824, cited in Bancroft, *History of California*, II, 516.

62 C. Alan Hutchinson. *Frontier Settlement in Mexican California: The Híjar-Padrés Colony and its Origins, 1769–1835* (New Haven, 1969), 172.

63 José Fernandez, Cosas de California (Bancroft Library MS, 1874), 33. He also related an amusing incident on the subject: "The majority of those who established commercial houses in Alta California were citizens of the state of Massachusetts and when the Indians asked them from where they had come, they replied that they were from Boston; the Indians, whose knowledge of geography was very limited, believed that all white men came from a single place, and for this reason whenever they saw an Englishman, or a German, or an American, they would exclaim, 'There goes a Boston!'" Fernandez, 33–34.

64 Sir George Simpson, *Narrative of a Journey Round the World during the Years 1841 and 1842*, 2 vols. (London, 1847), I, 293.

65 Tiburcio Tapia to Los Angeles Ayuntamiento, Los Angeles, July 19, 1839, CA, Departmental State Papers: Angeles, II, 44. Los Angeles Ayuntamiento to Tapia, Los Angeles, July 25, 1839, CA, Departmental State Papers: Los Angeles, II, 57.

66 Eugéne Duflot de Mofras, *Exploration du Territoire de l'Orégon, des Californies, et de la Mer Vermeille*, 2 vols. (Paris, 1844), I, 232.

67 Lansford W. Hastings to Larkin, New Helvetia, March 3, 1846, Larkin, *Larkin Papers*, IV, 221.

68 Mariano Vallejo to Manuel Castro, Sonoma, May 25, 1846, Departmental State Papers, V, 59.

69 Quoted in Frederic Hall, *The History of San Jose and Surroundings* (San Francisco, 1871), 143.

70 José Arnaz, Recuerdos (Bancroft Library MS, 1878), 38.

71 Richard Henry Dana, *Two Years Before the Mast* (New York, 1909), 79.

72 Hastings to Larkin, New Helvetia, March 3, 1846, Larkin, *Larkin Papers*, IV, 221.

73 Leonard Pitt, *The Decline of the Californios: A Social History of the Spanish-Speaking Californians, 1846–1890* (Berkeley, 1966) 14.

74 Pitt, *Decline of the Californios*, 14–15.

75 Larkin to Abel Stearns, San Francisco, April 24, 1856, *Larkin, Larkin Papers*, X, 263.

Spain's fall from prominence was a precipitous one after *El Siglo de Oro*. But her sovereignty over innumerable territories and peoples persisted well beyond her capacity to control them and the empire remained a remarkable, though often passive, fact depending for its existence on inertia, its incalculable vastness and distance from would-be predators, and a rich and cohesive fabric of cultures and institutions.

This was not sufficient to shield Spain itself from the voracious appetites of her European confrères, who could exploit her vulnerability when timing, circumstance, and diplomacy permitted. The Bourbon Family Pact, a by-product of the War of the Spanish Succession, proved to be a mixed blessing. Established in 1733, it at once invited the protection of France and the wrath of her rivals, principally England. As a result, by the time of the California colonization during the reign of Charles III (1759–1788), the debits of unproductive military commitments had more than offset the revitalizing effects of economic reforms instituted under the guidance of French administrators.

In the American colonies, Spain, with the encouragement of her Gallic ally, formed in 1765 a permanent colonial army. Costly as it was, it was never able to meet the challenge of subduing the northern frontier of New Spain, a region characterized by sparse settlement, vast and unyielding terrain, and mobile, predatory, and, ultimately, indomitable Indian tribes. These guerilla bands had held sway over the arid expanses of Durango, Chihuahua, Sonora, and the United States's southwest desert since the midsixteenth century when Iberian explorers and miners had first challenged them. It was no wonder that elements at the royal court were to argue at this time that most of the American colonies had become an unsupportable burden and should be jettisoned. If this harsh and dangerous frontier was to be so easily parted with after three centuries of sacrifice, exploitation, and settlement, it helps suggest why its existence was at best a peripheral and even incomprehensible idea to most individuals resident in the cosmopolitan and cultured capitals, ports, and haciendas of New Spain.

Yet the inexorable advances of England—which often were gained at the expense of Spain's major partner to the north of the Pyrenees—and the quiet incursions of Russian hunters and military south from Alaska struck a responsive reflex in Spanish colonial policy. What might have been freely allowed to drift into oblivion became in the mid-1760s a focal point of diplomatic attention and the efforts of high-ranking colonial officials, notably José de Gálvez. This dynamic administrator envisioned a productive and self-sufficient colony in California that would also serve the purpose of discouraging foreign adventurism. The land had been scouted within fifty years of the first voyage of Christopher Columbus and judged to be potentially bountiful. It would be self-supporting because it was assumed that experienced Franciscan friars would be able to organize the Indian population in missions: agrarian-centered urban communities in which dogma, industry, the arts, and the tools of self-government would all be instilled when Indians were not laboring in the fields under the watchful eyes of the padres.

The desire for minimal stress on the viceroyalty treasury cast the Church as the dominant Spanish presence in California. But it was not to be only a spiritual conquest, for military protection would be needed. This combination at once created a rivalry and an inherent set of antagonisms that neither side would ever be able to ignore, a devilish symbiosis whose legacy of strife predated the 1573 *ordenanzas*. The lives of both military and religious were mutually dependent as both defense and sustenance (corporeal, if not spiritual) were to be gained from the arrangement. The soldiers could not (and would not) raise their own food because to do so would fatally damage the Indians' respect for them. The subsequent addition of civilian settlements (San José in 1777 and Los Angeles four years later) only served to increase Church-State tensions. Not only was populating the land a factor in government policy, but it was perceived by the Church as a challenge to its dominance over resources and peoples.

Colonial law was of no great value in mediating this set of conflicts, for either it was mute on important questions or effectively ignored them. For example, as the Church saw things, the presidio was a temporary affair whose longevity would depend on the establishment of a viable mission community. On the other hand, the strategic role of the presidio gave its location little flexibility and its tenure permanence. This consideration was especially im-

portant in California, where the Spanish sought to secure
key harbors and occupy surrounding territory. At Monterey and, much earlier, the fabled ports of the Spanish
Main (for example, Havana, Cartagena, and Santo Domingo), the importance of the site left no alternative but a
constant and sturdy presence. It was no coincidence that
two of the world's finest natural harbors, San Francisco
and San Diego, were key presidial sites in California. Monterey, which loomed larger in the Spanish imagination by
virtue of its spurious and archaic association with the
fabled Northwest Passage, became a presidio only because
the frequent and impenetrable fogs that funnel inland
from the Golden Gate had concealed the entrance to San
Francisco Bay from the eyes of seaborne coastal
explorations.

The strategic mandate of Monterey created problems.
First, the presidio and its soldiers did not evaporate as the
missionaries had hoped they would. Second, its existence
and development were not governed according to the accumulated wisdom of previous efforts codified in the *Recopilación*. Instead, a decentralized and improvisatory
authority determined the particulars of the presidio's existence. At Havana or Cartagena—key settlements in
Spain's halcyon sixteenth-century days—little had escaped
vice-regal or even royal attention. But Monterey, precari-
ously perched on the edge of a remote continent 2,000
laborious and often perilous miles from Mexico City,
might well have been in Tierra del Fuego or Siberia. Survival was a sufficient beneficence in the eyes of the viceregal government, for which there were far more pressing
problems much closer at hand. This attitude was evident
to any foreign eye casting covetous looks at the expanding
frontiers of Spanish colonization.

After about two decades of presidial life within the walls
of the garrison, Monterey began to show signs of becoming
a maturing community. Retired soldiers were pursuing the
agrarian life in an area which now excells all others in its
production of artichokes, brussels sprouts, and so forth.
By the 1780s Governor José de Arrillaga had granted lands
to deserving *inválidos* in order to encourage agriculture.
In 1792 he was given official sanction from Mexico to
grant house lots and lands for tillage within the limitation
of four square leagues (28.01 square miles), the standard

pueblo grant in California. Presidios, though not included
in the traditional urban canon, were now enjoying the
additional dimension of urban land grants, and the effect
of their growing populations was to add urban roles to
their military functions. Even without a pueblo grant, the
presidios were becoming nuclei complemented by agricultural production, all confined within the same area specified in the pueblo grants to civilian towns such as San José
and Los Angeles.

In Monterey, function superseded the formality that the
Recopilación had failed to define. By 1800 the California
presidios had virtually abdicated their military significance
and had become civilian and mercantile in outlook and
enterprise. At San Diego, this status precipitated a near-
revolt against military authority. Shortly after resolution
of this upheaval, San Diego joined Monterey in the creation of civilian municipal governments, which promptly
promulgated ordinances of environmental control and be-
havioral restraint.

However, the adherence to the traditional Hispanic plan
was not a concern of the emergent *ayuntamiento*. Planning
became an important issue only in the late 1840s, long
after Spanish sovereignty was terminated (circa 1812) and
shortly after Mexico's had evaporated (1846–1848). By
that time, the Anglo-American element had become the
dominant population group, and it was an Englishman
(William Robert Garner) and an American (Walter Colton)
who were "to regulate the streets in the town of Monterey." Finally, in 1849, the *ayuntamiento* created the first
plan and orderly blueprint for growth, a rather ironic
after-thought for the capital city of a Spanish colony.

If a formal lack of direction and definition was a factor
in presidial matters, there was certainly no juridical am-
bivalence in the mutually-exclusive domains of Church
and State. However, in practice the business of a vast
empire blurred the statutory distinctions between the
realms of Church and State that had been so carefully
crafted during the sixteenth century. By the time of the
California colonization, the parallel efforts that were to
have been made in both the religious and secular spheres
had been submerged in a long-standing legacy of acrimony.
The struggle centered on control of population and resources. First, the State sought to limit the tenure of mis-

sionary settlements by pressuring the Church to move toward the frontiers and allow older mission communities to enter the secular world of self-government and State taxation. Second, the State sought to limit Church control of the ample frontier territory acquired by missionary activity.

Secularization of the missions, the first of these State-sought goals, was to place mission communities in a status identical to that of civilian towns. The *Recopilación* was quite explicit on the ingredients of such a status, especially with regard to planning and municipal government. It was over the question of *when* secularization was to occur that a firm set of guiding principles was needed, and their absence invited opportunistic improvisation by government authorities. A highly sophisticated civilization, such as the Aztec realm in central Mexico, colonial officials reasoned, would require only a decade of missionary supervision to function successfully in Spanish society. On the frontier, Indian society—from the viewpoint of the Spaniards—was threadbare and primitive, lacking a tradition of quasi-permanent settlement and requiring, as Fr. Fermín Francisco de Lasuén phrased it, "denaturalizing." This was no mean task, for, the Friar wrote, "it requires them to act against nature." Since the Franciscan missionaries attempted to stem the inertial tendencies of many centuries of nomadic life, it is to be expected that this would require a period of time much longer than the secular authority would be willing to mandate.

Secularization of the missions was, of course, the abdication by the friars of control over population and territory. When the California missions were finally secularized in the 1830s, the cresting of popular opinion quickly swept away all vestiges of the Franciscan regime. After sixty years of stewardship, the persistence of the Franciscans had failed to create a viable Indian society, even by the most rudimentary of standards. Further, after more than three centuries of continuous study, experimentation and implementation, the mission community in California and in other parts of the Spanish empire, quickly withered in a secular milieu.

It was the cumulative missionary intransigence that invited the inexorable assault on their domain. The 1767 expulsion of the Jesuits from Spain's colonies should have signaled without any ambiguity that the fragile Church-State compromise that forged the 1573 *ordenanzas* was long since shattered. Although these regulations and their subsequent codification in the *Recopilación* clearly defined the rights and limits of civilian and mission settlements, by the eighteenth century the credibility of missionary interests had become little more than an illusion. Civilian settlement in California was an objective that could not be compromised. *The Recopilación*, then, represented an accommodation that had long since outlived its usefulness.

The need to populate the remote colony, like the establishment of San José and the Villa de Branciforte, was an action that no legal mandate could deflect. Although colonial officials attempted to adhere to the formal specifications concerning the type of individual to be sent to the frontier, the fractured and turbulent society of New Spain ensured that distant regions were utilized as a social safety valve to relieve the seething and often desparate circumstances of itinerant populations in Mexico's more important urban centers. Just as Philip II recommended that such undesirables be sent to the Philippines ("or other parts," the *Recopilación* noted), colonial and republican officials in Mexico saw California as just such an outlet.

The colonial army was the vehicle to achieve such a purge, missionary objections notwithstanding. The scarcity of women in California merely magnified the unruly circumstances of military coexistence with new mission settlements. Suggestions were frequently advanced for improving these circumstances, but no real measure of relief ever materialized. The chief victims of this state of affairs were the relatively small number of settlers and their families. They naturally questioned the introduction of undesirables into the province, and when Mexico attempted to introduce a colony of teachers and artisans in the mid-1830s, they vociferously blocked the group's efforts to settle. What the *Californios* wanted was social stability, and the policies of the Mexico City viceroys thwarted this aim. Once the province began to prosper, the ingredients of such a society were now unwelcome (and sixty years late) for they now could not help but impinge on the missionary domain whose gates were about to be opened by secularization. Impatient with the missionaries' tenacious opposition to the intrusions of secular society, and threatened by any perceived dilution of their long-awaited opportunity to carve up the sprawling mission lands, the old-line California settlers were the ultimate victims of Spain and Mexico's inability to develop California. Government policies of not-so-benign neglect limited the population, which found itself instantly overwhelmed when gold was discovered. After that, the *Californios'* hold on land, livelihood, and lifestyle was shattered to smithereens.

In conclusion, then, the Laws of the Indies provided a firm statutory guide to the implanting and development of colonial society. They represented a compromise among myriad interests whose often conflicting goals were melded in compromises wrought thousands of miles distant from the empire which they were to govern. As Spain's colonial holdings spread over two continents and the Philippines, improvisation took precedence over governance by statute. Yet, if the colonial official found he could not always comply with the laws, at least he could guide his actions by their spirit. Still, as time passed and circumstances changed, but the laws remained unchanged, the disparity between action and compliance grew. Perhaps the inflexibility of the Law of the Indies was inherent in the evolution of Spain in the course of four centuries from newly forged nation-state to unwieldy and ossified monarchy soon to be consumed by the spirit of Revolution from whose crucible emerged the Latin American nations.

In Hispanic America today the streets, plazas, and arcades, the Church, and a common culture signal the shared heritage that is a living testament to the struggle, sacrifice, and brutality of the quest for empire. In the *Recopilacion* the ideas and theories of building and regulating an empire are the yardstick against which all else is measured.

BIBLIOGRAPHY

"Actas de la Fundación de la Ciudad de Lima."
Revista de las Españas. November–December 1934.

La Administración de D. Frey Antonio Maria de Bucareli y Ursua.
Edited by Romulo Velasco Ceballos. 2 vols. Mexico, 1936.

Alberti.
Ten Books on Architecture.

Alvarado, Juan B.
"Historia de California." 5 vols. Manuscript in Bancroft Library, University of California, Berkeley, 1876.

de la Ascensión, Fray Antonio.
"Descubrimiento y Demarcación de la California." In *Colección de Documentos Inéditos Relativos al Descubrimiento, Conquista y Organización de las Antiquas Posesiones Españoles de América y Oceania sacados de los Archivos del Reino*, VIII, pp. 537–574.

Atherton, Faxxon Dean.
California Diary. Edited by Doyce B. Nunis, Jr. San Francisco and Los Angeles, 1964.

Ayuntamiento Records.
In *California Archives, Los Angeles Archives.*

Bancroft, Hubert Howe.
History of Arizona and New Mexico, 1530–1885. 1889. Reprint. Albuquerque: Horn and Wallace, 1962.

Bancroft, Hubert Howe.
History of California. 7 vols. San Francisco, 1884–1890.

Bancroft, Thayer and Brooks.
Map of Los Angeles (a composite of Ord, Hancock and Hansen). California Room, Los Angeles City Library.

Bandini, José.
Descrisción de l'Alta California en 1828. Translated by D. M. Wright. Berkeley: University of California Press, 1951.

Banham, Reyner.
Los Angeles: The Architecture of Four Ecologies. New York: Harper and Row, 1971.

Barreiro, Lic. Antonio.
The Ojeada. In *Three New Mexico Chronicles.* Translated and annotated by H. Bailey Carroll and J. Villasana Haggard. Albuquerque, NM: The Quivira Society, 1942.

Bartlett, John Russell.
Personal Narratives of Explorations and Incidents in Texas, New Mexico, California, Sonora, and Chihuahua. 2 vols. New York, 1854.

Beilharz, Edwin A.
Felipe de Neve: First Governor of California. San Francisco, 1971.

Bernal, Ignacio.
"Mexico Tenochtitlan." In *Cities of Destiny.* Edited by Arnold Toynbee. New York: McGraw-Hill, 1967, pp. 204–206.

Beyer, Glenn H.
The Urban Explosion in Latin America. Ithaca, NY: Cornell University Press, 1967.

Bobb, Bernard E.
The Viceregency of Antonio Maria Bucareli in New Spain, 1771–1779. Austin, 1962.

Bolton, Herbert E.
Texas in the Middle 18th Century: Studies in Spanish Colonial History. Berkeley: University of California Press, 1915.

Bolton, Herbert E.
The Mission as a Frontier Institution in the Spanish-American Colonies. American Historical Review, 1917. Reprint. El Paso, 1962.

Bolton, Herbert E.
The Spanish Borderlands: A Chronology of Old Florida and the Southwest. New Haven: Yale University Press, 1921.

Bolton, Herbert E., and Marshall, T. M.
The Colonization of North America. New York: Macmillan, 1930.

Brevoort, Elias.
"Santa Fe Trail 1884." Manuscript in Bancroft Library, University of California, Berkeley.

Bryant, Edwin.
"What I Saw in California in the Years 1846–1847." Manuscript in Bancroft Library, University of California, Berkeley.

California Archives.
The following are used here:
1. *Departmental State Papers.* 2 vols. San Jose.
2. *Legislative Records.*
3. *Los Angeles Archives* including *Ayuntamiento Records.*
4. *Provincial State Papers.* 13 vols.
5. *State Papers: Missions and Colonization.* 2 vols.
6. *Unbound Documents.*

Caplow, Theodore.
"The Modern Latin American City." In *Acculturation in the Americas—Proceedings and Selected Papers of the XXXIX Congress of Americanists*, edited by Sol Tax, pp. 255–260. Chicago: University of Chicago Press, 1952.

Carrillo, Raymundo.
"Los Edificios de Monterey, December 31, 1800." In *Provincial State Papers, Benicia, Military II*, pp. 126–127.

Carroll, H. Bailey, and Haggard, J. Villasana, trans. and annotated *Three New Mexico Chronicles*. Albuquerque, NM: The Quivira Society, 1942.

Chapman, Charles E.
"The Alta California Supply Ships, 1773–1776." *Southwestern Historical Quarterly*, XIX, October 1915, 184–194.

Chapman, Charles E.
The Founding of Spanish California. New York, 1916.

Chapman, Charles E.
A History of California: The Spanish Period. New York, 1939.

Charles III.
"Reglamento e Instrucción para los Presidios que se han de formar en la linea de frontera de la Nueva España." Quoted in *History of California*, Vol I, by Hubert Howe Bancroft, pp. 206–207.

Chevalier, Francois.
Land and Society in Colonial Mexico. Translated by Alvin Eustis and edited by Lesley Byrd Simpson. Berkeley and Los Angeles: University of California Press, 1963.

Colección de Documentos Inéditos Relativos al Descubrimiento, Conquista y Organización de las Antiquas Posesiones Españoles de América y Oceania sacados de los Archivos del Reino.
42 vols. Madrid, 1864–1884. Vol. VIII contains "Ordenanzas sobre descubrimiento nuevo y Población" (Segovia, July 13, 1573), pp. 484–537.

Compendium of Seventh United States Census, 1850.

Corney, Peter.
Early Voyages in the North Pacific, 1813–1818. Fairfield, Washington, 1965.

Costansó, Miguel.
"Informe de Don Miguel Costansó al Virrey, Marqués de Branciforte, sobre el Proyecto de Fortificar los Presidios de la Nueva California." In *Noticias y Documentos acerca de las California, 1764–1795.* Madrid, 1959. Translated by Manuel P. Servin, in *California Historical Society Quarterly*, 49, September 1970, pp. 221–230.

de la Croix, Horst.
Military Considerations in City Planning. New York: Braziller, 1971.

Crouch, Dora P., and Axel I. Mundigo, "The City Planning Ordinances of the Laws of the Indies Revisited, II", *Town Planning Review*, vol. 48, Oct. 1977, pp. 397–418.

Culleton, James. *Indians and Pioneers of Old Monterey*. Fresno, 1950.

Dakin, Susanna Bryant. *The Lives of William Hartnell*. Stanford, 1949.

Dana, Richard Henry. *Two Years Before the Mast*. New York, 1909.

Davis, William Heath. *75 Years in California*. San Francisco, 1929.

Davis, William Heath. *El Gringo, or New Mexico and Her People*. Santa Fe: Rydal Press, 1938.

Departmental State Papers. 2 vols. in *California Archives*. San Jose.

"Descripción Anónima del Peru y de Lima a principios del Siglio VII, compuesta por un Judio Portugués y dirigida a los Estados de Holanda." *Revista Archivo Nacional*, Vol. XVII, Lima (1944), pp. 3–44.

Documentos para la Historia de California, 1826–1850: Originales y copiados de los Archivos del Condado de San Diego. "Documentos para la historia de Nuevo Mexico." 3 vols. P-E, 2–4, Bancroft Library, University of California, Berkeley. Transcripts of Vols. 25 and 26 of the Historia in Mexican archives.

Dominguez, A. *The Missions of New Mexico, 1776*. Trans. and annotated by E. B. Adams and A. Chavez. Albuquerque, NM: University of New Mexico Press, 1956.

Duflot de Mofras, Eugene. *Exploration du Territoire de l'Oregon, des Californies, et de la Mer Vermelle*. 2 vols. Paris, 1844.

Duhaut-Cilly, Auguste. *Voyage Autour de Monde*. 2 vols. Paris, 1834–1835.

Emory, William R. *Notes of a Military Reconnoissance from Fort Leavenworth in Missouri to San Diego in California*. New York, 1848.

Encyclopedia Britannica. 14th ed. "St. Louis."

Engelhardt, Zephyrin, O.F.M. *The Missions and Missionaries of California*. 4 vols. San Francisco, 1908–1915.

Escudero, Don José Agustin. Additions to the *Exposición* by Don Pedro Bautista Pino and the *Oljeada* by Lic. Antonio Barreiro. In *Three New Mexico Chronicles*. Trans. and annotated by H. Bailey Carroll and J. Villasana Haggard. Albuquerque, NM: The Quivira Society, 1942.

Esquer. Ignacio, and Gomez, Ambrosio, Monterey, August 27, 1849. In *Unbound Documents*, volume of *California Archives*, pp. 181–182.

Font, Fray Pedro. *Diary of an Expedition to Monterey by Way of the Colorado River, 1775–1776*. Edited and translated by Herbert E. Bolton. Berkeley: University of California Press, 1933.

Forbes, Alexander. *A History of Upper and Lower California*. San Francisco, 1937.

Forrest, E. R. *Pueblos and Missions of the Old Southwest*. Cleveland: A. H. Clark, 1929.

Foster, G. M. *Culture and Conquest: The American Spanish Heritage*. New York: Viking Fund Publications in Anthropology, Quadrangle Books, 1960.

"Fundación de Pueblos en el Siglo XVI."
Boletin del Archivo General de la Nación, Vol VI, No. 3, May–June 1935, pp. 321–360.

Gakenheimer, Ralph.
"The Spanish King and his Continent: A Study of the Importance of 'The Laws of the Indies' for Urban Development in Spanish America." Master's Thesis, Cornell University, 1959.

Garner, William Robert.
Letters from California, 1846–1847. Edited by Donald Munro Craig. Berkeley, Los Angeles, and London, 1970.

Garr, Daniel J.
"Hispanic Colonial Settlement in California: Planning and Urban Development on the Frontier, 1769–1850." Ph.D. dissertation, Cornell University, 1971.

Garr, Daniel J.
"Planning, Politics and Plunder: The Missions and Indian Pueblos of Hispanic California." *Southern California Quarterly*, 54, Winter 1972.

Garr, Daniel J.
"Villa de Branciforte: Innovation and Adaptation on the Frontier." *The Americas*, Summer 1978.

Garr, Daniel J.
"Los Angeles and the Challenge of Growth, 1835–1849." *Southern California Quarterly*, Vol. 61, Summer 1979, pp. 147–158.

Geiger, Maynard J., O. F. M.
The Life and Times of Fray Junipero Serra. 2 vols. Washington, D.C., 1959.

Gibson, Charles.
Spain in America. New York, 1967.

Guest, Florian F., O.F.M.
"The Establishment of the Villa de Branciforte." *California Historical Society Quarterly*, 41 (March 1962).

Guinn, J. M.
"From Pueblo to Ciudad, the Municipal and Territorial Expansion of Los Angeles." *Historical Society of Southern California*, vol. 7, 1908, 216–221.

Guinn, J. M.
History of California and an Extended History of Los Angeles and Environs. 2 vols. Los Angeles: Historical Record, 1916.

Hackett, C. W.
Historical Documents Relating to New Mexico Nueva Vizcaya and Approaches Thereto, to 1773. Washington, D.C.: Carnegie Institute, 1923.

Hanke, Lewis.
The Spanish Struggle for Justice in the Conquest of America. Boston, 1965.

Hansen, Woodrow, J.
The Search for Authority in California. Oakland, 1960.

Harris, Walter D., Jr.
Growth of Latin American Cities. Athens, Ohio: Ohio University Press, 1971.

Hastings, Lansford W.
The Emigrants' Guide to Oregon and California. Cincinnati, 1845.

Hollenbeck, Clive.
Spanish Missions of the Old Southwest. New York: Doubleday, Page and Company, 1926.

Horgan, Paul.
Laney of Santa Fe. New York: Farrar Straus and Giroux, Inc., 1975.

Humboldt, Alexander von.
Political Essay on the Kingdom of New Spain.
4 vols. Translated by John Black. London, 1811.

Hutchinson, C. Alan.
Frontier Settlement in Mexican California: The Hijar-Padres Colony and Its Origins, 1769–1835. New Haven and London, 1969.

Hutton, William Rich.
Glances at California 1847–1853.
Edited by Willard O. Waters. San
Marino. 1942.

Kelsey, Harry.
"A New Look at the Founding of
Old Los Angeles." *California His-
torical Quarterly*, LV, No. 4,
Winter 1976, pp. 326–339.

Knowles, Ralph K.
Energy and Form. Cambridge,
Mass.: MIT Press, 1978.

Kotzebue, Otto von.
*A Voyage of Discovery into the
South Sea and Bering's Straits.* 3
vols. London, 1821.

Kubler, George.
"Mexican Urbanism in the 16th
Century." *Art Bulletin*, Vol. 24,
June 1942, pp. 160–177.

Kubler, George.
*Mexican Architecture of the 16th
Century.* New Haven: Yale Uni-
versity Press, 1948.

Kubler, George.
*The Religious Architecture of
New Mexico.* 4th ed. Albuquer-
que, NM: University of New
Mexico Press for School of Amer-
ican Research, 1972.

La Farge, Oliver.
Santa Fe. Norman, OK: University of Oklahoma Press, 1970.

Lafond, Gabriel.
Voyages Autour du Monde. 2
vols. Paris, 1843.

Laplace, Victor.
*Campagne de Circumnavigation
de la Fregate L'Artémise pendant
les années 1837, 1838, 1839 et
1840.* 6 vols. Paris, 1840–1854.

Larkin, Thomas O.
The Larkin Papers. 10 vols.
Edited by George P. Hammond.
Berkeley and Los Angeles: Uni-
versity of California Press, 1951–
1964.

Lasuén, Fermin Francisco de.
Writings. 2 vols. Edited and
translated by Finbar Kenneally,
O.F.M. Washington, D.C., 1965.

Lawrence, Eleanor.
"Mexican Trade Between Santa
Fe and Los Angeles 1830–1848."
California Historical Quarterly,
10 (1931), pp. 27–39.

Legislative Records.
In *California Archives.*

Los Angeles Archives (includes
Ayuntamiento Records).
In *California Archives.*

Lowery, W.
*The Spanish Settlements within
the Present Limits of the United
States, 1513–1561.* New York:
G. P. Putnam's Sons, 1901.

Manning, William Ray.
"The Nootka Sound
Controversy." In *Annual Report
of the American Historical Association.* Washington, D.C., 1905.

Maps of Los Angeles.
In California Room, Los Angeles
City Library. Included are the
following:
1. Bancroft, Thayer and Brooks.
2. Rowan and Koeberle, 1887.
3. Sanborn-Perris Map Company,
Insurance Map of Los Angeles.
4. A. J. Stahlberg, 1876.
5. H. J. Stevenson, 1884.

Mason, Jesse D.
*History of Santa Barbara and
Ventura Counties, California.*
Oakland, 1883.

McBride, George.
The Land Systems of Mexico.
American Geographical Society,
1923. Reprint. Octagon Press,
1971.

Meem, J. G.
Preface to *Old Santa Fe Today.*
Albuquerque, NM: University of
New Mexico Press for Historic
Santa Fe Foundation, n. d.

Miro-Quesada, Aurelio.
Lima, Ciudad de los Reyes. Buenos Aires: Ernece Editores, 1946.

Moore, J. Preston.
*The Cabildo in Peru Under the
Hapsburgs, 1530–1700.*
Durham, NC, 1954.

Morrison, Hugh.
Early American Architecture.
Oxford University Press, 1952.

Morse, Richard.
"Latin American Cities: Aspects
of Function and Structure." *Comparative Studies in Society and
History*, IV, July 1962, pp. 473–493.

Morse, Richard.
"Some Characteristics of Latin
American Urban History." *American Historical Review*, Vol.
LXVII, October 1961–July 1962,
pp. 317–338.

Mundigo, Axel I., and Dora P.
Crouch,
"The City Planning Ordinances of
the Laws of the Indies Revisited,
I", *Town Planning Review*, Vol.
48, July 1977, pp. 247–268.

Musick, James B.
St. Louis as a Fortified Town. St.
Louis, 1941.

Nelson, H. J.
"Walled Cities of the United
States." *Annals* of the American
Association of Georgraphers, 51
(1961).

Neuerburg, Norman.
"Painting in the California Missions." *American Art Review*, IV,
No. 1, July 1977, pp. 72–88.

Neuerburg, Norman.
"Indian Carved Statues at Mission Santa Barbara." *The Masterkey*, Vol. 51, No. 4, October-
December 1977, pp. 147–151.

Neumeyer, Alfred.
"The Indian Contribution to
Architectural Decoration in Spanish Colonial America." *Art Bulletin*, Vol. 30, No. 1, March 1948,
pp. 104–121.

Newcomb, Rexford.
*Spanish Colonial Architecture in
the United States*. New York: J. J.
Austin, 1937.

Newmark.
*Sixty Years in Southern California
1853–1913.*

Nuttall, Zelia.
"Royal Ordinances Concerning
the Laying Out of New Towns."
*The Hispanic American Historical
Review*, Vol. 4, No. 4, November
1921, pp. 743–753.

Nuttall, Zelia.
"Royal Ordinances Concerning
the Laying Out of New Towns."
*The Hispanic American Historical
Review*, Vol. 5, No. 2, May
1922, pp. 249–254.

Nuttall, Zelia.
"Royal Ordinances Concerning
the Laying Out of New Towns."
Reprinted in *Planning and Civic
Comment*, Vol. V, pp. 17–20.

Ogden, Adele.
*The California Sea Otter Trade,
1784–1848*. Berkeley and Los
Angeles: University of California
Press, 1941.

Ord, Lt. Edward.
"Diary 1850–1856." Manuscript
in Bancroft Library, University of
California, Berkeley.

"Ordenanzas sobre descubrimiento nuevo y Población."
Segovia, July 13, 1573. In Vol.
VIII of *Colección de Documentos
Inéditos Relativos al Descubrimiento, Conquista y Organizacion de las Antiquas Posesiones
Españoles de América y Oceania
sacados de los Archivos del
Reino*. 42 vols. Madrid, 1854–
1884.

Palou, Francisco.
Noticias de la Nueva California.
4 vols. Edited and translated by
Herbert E. Bolton. New York,
1966.

Parry, J. A.
*The Audiencia in Nueva Galicia
in the 16th Century: A Study in
Spanish Colonial Government.*
Cambridge, 1948.

Paz-Soldan, J. P.
*La Ciudad de Lima bajo la
Dominación Española*. Lima:
Imprenta Gil, 1908.

Péron, M, "Monterey in 1796."
Translated by Henry R. Wagner.
*California Historical Society
Quarterly*, I, October 1922, p.
176.

Peterson, Charles E.
*Colonial St. Louis: Building A
Creole Capital. St. Louis Missouri
Historical Society Bulletin*, 1947.
Reprint, St. Louis Missouri His-
torical Society, 1949.

Petit-Thouars, Abel du.
Voyage Autour de Monde. 10
vols. Paris, 1840–1844.

Phelan, John Leddy.
*The Millennial Kingdom of the
Franciscans in the New World*.
Berkeley: University of California
Press, 1956.

Pierce, Richard A., and Winslow,
John H., eds.
*H.M.S. Sulphur at California,
1837 and 1839*. San Francisco,
1969.

Pike, Frederick B.
*The Conflict Between Church and
State in Latin America*. New
York, 1964.

Piñart, A. L.
(collector) "Colección de documentos sobre Nuevo Mexico,
1681–1841." 25 portfolios in
Bancroft Library, P-E, 37–61,
University of California, Berkeley.

Pino, Don Pedro Bautista.
The Exposición, 1812. In *Three
New Mexico Chronicles*. Trans-
lated and annotated by H. Bailey
Carroll and J. Villasana Haggard.
Albuquerque, NM: The Quivira
Society, 1942.

Portolá, Gaspar de.
"Diario del Viaje a la California."
Quoted in *History of California*
by Hubert Howe Bancroft, I, p.
151.

Pourade, Richard F.
The History of San Diego. 5 vols.
San Diego, 1960–1965.

Powell, Phillip W.
Soldiers, Indians and Silver.
Berkeley and Los Angeles: Uni-
versity of California Press, 1952.

Prescott, William H.
History of the Conquest of Peru.
New York: Dutton, 1921.

Priestley, Herbert I.
*José de Galvez, Visitor-General of
New Spain, 1765–1771*. Berkeley: University of California Press,
1916.

Priestley, Herbert I.
The Mexican Nation, A History.
New York, 1924.

Provincial Records.
5 vols. In *California Archives*,
Bancroft Library, University of
California, Berkeley.

Provincial State Papers.
13 vols. In *California Archives*.

*Recopilación de leyes de los Rey-
nos de las Indias*. 3 vols. 4th ed.
Madrid, 1791.

Reps, John.
The Making of Urban America.
Princeton, NJ: Princeton Univer-
sity Press, 1965.

Revillagigedo, Juan Vicente
Güemes y Pacheco de Padilla,
Segundo Conde de.
*Instruccion Reservada al Marqués
de Branciforte*. Mexico, 1966.

Richman, I. B.
*California Under Spain and Mex-
ico 1535–1847*. Boston: Hough-
ton Mifflin, 1911.

Ritch, William G.
"History of New Mexico."
Manuscript, P-E, 12, in Bancroft
Library, University of California,
Berkeley, 1884.

Robinson, Alfred.
Life in California. Oakland,
1947.

Robinson, William Wilcox.
The Story of Pershing Square. Los
Angeles: Title Guarantee and
Trust Company. 1931.

Robinson, William Wilcox, ed.
"The Story of Ord's Survey as
Disclosed by the Los Angeles
Archives." *Historical Society of
Southern California Quarterly*,
September, December 1937.

Robinson, William Wilcox.
Maps of Los Angeles. Los Angeles: Dawson's Bookshop, 1966.

Rockwell, John A.
*A Compilation of Spanish and
Mexican Law in Relation to
Mines, and Titles to Real Estate,
in force in California, Texas, and
New Mexico*. 2 vols. New York,
1851.

Rowan and Koeberle.
Map of the City of Los Angeles,
1887. California Room, Los
Angeles City Library.

Ruschenberger, William S. W.
*A Narrative of a Voyage Round
the World During the Years
1835, 36 and 37*. 2 vols. London,
1838.

Sanborn-Perris Map Company.
Insurance Maps of Los Angeles,
Vol. 4, 1900. California Room,
Los Angeles City Library.

Santa Barbara Archives.

Schurz, William Lytle.
The Manila Galleon. New York,
1939.

Serra, Junipero.
Writings. 4 vols. Edited by
Antonine Tibesar, O.F.M. Wash-
ington, D.C., 1955–1966.

Sherman, William Tecumseh.
*Recollections of California,
1846–1861*. Oakland, 1945.

Sierra, Justo.
*The Political Evolution of the
Mexican People*. Translated by
Charles Ramsdell. Austin and
London, 1969.

Simpson, Sir George.
*Narrative of a Journey Round the
World During the Years 1841
and 1842*. 2 vols. London, 1847.

Simpson, L.
The Encomienda in New Spain.
Berkeley: University of California
Press, 1929.

Smith, Adam.
*An Inquiry into the Nature and
Causes of the Wealth of Nations*.
2 vols. 2nd ed. Edited by James
E. Thorold Rogers. Oxford,
1880.

Smith, Robert C.
"Colonial Towns of Spanish and
Portuguese Americas." *Journal of
the Society of Architectural Historians*, XIV, No. 4, December
1955, pp. 3–12.

Spicer, E. H.
Cycles of Conquest. Tucson: University of Arizona Press, 1962.

Stahlberg, A. J.
Los Angeles Map, 1876. Califor-
nia Room, Los Angeles City
Library.

Stanislawski, Dan.
"The Origin and Spread of the
Grid Pattern Town." *The Geo-
graphical Review*, XXXVI, No. 1,
January 1946, pp. 105–120.

Stanislawski, Dan.
"Early Spanish Town Planning in
the New World." *The Geographical Review*, XXXVII, No. 1, January 1947.

*State Papers: Missions and Colo-
nization*. 2 vols. In *California
Archives*.

Stevenson, H. J.
Map of the City of Los Angeles,
California, 1884. California
Room, Los Angeles City Library.

Storke, Yda A.
*A Memorial and Biographical
History of the Counties of Santa
Barbara, San Luis Obispo and
Ventura, California*. Chicago,
1891.

Stubbs, S. A.
Bird's-Eye View of the Pueblos.
Norman, OK: University of Okla-
homa Press, 1950.

Taylor, Bayard.
Eldorado, or Adventures in the Path of Empire. 2 vols. New York, 1850.

Thomas, Alfred Barnaby.
Teodoro de Croix and the Northern Frontier of New Spain 1776–1783. Norman, OK: University of Oklahoma Press, 1941.

Three New Mexico Chronicles. Trans. and annotated by H. Bailey Carroll and J. Villasana Haggard. Albuquerque, NM: The Quivira Society, 1942.

Trent, Sanford.
Architecture of the Southwest. New York: W. W. Norton, 1950.

Tuan, Ye-Fu.
Topophilia. Englewood Cliffs, NJ: Prentice-Hall, 1974.

Tyson, Philip T.
Geology and Industrial Resources of California. Baltimore, 1851.

Underhill, Reuben L.
From Cowhides to Golden Fleece: A Narrative of California, 1832–1858. Stanford, 1939.

Vallejo, José de Jesus.
"Reminiscencias Historicas de California." Manuscript, Bancroft Library, University of California, Berkeley, 1874.

Vancouver, George.
Voyage of Discovery to the North Pacific Ocean and Round the World. 3 vols. London, 1798.

Villa gutierre Soto-Mayor, Juan de.
"Historia de la Conquista . . . Nuevo Mexico" (ca. 1703). P-E 232 (film), Bancroft Library, University of California, Berkeley.

Violich, Francis.
Cities of North America. New York: Reinhold, 1944.

Violich, Francis.
"Evolution of the Spanish City: Issues Basic to Planning Today." *Journal* of the American Institute of Planners, 28, No. 3, August 1962, pp. 170–179.

Vitruvius.
Ten Books on Architecture.

Vizcaino, Sebastian.
"Relación del Viaje hecho para el Descubrimiento de las Islas llamadas 'Ricas de Oro y Plata,' situadas en el Japon. Japón . . .," January 22, 1614. In *Colección de Documentos Inéditos Relativos al Descubrimiento, Conquista y Organización de las Antiquas Posesiones Españoles de América y Oceania sacados de los Archivos del Reino.* Vol. VIII, pp. 101–199.

Wade, R. C.
The Urban Frontier: The Rise of Western Cities 1790–1830. Cambridge, Mass.: Harvard University Press, 1959.

Walpole, Frederick.
Four Years in the Pacific . . . from 1844 to 1848. 2 vols. London, 1849.

Walter, P. A. F.
"El Palacio Real." In *Old Santa Fe*, pp. 333–334.

Watts, J.
"Santa Fe Affairs." Manuscript, Bancroft Library, University of California, Berkeley.

White, Leslie A.
"The Pueblo of Santa Domingo, New Mexico." *Memoirs of the American Anthropological Association*, 43 (1935).

Wilgus, A. Curtis.
The Development of Hispanic America. New York: Farrar, Rinehart, 1941.

Wilkes, Charles.
Narrative of a United States Exploring Expedition During the Years 1838, 1839, 1840, 1841, 1842. 5 vols. Philadelphia, 1845.

World Book Encyclopedia. Vol. 12. "Los Angeles."

Zubrow, Ezra B. W.
Population, Contact, and Climate in The New Mexican Pueblos. In Anthropological Papers of the University of Arizona, No. 24. Tucson: University of Arizona Press, 1970.